QUEERING FAMILY TREES

T0375084

Queering Family Trees

Race, Reproductive Justice, and
Lesbian Motherhood

Sandra Patton-Imani

NEW YORK UNIVERSITY PRESS
New York

NEW YORK UNIVERSITY PRESS
New York
www.nyupress.org

References to Internet websites (URLs) were accurate at the time of writing. Neither the author nor New York University Press is responsible for URLs that may have expired or changed since the manuscript was prepared.

Library of Congress Cataloging-in-Publication Data
Names: Patton-Imani, Sandra, author.
Title: Queering family trees : race, reproductive justice, and lesbian motherhood / Sandra Patton-Imani.
Description: New York : New York University Press, [2020] | Includes bibliographical references and index.
Identifiers: LCCN 2019039534 | ISBN 9781479865567 (cloth) | ISBN 9781479814862 (paperback) | ISBN 9781479866595 (ebook) | ISBN 9781479828548 (ebook)
Subjects: LCSH: Lesbian mothers—United States. | Families—United States. | Reproductive rights—United States. | Race discrimination—United States.
Classification: LCC HQ75.53 .P38 2020 | DDC 306.874/308664—dc23

LC record available at https://lccn.loc.gov/2019039534New York University Press books are printed on acid-free paper, and their binding materials are chosen for strength and durability. We strive to use environmentally responsible suppliers and materials to the greatest extent possible in publishing our books.

Manufactured in the United States of America

10 9 8 7 6 5 4 3 2 1

Also available as an ebook

In memory of my first "baby," my sister

Nancy Lynn Patton

I learned more from her than anyone else in the universe.

Her life gave me a window onto oppression and othering

that built feminist consciousness into the foundation of my being:

my sister's struggles are my struggles.

CONTENTS

Introduction: Family Legibility and Legitimate Citizenship   1

1. Family-Making and Citizenship: "Life, Liberty, and the Pursuit of Freakin' Happiness . . ."   23

2. Reproductive Allegories: Family Trees and National Belonging   49

3. Making Family: Origin Narratives and Stratified Reproduction   79

4. What about the Children?: Genealogies of Illegitimacy and Reproductive Injustice, 1990–2000   109

5. Navigating Illegitimacy: Socialization, Race, and Difference, 2000–2003   137

6. Making Family Legal: Border Crossings and Other Perils, 2004–2007   165

7. Irreconcilable Differences: Socialization, Religion, and Race, 2008   195

8. Queer in the "Heartland": Allegories of Family, Race, and Equality, 2009   221

Conclusion: Grafted Trees and Other Allegories, 2015–   247

Acknowledgments   273

Notes   275

Bibliography   285

Index   303

About the Author   315

SAME-SEX MARRIAGE, 1970–2015

May 18, 1970   Same-sex couple applies for marriage license

Dec. 4, 1984   Nation's first domestic partnership law passed

Oct. 10, 1987   First mass same-sex wedding ceremony

May 7, 1993   Hawaii Supreme Court rules on same-sex marriages

Sep. 21, 1996   Defense of Marriage Act (DOMA) passed

Apr. 26, 2000   Vermont civil union bill becomes law

Nov. 18, 2003   State Supreme Court decision makes Massachusetts first US state to legalize gay marriage

Spring 2004   Same-sex couples in cities in California, New Mexico, Iowa, Oregon, and New York attempt to get legally married, with varied results

November 2008   California voters approve Proposition 8 banning same-sex marriage

April 2009   Iowa Supreme Court overturns ban on same-sex marriage

June 2015   US Supreme Court legalizes same-sex marriage federally

Adapted from https://gaymarriage.procon.org

Introduction

Family Legibility and Legitimate Citizenship

The questions at the heart of this book—about the relationships between definitions of *family, civil rights,* and *belonging*—became pointedly personal for my spouse, Melanie, and me in the fall of 2002 at the YMCA in downtown Des Moines, Iowa. We had signed up for a family membership when we moved to town the year before. One warm October night, we arrived at the gym to work out, but found that we had forgotten our membership cards. The manager behind the front desk casually typed our names into the computer to verify that we belonged. When she looked up from the screen her gaze pierced us. Something about what she saw stopped her short: A Black woman. A white woman. The same last name. A lifetime of stories about what makes a family seemed to animate the disdain on her face. She looked at the computer screen again and asked sharply, "How do *you* have a family membership?" I replied, "We're domestic partners. That means we're a family." Shaking her head, she objected, "We don't honor *that kind* of family here." Then, less than graciously, she let us pass that night, but she also let us know she would have to report our illegitimate status to YMCA authorities.

When the manager called us early the next morning, she reported tersely, "I consulted with my superiors, and you will not be allowed to return to the Y." She didn't say we could change our membership from family to individual status. She simply said, "You will not be allowed to return to the Y." Melanie reminded her that we had already paid for the month ahead, and again, less than graciously, she conceded that we could use the gym until the end of the month. We were stunned that a publicly supported organization could discriminate against us so blatantly. Melanie had been a member of the YMCA of Minneapolis-St. Paul since she was a child, and the two of us had shared a family membership there before moving to Des Moines. Each metro-area YMCA, it turned out, determined its own membership policies.[1]

The Des Moines YMCA defined family according to Iowa state law, which, like US federal law at that time, held that marriage was a legally sanctioned relationship between one man and one woman. We contacted a YMCA senior manager to discuss the situation. We explained to him that we had been granted civil union status from the state of Vermont, where we had gone to take advantage of one of the few opportunities available for our relationship to be legally recognized. He was clear that the YMCA's policy would not bend.

The YMCA's official position that "family" depends on legal marriage rendered us illegitimate, and thus, illegible as family. At this time we had not yet become parents. But we had included my youngest sister, Nancy, who had Down syndrome, in our family membership (another violation of Y policy, it turned out), because she was spending several months each year living with us. As ordinary members, we three had been using the gym with no problem for a year. Had we not forgotten our membership cards the manager might never have discovered that, in her view, we had been illegitimately passing as a family. The moment of outing—of becoming visible as an interracial lesbian couple with a sibling—made us into a problem that had to be reported to institutional "superiors." As we moved into conflict with the Y, we learned that a broad range of families were affected, including unmarried cohabitating couples, siblings, "chosen" kin, multigenerational families, all of whom were denied the privileges of family membership.[2]

Just a few days after the incident, Melanie and I filed a complaint with the Des Moines Human Rights Commission under a recently enacted city ordinance prohibiting discrimination in public accommodations based on sexual orientation. We were furious because of the way we had been treated and decided to document the process on video and to make a documentary. That would turn out to require a long-term commitment. A combination of budget cuts to the Human Rights Commission, poor leadership, and homophobia created a five-year delay in the processing of our case. We tried to resolve the issue using other legal remedies but found that, while we were part of a protected class in the city of Des Moines, we had no state or federal protection. Our only legal protection against discrimination was at the city level. This meant that if the Des Moines Human Rights Commission did not resolve the case, we had no recourse. Once the commission did investigate the case, they ruled in our favor and required the Des Moines YMCA to change its definition of "family membership." Now family status would not require legal marriage (not yet legal for gays and lesbians in Iowa); it would only require cohabitation.

The inconsistencies in federal, state, county, and city laws governing family relationships and access to social resources make clear how profoundly family policy shapes access to the full rights of citizenship in the United States. Legal marriage was the only avenue for accessing fundamental rights of citizenship—in this case, to be guaranteed the same public accommodations as any other family. Yet we were effectively prohibited from marrying each other anywhere. Lack of reciprocal recognition of same-sex marriages between states and by the federal government rendered the one option we had in 2000—our Vermont civil union—legally meaningless. We were caught within irreconcilable tensions over social and legal definitions of family that, I would suggest, characterized the politics of kinship and queerness at the turn of the twenty-first century.

The experience of basically being kicked out of the YMCA for being lesbians and for calling ourselves a family, and then having the civic institution created to protect our rights fail to do so for five years, caused us to rethink our social and political location in Des Moines, in Iowa, in the United States, as well as transnationally. Faced with fundamental questions about what constitutes a family and who decides it, we started thinking about how other families like ours might be navigating the uneven legal and social terrains of marriage and family in the United States. Melanie and I expanded the focus of our research; we decided to include interviews with lesbian mothers in states with a range of laws and policies regulating family.

This interdisciplinary exploration of queer mothering and family-making draws on the ethnographic interviews Melanie and I conducted in different states with over one hundred lesbian and queer mothers across a broad range of racial-ethnic identities.[3] These interviews include African American, Latina, Native American, white, and Asian American mothers living in a range of socioeconomic circumstances. Between 2004 and 2010, I conducted participant observation, and together we conducted in-depth interviews in a number of states, each with its own laws regulating marriage, adoption, and other family policies.[4] In this book I apply a reproductive justice analysis to family-making among queer mothers in the United States at the turn of the twenty-first century. I draw on critical race theory, queer theory, queer of color critique, and feminist research on reproduction and family to explore the ways lesbian mothers navigate family-making in social and legal contexts that define queer families as illegitimate.[5] I turn now to an overview of the arguments I make here, followed by a consideration of queer family trees. I conclude with a discussion of the research process and my family's location in it.

How Did This Happen and What Does It Mean?

The question of what effect legalizing same-sex marriage may have on the future of the nation was the topic of fierce public discussion in the United States between 1991 and 2015. In 1991 three same-sex couples sued the Hawaiian director of health in an (ultimately unsuccessful) attempt to require the state to issue them marriage licenses. Conservative politicians responded with alarm. The introduction of the federal Defense of Marriage Act (DOMA) in 1996 ushered same-sex marriage, along with welfare and immigration "reform," into a particularly vicious political dialogue about "family values." The floor of Congress hosted unprecedented debates focused on "deviant" mothers and their children as a threat to the nation. The children's book *Heather Has Two Mommies* was held up by members of Congress as a prime example of the corrupting influence of gays and lesbians on "innocent" children. Having two mothers and no father was represented as a threat to family values, as was being a single mother receiving AFDC or an immigrant mother without government documentation. "Illegitimate" mothers were represented as the villains in a sociopolitical narrative about family, race, reproduction, and citizenship in political debates, news media, and social interactions. These debates continued through a series of court cases, legislative proposals, and laws regarding same-sex marriage in the United States that culminated in the 2015 US Supreme Court ruling in *Obergefell v. Hodges*, overturning DOMA as unconstitutional. The lived experience of these years felt, at times, slow and plodding in regard to legislative changes. In 1991 the prospect of same-sex marriage becoming legal seemed far-fetched. Yet when we look back historically, it was a remarkably short period of time for such dramatic shifts in social definitions of legitimate family.

If we are to believe the most pervasive political tales in this era about families headed by lesbians and gay men, then legalizing same-sex marriage should be *either* the panacea for all the constitutional vulnerabilities of LGBT citizenship *or* the downfall of civilization due to the crumbling of the institution of marriage. While these views clearly differ, they share an emphasis on family, citizenship, and the future of the nation. The debate was about "inclusion" in legal marriage, and the arguments were often virulent.[6] Yet neither side in the mainstream debate challenged the premise that "marriage is a keystone of the Nation's social order" (*Obergefell v. Hodges*, 2015). For the most part, neither "pro" nor "con" arguments questioned the fact that it was only through marriage that some rights and privileges of citizenship could be accessed.[7] These debates about equality emphasize government neutrality and individual choice. The denial of structural inequality based on race and gender is crucial to this story about American equality. News media and policy dialogues about same-sex marriage primarily focus on sexuality and equality, suggesting that "differences" between queer folks are irrelevant.[8] I argue that these national narratives emphasizing "colorblindness," "gender-neutrality," and "choice" obscure inequalities of access to various forms of social recognition and resources for socioeconomically vulnerable families in the United States.[9] In other words, focusing on the "choices" made by individual people, rather than the ways governmental structures shape access to family-making rights and protections, creates an illusion of equality.[10]

One might be tempted, in the afterglow of *Obergefell v. Hodges*, to believe that the battle is over for equality through access to legal marriage, that gays and lesbians fought a tough fight and finally won. Indeed, the legalization of same-sex marriage is often celebrated as the capstone of "American equality" in a progression from the civil rights movement forward.[11] It may look like that from a certain angle, but this only shows one side of a very complex story about family and citizenship. This narrative of progress toward full equality is appealing, but a closer exploration of the complex negotiations between LGBTQ families, legal inequities, and public stories about citizenship demonstrates that the foundational structures of inequality remain intact. Same-sex couples are now allowed to marry, and this change, without a doubt, provides new legal protection and recognition to some families, a recognition that shapes daily life experiences of social legibility and legitimacy. Yet, as this research makes clear, the social and legal structures that regulate citizenship through family policy still revolve around legal marriage, adoption, and family legitimacy.

Obergefell v. Hodges does not challenge the nuclear family ideal; legal marriage has simply become more inclusive. Yet we must ask: Inclusive for whom and on what terms? As this book will show, the experiences of the mothers we interviewed challenge the ways these issues are typically represented in policy and news discussions. These mothers' central arguments are not only for inclusion in legal marriage, but for a redefinition of what determines inclusion. While some parents wanted recognition for being "just like any other family," other mothers criticized social and legal definitions of legitimate kinship. Some articulated both of these conflicting perspectives. The liberal view of expanding who is allowed to marry is one way to provide rights and protections, and most of the women we interviewed wanted access to such rights. Another strategy, embraced by leftists, would be to divorce rights from marriage.[12] This view was also articulated by some of the same mothers that wanted access to those rights.

Views of marriage as either assimilation or resistance characterize the activist and academic views of same-sex marriage throughout this public debate. As sociologist Amy L. Hequembourg makes clear, the debate among LGBTQ academics over same-sex marriage has primarily focused on tensions between the belief that marriage will lead to equality for gays and lesbians (or at least that the institution of marriage will be changed by including same-sex couples), and the argument that same-sex marriage will lead to assimilation.[13] Intellectually, I lean to the left, yet, like many of the mothers I interviewed, that stance conflicts with my social location as a queer mother whose family is not fully recognized or protected within the framework of the white supremacist patriarchal status quo. Mothers both desired access to same-sex marriage and critiqued it as a patriarchal institution. These tensions challenge the "for or against" framework presented in mainstream news media, as well as tensions between views of same-sex marriage as assimilationist versus resistant. The family-making narratives of the queer mothers we interviewed complicate both representations of same-sex marriage—as a panacea for all of the legal inequities associated with being gay in the United States *and* as a purely assimilationist institution. Indeed, they challenge the solvency of the categories of assimilation and resistance for understanding the ways people respond to power inequalities.

The lives of the mothers we interviewed demonstrate that intersections of geography, socioeconomic status, gender, sexuality, tribal affiliation, and racial-ethnic identity profoundly shape access to family protections, rights, and privileges in this era. In the absence of federal recognition of same-sex marriage, parents have had to purchase legal protection—second-parent adoptions, powers-of-attorney, wills—even in states where marriage is legal. These transactions make visible social structures and inequalities that keep some parents from being able to financially access these seemingly available choices. Indeed, many of the families we interviewed could not afford second-parent adoptions or other legal measures available through lawyers at a cost, and so their families are effectively rendered illegitimate and vulnerable.

Reproductive justice and critical race theorists make clear that social inequalities organized through race, gender, class, sexuality, and disability fundamentally influence the ways *all* families interact with and access the law.[14] Putting race and gender at the center of research on queer mothers challenges the whitewashing of public images of families and demonstrates that structural inequalities are magnified by laws regulating access to family protections through legal marriage. As reproductive justice scholar Rickie Solinger argues, in a capitalist society organizing access to social rights through (consumer) choice effectively makes motherhood a class privilege. If one cannot afford the lawyer fees for second-parent adoptions, wills, or powers of attorney, then that choice is unattainable. In the case of the mothers we interviewed, this stratification was, at least in part, maintained through the commodification of legal family protections. Basic protections that heterosexually married couples take for granted became high-cost consumer goods that were out of reach for many of the families we talked with.

The consequences of these inequalities go beyond the level of individual experience. What kinds of relationships are recognized, supported, and legitimated shapes who is able to construct families and how. Compulsory heterosexuality positions lesbians, gay men, bisexuals, and trans* people outside the legitimate channels of family-making. Yet LGBT people do not experience this "outsiderness" in the same ways. Gender profoundly shapes how people become parents and whether and how family relationships are recognized. Race and class intersect in complex ways to regulate relationships and foster the reproduction of ideal American families that help maintain the status quo. The stakes in these family policy debates speak to questions about how inequality is reproduced in stealthy ways that deny structural power and blame individual actions for social problems. Patriarchy, compulsory heterosexuality, white supremacy, and socioeconomic inequality are actively *reproduced* through the social and legal construction of legitimate families.

How we understand this history matters for how we move forward. The stakes in reproductive policy discussions continue to heighten in the contemporary political moment. The 2015 federal legalization of same-sex marriage was celebrated in news media as evidence that the nation was moving toward its promise of full equality. Just over a year later backlash reared his orange head. Overnight, with the November 2016 presidential election outcome, the United States no longer felt like a safe place for far too many of us. Since 2016 there has been a systematic attempt to roll back civil rights across the board. How will we ever work together to survive the deluge of reactionary politics impacting the current political moment if we do not grasp the complexities of how same-sex marriage was legalized and what it means for different families? It is crucial that we understand how it is that a law purporting to create equality could actually further entrench structural oppression. The history I explore in this book pushes us to consider how power hides, reappropriates, and reframes the ways we understand ourselves and each other, in relation to larger notions of community and coalition.

Understanding how race, gender, and socioeconomic status shape LGBTQ family-making requires broadening the scope of analysis to include other arenas of family policy and law. Same-sex marriage is only part of this story. I contend that exploring this debate in the larger political context of family policy—particularly welfare, immigration, and adoption—makes clear the insidious politics of gendered racism undergirding US family policy between 2001 and 2015. One of the central beliefs driving the movement was the illusion that same-sex marriage was the key to equality. I critique this premise throughout. Yet it is important to think beyond the question of whether or not this is true, to consider how this understanding became so broadly accepted. Race, gender, sexuality, and class were simultaneously utilized and denied in these political dialogues.

Exploring same-sex marriage debates alongside other arenas of regulation helps us understand how multiple kinds of oppression and privilege are mutually reinforcing. This multifaceted, decades-long debate masterfully crafted a mainstream media story that framed access to marriage for same-sex couples as "equality" for LGBT families, while silently entrenching racism, sexism, and economic inequality. Part of how power succeeds is by pitting people against each other. We must be willing to consider the ways we are shaped by and embroiled in the system at the same time that we attempt to resist it.

Critical race theory is a useful framework for exploring the ways that laws and policies both draw on and contribute to sociopolitical narratives supporting the status quo. As critical legal scholar Peggy Cooper Davis explains, "All legal doctrines are stories, structured upon formal but ambiguous texts and nourished by history and culture" (1997, 6). The legalization of same-sex marriage in the United States was accomplished, at least in part, through racialized narratives about mothers and children in news and public policy discussions. I argue that the virtual exclusion of lesbians of color from public narratives about LGBTQ families is crucial to maintaining the belief that legal marriage for same-sex couples provides access to full equality as citizens.

In the absence of attention to the voices and experiences of queers of color in mainstream political debates, two narratives prevailed. One story was about good mothers raising innocent children to be productive citizens. The other story was about bad mothers who were incapable of properly socializing their children. Each of these fables was discussed in terms of the future of the nation. Narratives about illegitimate mothers and innocent children were used to convey racial meaning without explicitly mentioning race or ethnicity. Mainstream understandings of adoption, particularly transracial adoption, were used to covertly erase and silence mothers of color while celebrating white mothers. These ancient sociopolitical narratives about illegitimacy were key to the legalization of same-sex marriage. I turn now to the story of one family that we interviewed, to explore the ways that LGBTQ family-making both supports and subverts social and political power inequalities.

Queering Family Trees: Recognizing Multiple Mothers

Sophie was born to an unknown mother in rural Cambodia in 1999 and adopted as an infant by Kimberly, a single white woman living in the United States.[15] When that adoption was complete Kimberly's partner, also white, went through a second-parent adoption in Iowa to legalize her relationship with Sophie. After the couple split up, each of them became involved in another long-term relationship. Now Sophie lives part-time in one house with Kimberly and Mischa (whom we interviewed in 2007) and part-time in another house with her other two moms; all four of the mothers she lives with are white. Her family includes a sister adopted from Russia, a brother adopted from Cambodia, a brother adopted from Haiti, and an African American foster brother. Her siblings have birth mothers who were unable to care for them, primarily because they were poor, many of them unmarried. One of the challenges adoptees often discuss is conceptualizing, recognizing, and imagining two mothers in a social context that only recognizes one.[16] The children of lesbian couples also experience having two mothers in a world that expects people to just have one. Sophie's story pushes us beyond the typical birth mother/adoptive mother dyad. Sophie has *five* mothers.

Adoption is important in this research in multiple ways that run through the stories of all the families we interacted with and speak allegorically to larger social connections between family and nation. At the most practical level, nonrelative adoption—what social workers often refer to as "stranger adoption"—is the way many of these families were formed. Adoption also functions in particular ways for queer families in regards to the legal and social necessity of second-parent adoptions. Under the patchwork assemblage of legal restrictions on same-sex marriage and adoption both in the United States and transnationally, second-parent adoption is the legal means through which many parents codified their relationships with the children their partners had given birth to or adopted.

The somewhat unique social location of adoptees illustrates tensions between social narratives of legitimate family and biological inheritance. I connected with the people we interviewed as queer mothers, but my social location as an adoptee also fundamentally shaped the interview process and informed my understanding of family-making in this context. I was born illegitimate to an unwed mother, and legitimated through the sociolegal practice of adoption. My birth mother is not, by law, my mother, and is rendered invisible in my family tree. Two mothers can only squeeze into genealogical templates if there are no fathers. As an adoptee, I have two mothers and two fathers, whether or not I know who they are. My status as a "legitimate" person and citizen depends upon the erasure—through the sealing of my birth records—of my unwed birth parents and the circumstances of my birth.

Unwed mothers are expunged from new birth certificates issued through closed adoptions, and sentimental narratives of children redeemed as legitimate through placement in "forever families." Queer adoptive parents, too, often seem invisible in the adoption application process; partners and spouses are often represented as "roommates" in the formal family narratives presented to social workers in application materials and home studies. The US and transnational adoption systems are grounded in erasures, and the most glaring absence in this mainstream narrative is the acknowledgement of power regulating the reproductive options available to different populations of women.

The recognition of Sophie's two legal mothers through adoption depends on the termination of parental rights between Sophie and her Cambodian birth parents. These original parents are symbolically deleted by adoption laws and by widely embraced media narratives about transnational adoption to the United States that promote the "salvation" of orphans through adoption. Her birth parents are quite literally erased from her family tree through the creation of a new birth certificate, listing her legal parents *as if* she had been born to them—a sort of legal passing that is commonly practiced in adoption. This version of "passing" depends upon the denial of racial difference, or at least of the salience of racial difference. Sophie has three birth certificates: the first, in Cambodia, likely lists her Cambodian parents; her first US birth certificate legalizes Kimberly as her sole parent; and her third birth certificate lists both her legal mothers.

It would be easy to cast her adoptive parents as privileged and her birth parents as oppressed, and that would not necessarily be incorrect. Yet these categories are too neat to account for the multiple and complex ways the reproductive experiences of each of these parents is stratified differently based on their social locations in relation to definitions of legitimate nuclear families. Stratified reproduction is a useful analytical tool for exploring how some women's reproductive practices are valued and supported and other women's families are actively denigrated and even dismantled.[17] Intersectionality—another central tenet of reproductive justice—is key to recognizing the ways race, poverty, gender, sexuality, and nation locate each of Sophie's parents in positions of inequality and privilege in relation to patriarchal definitions of family in Cambodia and the United States. The relational character of oppression is not lost on Kimberly and Mischa; they share the details they learned about their children's original mothers and the horrific circumstances that prevented each of them from keeping their children. And while they told stories about scrimping and saving in order to afford adoption, they acknowledge that their social locations as middle-class white women in the United States allow them the privilege, the cultural and economic resources, to adopt their children. These origin stories are part of their navigation of family in a transnational context of stratified mothering, and their complexities embody some of the irreconcilable tensions at the core of contemporary family-making.

My family tree, like that of most adoptees, is haunted by multiple mothers, whether or not they are known or acknowledged. "Birth mother" has always been a magical term for me. As long as I can remember, I have been longingly imagining my first mother—the one that did not keep me. I loved the mother that raised me; though she was by no means perfect, I never doubted her love. Yet she could never be everything I needed or wanted or imagined I needed in a mother, because she was not my birth mother. There was always another mother out there, though I knew better than to speak this aloud. Secrecy and denial are required for symbolic inclusion in legitimate family trees. My birth mother was a magical shape-shifter, whom I could narrate in whatever way suited my needs at the moment. Her absence a palpable presence, I have imagined her as many people throughout the years. When I actually met the woman who gave birth to me, I found that she could not live up to the multiple versions I had imagined. No one could.

It was a great surprise to me when I gave birth to our twins that I began to be referred to as their "birth mother" because my spouse, their other mother, did not give birth to them. I encountered this at doctor's visits, in casual settings, and, most surprising of all, in social interactions with other queer moms. As I began paying attention to the language lesbians employed to describe their families and others like them, I noticed that the terms for two mothers in adoption had slipped into the lexicon of lesbian-headed families. In some ways, it makes perfect sense. One mother gives birth; the other mother must go through the legal channels of adoption in order to be considered a legitimate parent by the state. Public narratives about motherhood rarely make room for two mothers, and, thus, qualifiers and descriptors are attached to delineate social definitions of legitimate motherhood.

The use of the term "birth mother" proves to be remarkably flexible depending on context and the families' relationships to the state. In contrast to the way it is used in the realm of adoption, the term "birth mother" in lesbian-headed families refers to a mother who has given birth and is raising the child. "Birth mother" is used to distinguish between two queer moms raising a child or children. In traditional US adoptions the birth mother is legally defined as *not-the-mother*. Adoptive mothers do not give birth, but once they are declared legal parents by the state, they assume the role of legitimate mother. In lesbian-headed families birth mothers are legally defined as *the only* legitimate mother—until or unless the not-legal-mother adopts her own child, becoming a legally defined "second parent." As I and others have argued, a feminist analysis of adoption requires attention to the ways that some mothers are deemed legitimate and others illegitimate, through the complex transnational inequalities of capitalism, patriarchy, and white supremacy.[18] These family-making stories, in dialogue with public discourse as well as social law and policy, reveal conflicting ideologies and power relations governing the social category of mother and the social reproduction of particular kinds of families in a transnational context of stratified mothering.

In her now-classic essay "Punks, Bulldaggers, and Welfare Queens: The Radical Potential of Queer Politics?" political scientist Cathy Cohen urges a politics of coalition among folks positioned outside definitions of legitimate families and citizens.

> I envision a politics where one's relation to power, and not some homogenized identity, is privileged in determining one's political comrades. I'm talking about a politics where the *non-normative* and *marginal* position of punks, bulldaggers, and welfare queens, for example, is the basis for progressive transformative coalition work. Thus, if there is any truly radical potential to be found in the idea of queerness and the practice of queer politics, it would seem to be located in its ability to create a space in opposition to dominant norms, a space where transformational political work can begin. (Cohen 1997, 438)

I draw on Cohen's definition of "queerness" to imagine coalitions among folks deemed *illegitimate*. As I discuss in chapters 2 and 4, the politics of queer motherhood cannot be separated from public policy dialogues about welfare and immigration "reform" in the 1990s. Exploring debates about legitimate and legal motherhood together encourages our understandings of intersectionality to grapple with the profound complexities of power relations—not only the ways that individuals and families are shaped by multiple axes of power, but also the ways that families in different social locations are positioned strategically in relation to each other in public narratives about equality and citizenship. Historian Siobhan Sommerville explains: "The challenge is to recognize the instability of multiple categories of difference simultaneously rather than to assume the fixity of one to establish the complexity of another" (Sommerville 2000, 5).

In this racially comparative research, I narrate the politics of illegitimate kinship through the family-making stories of the mothers we interviewed. Putting queer mothers of color at the center changes what the story looks like. Focusing on adoption changes our views of same-sex marriage. Paying attention to the politics of welfare and immigration policy provides a broader context for exploring patterns of race, gender, sexuality, and socioeconomic inequalities. The relationships of the queer mothers we interviewed to the state speak to issues that affect mothers across a broad range of social locations. Indeed, these stories intersect with the circumstances of mothers located outside the normative model in a variety of ways. The families whose stories I share here articulate definitions of kinship that challenge social understandings of legitimate family and citizenship.

Queerly Legible: Recognition and Passing

When I began the research for this book, in the early years of the new millennium, the "gayby boom" was in full swing.[19] DOMA had been passed in 1996, barring federal recognition of same-sex marriages. Hawaii and Alaska had protracted legal battles over same-sex marriage, each ending with state constitutional amendments defining marriage between one man and one woman in 1998. My partner Melanie and I were "civilly unified" in the state of Vermont in 2000, the year civil unions became available there. The Netherlands became the first country in the world to legalize same-sex marriage in 2001, followed by Belgium in 2003. Our twins were born in 2003. Massachusetts became the first state in the United States to legalize same-sex marriage in 2004. Five years later, in 2009, same-sex marriage became legal in Iowa, where we live. Our family-making, like that of the mothers we interviewed, occurred in this historical context of shifting social definitions of legitimate family, laws regulating marriage and adoption, and social and legal recognition of same-sex relationships.

In some senses, the participant observation for this project began when Melanie and I moved to Iowa in 2001 so I could accept a position at Drake University. Des Moines was the smallest city either of us had ever lived in, and, predictably, we experienced more than a bit of culture shock. We were troubled by the messages we received about how our performance of couplehood challenged the cultures of the spaces we moved through socially. "You're not from here, are you?" was the most commonly repeated phrase in casual interactions out in public. Or, I should say, OUT in public. As an interracial lesbian couple we were both out and passing all the time. We didn't get to define how people saw us, and we were often perplexed by how they did. I grew up in California, went to graduate school in the Washington, DC, area, and had spent several years in the Minneapolis-St. Paul area. Melanie grew up in the Twin Cities and had also lived in Texas and Florida. Des Moines provided us with daily doses of culture shock—going in both directions—that in many ways continue to this day.

We are a family of two moms—one African American and Indigenous-descended, one white with red hair—and twin biracial kids with pale skin and red hair. How, or whether, we are seen depends on where we are and who is watching us. In predominantly white settings in the Midwest, when our children were little, people would often say things to them like: "Look at those red curls! We can see who your mother is!" Did they see my wife as some random Black woman standing near us? Or did they not *see* her at all? In brief exchanges like this we experience a sort of social efface-ment, refracted through race and gender. People learn not to see as real or legitimate families that do not meet the heternormative patriarchal struc-ture, and they learn not to acknowledge as family members kin not rec-ognized by law. We did not fit the template for "normal" families, and this gave strangers ample opportunities for letting us know we didn't belong. Mainstream narratives about kinship and heredity teach people to look for one mother and one father, with "likeness" the sign of relatedness. Red hair functions as a mark of heritability and of whiteness, obscuring our children's biracial identity, and, thus, my spouses' status as their mother. White middle-class heteronormativity is reproduced through the erasure of queers of color; white motherhood (attempts to) reclaim me symboli-cally from the deviance of queerness, but only when my Black wife is in-visible in social and legal interactions.[20]

Social performances of kinship—and their interpretations—are shaped by legal definitions of family like those employed by the YMCA, media discussions of politics, and social policies focused on kinship at multiple levels of jurisdiction.[21] The patriarchal nuclear family structure is broadly represented in mainstream news media as natural and nor-mal, influencing the ways that all kinds of people learn to see and rec-ognize families in social interactions. Whether one accepts such views as true, or resists such narrow representations, these ideological scripts affect our lives. Resistance is shaped by what one resists.

In other social spaces, people look at us and see a family. Melanie and I only pass as straight, our children only pass as white, when we aren't recognized as a family. People that do recognize us typically draw on heritability as well, to affirm their view of us as kin, their comments emphasizing how our children look like a perfect blend of the two of us. We are *queerly legible*. I engage the term "queer" as a position of critical resistance in relation to "legitimate" family structure and the social narratives employed to support it. Sociologist Jane Ward argues that, while it has many meanings, queer is most usefully defined as "a metaphor that describes various modes of challenge to the institutional and state forces that normalize and commodify differences" (2008a, 3). It is a stance in relation to power that is defined by critique and resistance.

Queer of color scholar David L. Eng discusses "a new form of passing in our putatively colorblind age, which is less about concealment of difference than about our collective refusal to acknowledge it" (2010, 117). Passing feels different when you don't intend to hide. In both social interactions and legal regulations, enactments of "colorblindness" depend upon the denial and erasure of any reference to race, foreclosing social recognition of racial "difference" (from whiteness, the unmarked norm). Within this system of racial meaning, noticing race is equated with racism, and this unfortunately translates too often to both the denial of racism as a structural issue, and the erasure of the ways that race informs people's senses of self, others, and society. Passing and legibility are two sides of the same coin, articulated through social narratives of normal and legitimate families.

Who sees you and how, depends on where you are, who you are with, what the other people around you look like, who might be calling you mommy at that moment—the list goes on. Context (social, legal, cultural, historical) shapes which people pass as what, or, rather, who is socially legible to whom. Colorblindness, grounded in erasure and evasion, intersects with patriarchy, heteronormativity, and capitalism to naturalize and normalize the family forms that support contemporary boundaries of legitimacy and citizenship.

Our insider-outsider social location, as an interracial lesbian couple with biracial twins, is structured through this genealogical narrative. The complexities of families like ours—regarding gender, sexuality, and race—reinforce understandings that social definitions of legitimate family are not so much representations of biological family relationships as of ideological, socially sanctioned lines of descent and inheritance. These stories about kinship are culturally, socially, politically, and historically specific. We are not alone among families who are misread or not seen.

The legal issues raised in our YMCA case intersected with another "ethnographic moment" during our first family vacation with our then-seven-month-old twins. In July 2004 we travelled to Family Pride Week in Saugatuck, Michigan, for reasons similar to most of the people we talked with there: to be with other families like ours. Particularly in the context of our battle with the YMCA, it was a powerful experience to be in a setting in which we were seen and recognized as a family. We felt "legit." We met three two-mom families with adopted children born in Guatemala, Ethiopia, China, Vietnam, and the United States. My earlier research is on transracial and transnational adoption, and I was interested in questions concerning race in same-sex adoption. We conducted in-depth interviews on videotape with six white lesbian mothers of adopted children of color. The stories they told about their families' interactions with the state were compelling, and they pointed me toward larger and deeper questions about the legal regulation of family.

We began interviewing mothers in different states with contrasting laws, to explore the ways that other queer mothers navigated the uneven and unequal terrain of family law and policy. We made sense of social and legal changes in dialogue with the families we interviewed. We marched in rallies and Pride parades together. We sat in workshops with other parents interested in teaching their children how to deal with homophobia, sexism, and racism. We listened. We learned from them. We gave talks and showed videos from our research; we listened to responses. We worked with others for social justice. We sat on boards of national and local nonprofits. We helped organize a queer community center. We listened to people's stories about power and inequality and race and gender and queerness. We celebrated legal and political victories even as we critiqued the forms they took.

I did not expect this to be a historical narrative, but somewhere along the way it became apparent that our struggles with the YMCA and with the limited legal system in place to protect our rights were part of a progression of change. Here in Iowa the movement was exciting and, frankly, astonishing. In the summer of 2007 our case was—after five years of struggle—successfully settled. In that same summer the State of Iowa passed a law protecting the civil rights of gays and lesbians. It seemed the momentum had begun. Just two years later, in April 2009, the Iowa Supreme Court ruled that limiting marriage to heterosexuals was unconstitutional.

Practical considerations shaped the research as well. When Melanie and I began looking for families to interview, we put out calls for

FIGURE I.1. Kathlyn and kids, berry picking, Family
Pride Week, Saugatuck, Michigan. Photo credit: Sandra
Patton-Imani.

LGBTQ families. Mostly women responded; very few men did. I did not
conduct this research alone, nor could I. Most of the interviews were
conducted together, though on a few occasions we met with people in-
dividually. Our children accompanied us on every research trip, and,
in fact, several of the destinations were Family Week or Pride events
designed for LGBTQ families. We were insider-outsiders in this research
because—like the other families we spoke with—that is who we are in
society. We participated and observed Pride events as a multiracial queer
family that always carried a camera and consent forms.

The interviews and participant observation for this research were
conducted over the course of several years in Iowa, where we live, as
well as in a number of different US locations, including Saugatuck,
Michigan; Albuquerque, Santa Fe, and Taos, New Mexico; Minneapolis-
St. Paul, Minnesota; Provincetown, Massachusetts; and Northern and

Southern California. We also interviewed lesbian mothers living in Missouri, Kansas, Indiana, Ohio, Illinois, New York, and Maryland. Distinct and specific narratives emerged in various geographic sites, but there were also commonalities in the negotiation and navigation required for family protection and everyday social life. This book explores complex relationships between family-making, law and policy, and national belonging. The life stories of the mothers we interviewed articulate the human consequences of laws that discriminate against queer families, emphasizing in particular the disproportionate effects of such discrimination on queer mothers of color and their children.

Outline of the Book

In chapter 1, "Family-Making and Citizenship: 'Life, Liberty, and the Pursuit of Freakin' Happiness . . . ,'" I draw on the voices of the mothers we interviewed to discuss navigations of citizenship and belonging, focusing in particular on how a range of lesbian-headed families have been positioned in a context of inconsistent and swiftly changing laws regulating same-sex marriage and adoption. In chapter 2, "Reproductive Allegories: Family Trees and National Belonging," I build a theoretical framework for examining conflicting narratives in ethnographic interviews, news media, and social policy and law grounded in a critical engagement of allegory. In chapter 3, "Making Family: Origin Narratives and Stratified Reproduction," I explore lesbian mothers' family-making stories in relation to the fertility and adoption industries. I use the stories of these mothers to explore the scaffolding of power that regulates motherhood, and the ways that it varies from state to state. Drawing on their family-making narratives, I look at the ways people navigated inequalities and made meaningful family lives.

Chapter 4—"What about the Children? Genealogies of Illegitimacy and Reproductive Injustice, 1990–1999"—begins a chronology of the 1990–2015 years; there, I consider the political context of family-making in the "family values" era. I explore public controversies over the children's book *Heather Has Two Mommies* by Leslea Newman (1989) in relation to political discourse on race, gender, and family values in the 1990s. I consider these narratives alongside political discussions of "welfare reform," immigration, disability payments, and the "fitness" of mothers. In chapter 5,

"Navigating Illegitimacy: Socialization, Race, and Difference, 2000–2003" I view the first few years of the twenty-first century through the stories of mothers navigating a sense of belonging and legitimacy in a socipolitical context of shifting laws and policies about same-sex marriage and adoption. I continue this chronology in chapter 6, "Making Family Legal: Border Crossings and Other Perils, 2004–2007." I use as a lens a series of same-sex marriage performances in 2004 in San Francisco, California; Bernalillo, New Mexico; and Iowa City, Iowa, exploring my interviewees' differing relationships to these local claims for legal same-sex marriage. Chapter 7, "Irreconcilable Differences: Socialization, Religion, and Race, 2008," focuses on public-private meanings of queerness, race, gender, and class in the public debate about same-sex marriage in California.

In chapter 8, "Queer in the 'Heartland': Allegories of Family, Race, and Equality, 2009," I explore the public marriage debate through an allegorical reading of social change in Iowa. Drawing on participant observation with a multiracial group of lesbians organizing a queer community center in Des Moines, I narrate the moment when the state granted new rights and a new sense of family legitimacy to lesbians and gays. In the conclusion, "Grafted Trees and Other Allegories, 2015–" I reexamine intersections of citizenship and family, gender and class, race and equality, drawing on this multiracial array of mothering experiences to envision coalitions and intersections between and among people and families whose lives are not valued. I consider the interactive narratives about kinship and belonging that emerged in my analysis and explore the symbolic and practical implications for the future of family and citizenship in the United States. These kinship stories redefine what counts as family and contribute to the larger public discussion about how best to meet the needs of families of all kinds.

The in-depth interviews articulate in rich detail the live tension between nation and family through the narratives of queer mothers in a range of circumstances. Not only does this contribute to mainstream and scholarly understandings of queer families and their relationships to law and policy, but it also provides an important reminder that *all* families are shaped by laws and policies. *Queering Family Trees* explores the voices and stories of queer mothers as lenses through which to understand, and to redefine, the complex interactions between race, gender, sexuality, family, public knowledge, media, and power in the contemporary United States.

1

Family-Making and Citizenship

"Life, Liberty, and the Pursuit of Freakin' Happiness . . ."

RAE: It is cost prohibitive to be gay. Life, liberty, and the pursuit of freakin' happiness is cost prohibitive if you are gay. It's set up so you can't
protect your family if you aren't of a particular socioeconomic class.

Rae is an African American queer mom living in Des Moines, Iowa,
who was single at the time of our interview in 2008. She articulates a
common sentiment among the mothers we interviewed, that connects
family-making with *citizenship*. Rae's comment explicitly links her
access to family protections with her rights of citizenship and economic
resources. Intersections of capitalism and politics circumscribe the
"inalienable rights" promised in the Declaration of Independence. Rae
declares her right to the American Dream of liberty and equality, while
making evident the economic and legal structures limiting the availability of tangible protections for her family.

The stories that emerged in this research process—through interviews, news media, and law and public policy—overwhelmingly focused
on citizenship and belonging. All of the mothers we interviewed were
apprehensive about protecting their families and expressed concerns
about equality and rights. Their family-making narratives emphasize interactions with social institutions, policies, and laws, but also with publicly available narratives about LGBTQ families as articulated in news
media, public policy discussions, and everyday social interactions.

Proponents of legalization have used the term *marriage equality* to
emphasize the demands of LGBT couples, as citizens, for dignity and
equal rights.[1] Supporters of prohibitions on same-sex marriage, in contrast, use language that suggests that the practice would damage the nation's moral fiber, shred the "traditional" family, and generally pollute

the worth of citizenship status for all. Law and policy discourse has also framed same-sex marriage with reference to questions about "American" identity and citizenship, positing proper socialization of children as key to the future of the nation (on both sides of the issue).[2] At the center of the political debate are questions of what constitutes American citizenship and who is included in the country's promise of equality.

Liberal narratives argue that same-sex marriage means full equality for gays and lesbians. Historian Siobhan Sommerville writes:

> In the past decade, popular and juridical debates about lesbian and gay civil rights in the United States have been driven primarily by a liberal discourse of inclusion, framed by the assumption that lesbians and gay men constitute one of the last groups of excluded "minorities" to be denied full citizenship under the law. Such a view tends to rely on an optimistic reading of the history of civil rights in the twentieth-century United States, a reading that moves gradually from discrimination against minority groups toward the fulfillment of an idealized democracy, in which all individuals have equal opportunities to inhabit the roles, rights, and responsibilities of citizens. (Sommerville 2005, 335)

This "optimistic reading" depends upon beliefs that racial inequality was eradicated by the success of the civil rights movement. This story both depends on and reinforces the narrative that the United States is now a colorblind society, and that this legal system constitutes equality.[3] Critically exploring colorblindness, or what sociologist Ruth Frankenberg calls "color evasiveness," is crucial to understanding the political story celebrating same-sex marriage as equality (1993). The simultaneous denial and recognition of power is at the center of this racial meaning system.

Critical race scholar Dorothy Roberts makes clear in her important book *Killing the Black Body* that "racism does not continue despite constitutional paradigms of liberty and equality; rather, racism is deeply embedded in these paradigms themselves" (1996, 373). This research is grounded in an interdisciplinary reproductive justice framework that moves beyond narratives celebrating individual choice to explore the ways that all family-making actions and decisions are shaped and regulated in negotiation with family laws and policies, as well as with public narratives that obscure inequalities constraining the varying options available to different populations of parents. Loretta Ross, founder of SisterSong Reproductive Justice Collective, explains: "Reproductive Justice says that the ability of any woman to determine her own reproductive destiny is linked directly to the conditions in her community—and these conditions are not just a matter of individual choice and access. Reproductive justice addresses the *social reality of inequality*, specifically, the inequality of opportunities that we have to control our reproductive destiny [emphasis added]" (2006, 14). As Ross makes clear, by drawing on an intersectional analysis of women's lives, reproductive justice emphasizes the ways that systemic inequality circumscribes the range of choices women in different social locations are able to exercise.[4]

Citizenship is not just a legal concept. The lived experience of citizenship involves both practical rights and protections, and *representational belonging* in the idea of the nation. As political scientist Melissa Harris-Perry makes clear, "Citizenship is more than an individual exchange of freedoms for rights; it is also a membership in a body politic, a nation, and a community. To be deemed fair, a system must offer its citizens equal opportunities for public recognition, and groups cannot systematically suffer from misrecognition in the form of stereotype and stigma" (2011, 36–37). Mothers reported experiencing "misrecognition" as their families interacted with social institutions like churches and hospitals. They told stories about personal interactions when they felt socially invisible. These moms articulate outrage at conservative representations of queers as perverts, of gays as sinners, of lesbian mothers as unfit, and of families headed by same-sex parents as signifiers of the breakdown of the family. The weight and significance of "stereotype and stigma" not only shapes how families are seen and treated socially, but functions in complex ways to justify legal inequalities and obscure the role of power in maintaining oppression. Families that conform to templates for patriarchal legitimacy through lawful marriage are legally recognized and thus provided concrete protections and supports. Families that cannot or will not assimilate to the social and legal terms of legitimacy are denied these supports.

In this chapter I consider the complex ways in which power shapes the lives of families while simultaneously hiding its very presence. The lived experience of citizenship that was shared in the interviews we conducted makes evident a set of power relations that are typically denied in mainstream news media. I argue that these public-private narratives linking family and citizenship reveal concealed fissures in US formulations of equality. I examine family negotiations of the lived experience of citizenship and explore the ways that families learn how and where we belong in society.

Religion, Race, and Belonging: "Violating Every Rule in the Book"

Laws and policies fundamentally shape the family-making experiences of these mothers. Yet that is only part of the story. As political scientist Paisley Currah reminds us, "Becoming swept up in the romance, or tragedy, of the electoral narrative, gets in the way of understanding the minute technologies of governance that regulate our lives" (2012, 9). So much of our negotiation of citizenship takes place in the spaces between laws, news media, and personal belief systems, in the "minute technologies of governance." The lived experience of citizenship is also shaped in daily life through interaction with social institutions outside the government. All LGBTQ families are affected by conservative Christian views of homosexuality as sinful, because these storylines have permeated public debates at every level of discourse. The oppressiveness of these stories about the wages of sin and deviance were particularly evident in the lives of mothers of color, who often sought a sense of racial-ethnic belonging in religious traditions they had been raised with.[5] These tensions were at the center of some families' navigation of the lived experience of citizenship and belonging.

Bekka and DeAnn are a Latina couple living in Albuquerque with two young daughters. Each of them was raised Catholic, and early on in their relationship they attended Catholic Church together.

> BEKKA: The thing I didn't like the most about it was that I couldn't hold DeAnn's hand, or I felt like I couldn't be with her. Or they make you feel like you're violating—well, everything they teach you, I've been through—my mom is like really religious, so I've been through like every CCD, catechism, confirmation, retreats, everything you could ever get pounded into your head about being Catholic, and it's always been such a *contradiction* from what I ended up being in my life. It was so hard to go and worship and to feel like I had a relationship with God that was accepting from him. So, I think that was my

FIGURE 1.1. DeAnn, DeNae, and Bekka, Albuquerque, New Mexico. Source: Sandra Patton-Imani.

> biggest issue with Catholic Church was that *I didn't feel like I could be who I was and be okay being Catholic.* And so that's where I was looking to still have a relationship with God and with Jesus and not feel like I was *violating every rule in the book.*[6]

Conflicts between religious teachings and queer existence are not unusual. Race adds another layer to these experiences for families of color. Bekka and DeAnn were raised in predominantly Latinx Catholic churches, and thus, at least some of their persistence in attending was rooted in a sense of racial-ethnic belonging.[7] But, as Bekka stressed, "I didn't feel like I could be who I was and be okay being Catholic." Her desire to feel at home in a spiritual community was thwarted by the constant reminder that she "was violating every rule in the book." These tensions were ultimately irreconcilable for them. They left the Catholic Church and joined the Albuquerque Metropolitan Community Church, a nondenominational LGBTQ-friendly church.

The quest for a sense of belonging for their families impacted mothers living in different social locations in particular ways. In Albuquerque,

New Mexico, the role of religion emerged as a central theme in interviews. A large Latinx population in New Mexico meant that a number of the women we interviewed had been raised in strict Catholic families. They talked about the tensions they experienced between, on the one hand, their desires for a fulfilling spiritual and community life, and, on the other, church doctrine labeling homosexuality as a sin. A number of white mothers—in Albuquerque and in other locations—discussed their negotiation of religious beliefs as well, though most of them did not explicitly connect their racial-ethnic identities to religious traditions.

Much of the rhetoric both for and against same-sex marriage suggests that the identity labels "person of color," "Christian," and "gay" are separate and monolithic categories. Christians are represented across all racial-ethnic categories, but queerness is typically represented as white. While whites are depicted as a diverse group of people regarding religion, African American, Latinx, and Asian American cultures are often characterized through homogenous adherence to religious traditions. In this narrative being gay is portrayed as incompatible with Christianity, and, thus, with the cultural and religious beliefs of communities of color. The family-making stories of the mothers we interviewed belie these representations. They speak from positions of intersection, as individuals negotiating the religious teachings they were raised with, as queer people of color desiring a faith community, as parents seeking to instill in their children a sense of spirituality and ethics, and as people of color seeking to challenge both religious and political systems of meaning that judge their families as illegitimate.

Bekka and DeAnn's struggle with the tenets of organized religion was similar to that of most of the mothers we talked with who were spiritual or wished to attend a church community. Whatever their beliefs, all the families we talked with had to engage with conservative Christian dogmas about homosexuality on some level, because public discourse was flooded with portentous tales of sinful queer families leading to the downfall of civilization. As Jessie, a young single white bisexual mother who lives in Minneapolis, told us:

JESSIE: I live with my grandparents and they're like all extra-Christian, so it's like a really bad thing. My grandparents grew me up really Christian and made me feel like I had to be with a guy, but I always liked girls. I was more comfortable with girls. They hate it. I think that it (the conservative Christian perspective on homosexuality) is wrong. I think it doesn't really matter who you're with as long as there's love. And they're saying that it's bad to be with the same gender as you.

Jessie articulates a common response to religious homophobia: *It doesn't really matter who you're with as long as there's love.* She was clearly still struggling with the judgments Christianity placed on her, regarding her attraction to women. She handles this tension by embracing the story that difference is not bad, as long as there is there is love. "Love" is represented as the commonality that unites every kind of relationship, gay or straight.

Like Bekka, Jessie found that the church she was raised in did not approve of the adult she had become. She did not want her four-year-old daughter to be taught that being gay is a sin. Jessie's struggles differed from those of the mothers of color we interviewed, in two ways. She was not seeking "a relationship with God," as Bekka put it. Nor was she seeking a sense of belonging in a racial-ethnic community or a church. In fact, Jessie found a sense of belonging in the LGBTQ community in Minneapolis. She talked about how important it was to bring her daughter to Twin Cities Pride, where we interviewed her. As many of the mothers we talked with emphasized, public gatherings celebrating LGBTQ Pride were important aspects of parenting where their children could feel a sense of acceptance and belonging in a community. "Pride" was fostered as resistance to homophobic views of LGBTQ folks as sinful, perverse, deviant threats to children.

While many of the white mothers we talked with left the churches in which they were raised, most of them found other, often better options in LGBTQ-friendly churches (if they were looking). Many others simply stopped attending or were never particularly invested. For mothers of color these options were often more complicated. Church has often functioned as a place of community belonging for people of color. Sociologist Mignon Moore explains:

In African American communities, religious structures provide direction for the language, rituals, and behaviors individuals incorporate in their lives. People participate in churches and mosques not just for spiritual guidance but also find a sense of community, and they use the teachings of these religious groups as a set of practices or blueprints by which to organize their lives, however loosely or stringently. Many Black religious institutions participate in public rule enforcement and policing of parishioners' lives, and they openly condemn behaviors deemed to fall outside of religious teachings. (2011, 205)

Several of the mothers we interviewed experienced a visceral sense of condemnation when they visited churches. I interviewed Iniece and Faith, who are both African American, at the Albuquerque Pride Festival. They explained to me that they did not attend church, though they would like to join one where they felt comfortable. They were angry that they were unable to find a Black church that was accepting of gays and lesbians.

> INIECE: I've had experiences with churches like that, where they don't accept us really because of their beliefs. And I feel that it's unfair because we need God just as much as they do. And I think that we really should have more lesbian and gay churches.
> FAITH: And no judgments toward us. 'Cause we're all God's people regardless of who we like and how we are.

They had visited predominantly Black churches, but felt uncomfortable.

> INIECE: They just really don't accept you. I mean, they look at you funny. They don't treat you like they would treat someone else who is not gay or lesbian.

They were treated as if they did not belong there. Melanie and I have had to navigate this terrain too. We were both raised in families that regularly attended church, and we had each drifted away from churchgoing in adulthood. Christian rhetoric about homosexuality and sin motivated us both to close those doors. Like many of the white mothers we interviewed, I feel no need to belong to a church community and am wary of the way mainstream Christian churches address LGBTQ families. Melanie was raised in a predominantly Black church, and her experience of community was profoundly different from mine. Like many of the women of color we interviewed, Melanie valued the sense of racial community she experienced in the church, as well as the spiritual grounding it provided her as a child. She appreciated in particular the survival skills for dealing with racism that she learned from this spiritual community that valued political resistance. Becoming parents is often the impetus for people returning to church, whether to instill in their children a sense of morality or for a sense of racial-ethnic community. Living in Des Moines, as an interracial queer couple with biracial children, has been challenging for us in multiple ways. One of the biggest issues for us has been finding a sense of community belonging in multiracial settings. We are not always legible as a family in predominantly white social settings in the Midwest.

When our kids were toddlers we explored the idea of going to church. We talked with a friend of ours—who is straight, African American, and Christian—about attending her predominantly Black church. She initially assured us we would be welcomed. We asked her how her minister talked about homosexuality and LGBTQ people. We asked her what our children would be taught about LGBTQ families in Sunday school. She was delighted that we were interested, but our questions gave her pause. She had never considered them. As a person committed to social justice for women and people of color she was determined to find the answers. She sat down with her pastor. He told her that all God's children are welcome in their church, *whether sinners or not*. He explained to her that it was important we understand however, that our children would learn about "God's truth" that homosexuality is a sin. His answers caused our friend a crisis of faith.

The LGBTQ-friendly churches we visited were predominantly white. People welcomed us, but we did not feel at ease, for a variety of reasons, even in the church held up by many in Des Moines as the most open and progressive. We felt like magical signifiers of the diversity this church celebrated. The few times we visited we were the only multiracial family, and Melanie was the only African American woman in the room. Before and after the service we received the hard-sell welcome from the membership director, who, ironically, made us feel like birds of prey being hunted for our colorful feathers. We tried to like it there. We wanted to feel like we belonged.

It didn't work. The final visit was defined by a typical, disconcerting experience. As we stopped to greet the minister on our way out, Melanie asked him a casual question. He answered it easily and without hesitation. But he directed his answer to me, not to her. I turned to my wife, trying to direct his gaze, but he was oblivious. Melanie and I looked at each other, knowing we were done there. We were able to walk away because neither of us is invested in Christianity or religion, but many of the mothers we talked with, like Bekka and DeAnn, wanted "a relationship with God."

Like Bekka and DeAnn, Betty and Edna were raised in predominantly Latinx Catholic churches, which they continued attending as adults. Their greatest challenges as lesbians raising children came from their participation in the Catholic Church, and their children's attendance at parochial school. They faced conservative representations of homosexuals as immoral sinners not only in political rhetoric, but also in regular encounters at church and school. They followed the Catholic tradition because that is what their parents did.

> BETTY: I went to parochial school for nine years. And so, you know that mindset, *dis is dis* and *dat is dat*, and you know, everything's black and white. There's no grey. And so, like when Edna and I would take our kids we'd sit our kids between us, you know. And I guess it was because, maybe we were hiding the fact that we were gay. I don't know.
>
> EDNA: Yeah, I don't think (shaking her head), you know the way the Catholics are with you know, the gay relationships and all that, you know, we knew that. Or how did they say that? "You're accepted— You're accepted as a Catholic as long as you don't practice."
>
> BETTY: As long as you don't *practice*.
>
> EDNA: So, what does that mean? You know, I'm gay but I'm not gonna live with a woman? I'm not going to you know, have a relationship, nothing like that? But I'm gay. Give me a break, you know? So, I guess you know, we never really talked about it. We just stopped going I think.

They left the Catholic Church for Albuquerque Metropolitan Community Church because they were weary of listening to sermons that condemned their relationship and wanted to be able to hold hands and express affection in that setting.

> BETTY: I think it was more because we wanted [thoughtful pause] our children raised Catholic, because we were raised Catholic. Because being naïve or blind to the fact that there is other churches out there that might accept us. We didn't know that. You know, so we put up,

you know, a front, I guess, for everyone in the Catholic Church. I mean, not that I'm bad-mouthing them, but I *am*. Because God created me. God created us. We're his children.

Betty employs a common response among LGBTQ folks discussing God and religion. She makes it clear that she is "bad-mouthing" the Catholic Church, not God. It is the religion they identify as discriminatory, not the deity. Catholicism demanded that they "put up a front." Betty has no doubts that "God created me." The distinction is important because it allows them to embrace other churches and maintain their faith that "God created us. We're his children." This common phrase, invoking a view of God as father and protector, is striking in this context. Conservative Christians focus on children and socialization to demonize queer folks as threats to innocence. Like many of the Christian mothers we talked with, Betty reappropriates this patriarchal model of family to envision a resistant version of spiritual community that emphasizes love and acceptance rather than sin and judgment. Edna continues:

EDNA: We didn't you know, show affection to each other, you know, or anything like that. You know, when they say, "Greet each other," or whatever we'd hug and kiss, you know. But we did with the kids the same. So, I guess maybe that's what it was. We just didn't show any affection. You know, like at MCC we can sit next to each other. We can hug.
BETTY: We can hold each other's hands.
EDNA: You know, and like that.
BETTY: And we can greet each other with a solid kiss. And not have to look over my shoulder, you know—*is someone going to hurt me*? Or did I *offend* someone?

They got tired of hiding their relationship in order to be accepted, or even safe. Like DeAnn and Bekka, they found a sense of belonging and spiritual community at MCC. Our family was welcomed, too, at MCC when we visited as part of this research project. The congregation appeared to be predominantly LGBTQ and was racially mixed. The church itself was adorned with rainbow sashes, candles, and banners celebrating God's love for all people. After the service the sense of fellowship continued at a barbeque celebrating Pride Week. The palpable sense of belonging we felt—even as nonchurchgoers—was grounded in a celebration of LGBTQ families of all races and ethnicities. This contrasted dramatically with conservative religious perspectives on queerness, race, and sin. It was clear from our interactions with the families there that they deeply valued the sense of community they felt.

"Extra Things": Navigating Inequality in Social Institutions

Governmental recognition of relationships determines the distribution of resources to citizens. Queer mothers we interviewed of all races, income levels, and geographic locations overwhelmingly cited family protection and both legal and social recognition as their primary motivations for desiring same-sex marriage. Tina and Cass are an interracial lesbian couple with five Black children who live in Des Moines, Iowa. Tina, who is African American, gave birth to their triplets via alternative insemination prior to meeting Cass, who later adopted the triplets through a second-parent adoption. They adopted their two youngest children together through the foster care system. Several years prior to our 2008 interview, they had a "sacred" commitment ceremony in their church celebrating their relationship that satisfied their need to declare their commitment to each other before God, family, and friends.

Their interest in the legalization of same-sex marriage was fundamentally about state recognition of family relationships and access to the social rights, protections, and benefits attached to such recognition. Tina and Cass are very clear that their ability to provide for their family in both the short and the long run are limited by fundamentally unequal laws.

> TINA: Really, I think that we love just like everybody else. If you don't want to call it a marriage, fine. But there should be something legally recognizing our relationships and our families. One of the things, for instance, is she's retired from the military, so until—Right now, while the children are young, if she should die they would receive her benefits. But if they were over twenty-one and grown, then as it stands right now, her social security and retirement benefits just cease. You know, just the same as with mine. And we had to do *so many extra things* just to secure our families, to make sure that they have all the rights and benefits of a heterosexual couple. And I don't believe that's okay.

As a military veteran Cass is eligible for a range of benefits through the US Department of Veteran Affairs, including a Death (Survivor's) Pension. These benefits are provided to the "surviving spouse or unmarried child of the deceased veteran" who meets the agency's income criteria. However, access to these benefits depends upon federal recognition of Cass's family relationships. The federal government did not recognize same-sex marriage as legal until the *Obergefell v. Hodges* ruling in 2015; thus Tina did not qualify as a "surviving spouse." Similarly, Cass's relationship with her children was not recognized by the Veteran's Administration, even as a stepparent, until she legally adopted them.[8] The legal fees for second-parent adoptions cost them several thousand dollars per child in the state of Iowa. "Extra things" are expensive. As retired military, Cass's social location challenges the promise of US citizenship. Being in service to the country implies a reciprocity of full protections and rights that she is not accorded because her family relationships are not deemed legitimate.

The Veteran's Administration application form and policies about benefit eligibility create and reproduce a template for legitimate family relationships. Unless you fit the family template you do not receive benefits. Sociologist Donilene Loseke suggests such policies create institutional narratives that serve the needs of the agency while ostensibly focusing on the client.[9] She argues for the importance of considering the complex ways power relations are embedded in narratives utilized by social institutions like the VA, and that such stories function as a means of obscuring the workings of power. As Cass's story demonstrates, institutional narratives function as gatekeeping mechanisms. The law does not need to say anything as blatant as "lesbians need not apply." Narratives regarding who counts as deserving of VA benefits are grounded in social understandings of family defined through heterosexual marriage. The narrow definitions of legitimate family relationships employed by the VA effectively disqualify Cass and Tina from inclusion. The policy functions subtly and with stealth: heterosexual family relationships are presented as natural and normal, thus deserving of benefits, and relationships outside legal marriage are considered illegitimate, therefore ineligible.

In *Arresting Citizenship*, political scientists Amy E. Lerman and Vesla M. Weaver explore the US criminal justice system's effect on democracy and citizenship. Their analysis provides an analytical framework for considering the ways interactions between individuals and the government shape the lived experiences of citizenship. They write, "Through experiences within particular policy domains and with various government agencies, we the citizenry draw general conclusions about how government works, its underlying values and core commitments, and the political standing of the various social groups to which we belong" (2014, 10). The lesbian mothers we interviewed learned through interactions with government at multiple levels of jurisdiction that queer families are not recognized consistently *as families* by the governing institutions, policies, and laws of this nation.

Indeed, historian Margot Canaday's important work argues that the state does not "simply encounter homosexual citizens, fully formed and waiting to be counted, classified, administered, or disciplined." She draws attention to the ways that heterosexuality is structurally enforced by the state through multiple arenas of regulation, including social welfare programs, immigration, and the military. "Rather," she argues, "the state's identification of certain sexual behaviors, gender traits, and emotional ties as grounds for exclusion (from entering the country, serving in the military, or collecting benefits) was a catalyst in the formation of homosexual identity. The state, in other words, did not merely implicate but also *constituted* homosexuality in the construction of a stratified citizenry" (2011, 4). In a sense, the state constructs the very category "queer families" by legally defining us as illegitimate in relation to narratives of ideal citizenship. Canady writes, "Over the course of the early to mid-twentieth century, the state crafted citizenship policies that crystallized homosexual identity, fostering a process by which certain individuals began to think of their relationship to the state" (10). These different negotiations with the state help us see the cracks in the promise of American citizenship. The array of voices and stories among the mothers here maps a broad range of complex relationships between families, social and cultural narratives about reproduction and kinship, and public laws and policies regulating marriage and adoption.

Experiences like Tina and Cass's with the Veteran's Administration taught mothers about where and how we belong in society. Anthropologist Aihwa Ong connects personal interactions with the state to a sense of national belonging. She uses the term "cultural citizenship" in reference to "the cultural practices and beliefs produced out of negotiating" with state power and ideologies employed to support it (1996, 738). Negotiations like those Tina and Cass engaged in, Ong argues, "establish the criteria of belonging within a national population and territory." Their family narratives, along with those of all the mothers we interviewed, speak volumes about whose citizenship is recognized, whose families are valued, and what it means to be "legitimate" in the eyes of the state. As Ong argues, "Cultural citizenship is a dual process of self-making and being made within webs of power linked to the nation-state and civil society" (1996, 738). In this case, interacting with the state was also a process of family-making and of being made.

Slippery Laws: "If We Were Able to Have a Civil Marriage . . ."

Tina and Cass told us another story about interacting with several governmental agencies regarding health benefits. They detailed the onerous process they underwent to have Tina and their children covered by the health insurance Cass's employer provided under the designation "domestic partner." Tina also worked for the state as a firefighter (and was insured), but she and Cass were excited about the prospect of state recognition of their family. When this lengthy process concluded, they discovered that their benefits were then to be classified by the Internal Revenue Service as "taxable income" because their relationship was not legally recognized at the federal level.

Without consistent marriage and adoption laws across states, lesbians and gay men in the United States have had to creatively piece together contracts in order to secure protection for our families. The stories mothers told about family-making were replete with interactions with lawyers, social workers, and judges, and with episodes of activism against unjust laws. "Family protection" has become linked with a set of commodities available (in some states) for those able to afford it. "Extra things" barely scratches the surface of the legal, financial, and emotional costs of family protection for same-sex parents: it includes powers of attorney, second-parent adoption, wills, guardianship papers, and other forms of legal recognition. In this social context of inequality, most mothers were diligent about securing every protection for their families that they could both access and afford.

Systemic power acts upon individuals and families in covert ways that make inequality practically invisible. "Like being mugged by a metaphor," is how critical race scholar Wahneema Lubiano describes interactions with state power that rob citizens of rights while simultaneously maintaining governmental illusions of equality and neutrality. Tina and Cass did not encounter any laws or policies that explicitly stated that domestic partners would cost more to insure than heterosexual married spouses. In fact, they were happy to have the opportunity for recognition and pursued the possibility of being insured as a family rather than as individuals as both a practical and a symbolic act. "Like a mugging," Lubiano writes, "this attack involves an exchange of assets." For Tina and Cass, the exchange of assets was literal in regards to the federal tax imposed on them, but it was also symbolic. Lubiano explains further that in such interactions with the state "some aspect of the social order is enriched" by reinforcing the narrative that the US government treats everyone the same way (Lubiano 1996, 64). Tina and Cass were caught between state laws recognizing same-sex relationships and federal laws defining them as illegitimate. The federal tax made the insurance more costly than its symbolic currency was worth; with a renewed sense of their status as second-class citizens, they canceled the family's coverage. The option for family recognition had a price tag beyond their means.

Like many of the mothers we interviewed, Tina and Cass talked about love in relation to marriage, but their more fundamental concerns were about the family protections, rights, and benefits provided to heterosexual families through legal marriage. They had done as many of the "extra things" they could financially afford "just to secure our families." They expressed anger and frustration at having to purchase legal protections that heterosexual families receive as a matter of course.

Rae's experiences, as an African American queer mom living in Iowa, illuminate the ways that rights, privileges, and protections depend on both financial resources and legal access:

RAE: When we first got together we had a ceremony at the Unitarian Church, and in retrospect I think back on that, and it frustrates me. Because if we were able to have a civil marriage like every other straight couple in the state of Iowa, this whole protection issue, when it comes to him being her son would be a nonissue.

The "whole protection issue" she references concerns her ex-partner's lack of legal relationship with their son. As Rae points out, if she and Jasmine had been allowed to legally marry prior to their son's birth, both of them would have been listed on his birth certificate. As it is, Rae is Jack's only legal parent; she and her partner conceived him via a sperm donor who relinquished all rights. In order for Jasmine to be Jack's legal parent, she and Rae would have had to go through a second-parent adoption. They could not afford this option, so they remain unrecognized and unprotected. In the context of the United States's piecemeal approach to legislating same-sex marriage, such protections as second-parent adoption, wills, and powers of attorney are financially prohibitive for many of the mothers we interviewed. This organization of rights as commodities has had a disproportionate effect on lesbian mothers, who lack the financial resources to secure their legal rights. Some of the mothers lived in what they described as precarious circumstances because of the expense.

Intersections of class, gender, and race are significant in shaping the level of legal protection families are able to purchase. As is true in the larger US population, women and people of color are more likely to experience discrimination in the labor market. Because lesbian-headed families are composed solely of women, they and their families are more likely to experience the economic effects of such discrimination. This is magnified for lesbians of color, who earn less, are less likely to own their own homes, and are twice as likely to be raising children as white lesbians (Cahill 2009, 219). Inequity is not evenly distributed.

A comparative framework is useful for exploring the ways that race and class in particular shaped the lived experience of citizenship for queer moms in this era. Access to family protection depended most fundamentally on local and state laws regulating marriage and adoption. Yet even in states with the most liberal laws, intersections of race, gender, and class circumscribed whether and how queer mothers were able to legitimize relationships among family members. In places where marriage and/or second-parent adoptions were not legal, access to protective documents were only available for those able to afford lawyers and other fees, yet even these legal roundabouts were insufficient for full legitimation of family relationships. Indeed, no matter where in the United States one lived prior to 2015, the protections acquired in one state were not necessarily recognized by other states, and no same-sex unions were considered legitimate under federal law.

The "Metalanguage" of Whiteness: Adoption and Stratified Mothering

Adoption often figured more prominently than marriage in the stories of legalization we heard. We met Patty, Jill, and their son Max at Family Pride Week in Saugatuck, Michigan, in 2004. They are a white lesbian couple that adopted their African American toddler through the US foster care system. In Patty's explanation of their views on same-sex marriage, "It's not a *procedure*—I guess is what it feels like to us—a ceremony that is important to us. The legal rights and the tax benefits and those sorts of things matter, but the actual marriage isn't important I don't think." Patty's choice of the word "procedure"—and the sneer on her face as she said it—articulate her critical distance from the institution of marriage. As a descriptor of marriage, the term sounds more like an invasive medical experiment than the storybook concept. Patty and Jill's social location as an unmarried lesbian couple that had, by legal necessity each separately and at different times, undergone the legal process of adopting their son demonstrated to them that family law and policy were not abstractions, but rather, arms of the state that exercise power in both personal and public ways that carry profound consequences. While Patty and Jill's family-making is limited through discriminatory same-sex marriage and adoption laws that tightly regulate LGBTQ couples' access to family protection and recognition, they are also racially and economically privileged within the child welfare system. There are restrictions on how they adopt, yet they did become parents.

For Patty and Jill, like many of the mothers we interviewed, adoption law carried particular weight because they had *lived* these policies through interactions with social workers, and through detailed application requirements, home studies, and financial expenditures. "That is to say," according to Lerman and Weaver, "American institutions, beyond merely reflecting social understandings, actively cultivate and structure racial membership, identity, and perceptions" (2014, 16). Child welfare policy not only dictated how Patty and Jill interacted with the system; it also conveyed institutional narratives about race, gender, class, and sexuality that shaped their experience.

Jill and Patty live in Ohio, a state where, at the time of our interview in 2004, single-parent adoption by gays and lesbians was allowed, second-parent adoption was not legal, and joint adoption by gay and lesbian couples was not clearly prohibited. They received and followed legal advice to adopt their son in two separate adoptions six months apart. They were neither strictly prohibited from legally protecting each of their parental rights, nor were they welcomed by the state with clear and facilitating laws. They finessed the level of legal protection for their family they were both legally and financially able to obtain. Ohio law states: "Only a union between one man and one woman may be a marriage valid in or recognized by this state and its political subdivisions" (Ohio Constitution, article XV), clearly positioning their union as (in)"valid" and (un)"recognized." Recognition is a legal concept intimately intertwined with questions of public representation: "Citizens want and need more than a fair distribution of resources: they also desire meaningful recognition of their humanity and uniqueness" (Harris-Perry 2011, 36). Family, relationships, parental status, identity, even love that is publicly labeled as "queer" is subject to the scrutiny and surveillance of the politically malleable concept of legitimacy. About people like Patty and Jill, the Ohio state constitution minces no words. Indeed, the mothers we interviewed were keenly aware of the politics of queer families because understanding the legal intricacies of local, state, national, and transnational laws has become a survival skill. Acts of political resistance are now necessary negotiations of family life.

Even as Jill and Patty experienced obstruction based on being a same-sex couple, their whiteness opened doors. The child welfare system welcomed them via the classic adoption paradigm of white women saving brown babies. Patty and Jill were construed as "fit" mothers after passing screening policies scrutinizing their adherence to institutional definitions of good parenting. In their family-making endeavors, they experience both discrimination and the unspoken privilege accorded to middle-class whiteness. The absence of attention to whiteness is central to its function as a silent signifier of legitimacy.

In her now-classic essay "The Metalanguage of Race," historian Evelyn Brooks Higginbotham contends: "First of all, we must define the construction and "technologies" of race as well as those of gender and sexuality. Second, we must expose the role of race as a metalanguage by calling attention to its powerful, all-encompassing effect on the construction and representation of other social and power relations, namely, gender, class, and sexuality. Third, we must recognize race as providing sites of dialogic exchange and contestation, since race has constituted a discursive tool for both oppression and liberation" (1992, 252). Higginbotham argues for the importance of intersectional analysis, but she also emphasizes the ways that race functions as a "metalanguage" that shapes representations of gender, class, and sexuality. In this instance, whiteness overrides queerness. Though being lesbians flags Patty and Jill as "different," their whiteness and middle-class status garners them approval as adoptive parents.

While this may help us to understand the stories of Patty and Jill, their son Max's brown skin reminds us that there is another mother in this story that is legally invisible. Unpacking Patty and Jill's privilege in relation to their child's birth mother is necessary. How does whiteness function with such stealth? How do Patty and Jill's race, gender, and class location position them in relation to the state? How does the absence of Max's birth mother narrate her relationship to the state? Why was she unable to care for him? Was he removed from her? Was poverty the primary factor shaping their separation? Her story is sealed in a closed adoption file. This absence is filled in by political narratives emphasizing "choice." Yet what options did she actually have? There are two primary versions of this story: in one, she voluntarily and selflessly relinquishes her son to give him a better life. In the other, her child is taken from her because she made bad choices. We do not know Max's mother's story. We only have her absence, and the pervasive sociopolitical narratives denigrating unwed mothers of color.

These narratives have been used in policy discussions to represent the dangers to society that illegitimate births pose. Adoption policy, particularly transracial adoption, figured prominently in congressional discussions about how to save the nation from the supposed breakdown of the family that conservatives attributed to "illegitimacy."[10] White middle-class mothers, of whatever sexuality, were cast as the saviors of at-risk children. Once adopted, the story goes, the transformational love of ideal white motherhood will socialize at-risk children into productive citizens. Historian Robin Bernstein's important work demonstrates "that the idea of childhood innocence and the bodies of living children have historically mystified racial ideology by hiding it in plain sight" (2011, 18). This subterfuge is at the center of neoliberal race-gender ideology. Contemporary narratives about transracial adoption are important to understanding the lived experience of citizenship for LGBTQ families. Yet these stories of white salvation are also, I contend, central to consideration of how same-sex marriage came to be legalized in such a short period of time. A critical consideration of race, including the role of whiteness as a redemptive discourse of motherhood, is necessary for illuminating queer family-making at the turn of the twenty-first century.

Structural Critiques: "It Seems Sort of Archaic to Me"

The most pervasive mainstream public discussions about equality for LGBTQ people in recent decades have largely focused on marriage, yet outside this tug-of-war live large numbers of US families who are critical of the heterosexual-married-parents ideal. Vanessa and Cathy, an interracial couple—African American and white—live in Albuquerque, New Mexico, where no form of same-sex marriage was legal at the time of our interview, in 2008. They discuss their ambivalent views of marriage:

> VANESSA: The importance of just having those sort-of-rights that come along with marriage, so that we don't have to put it in our wills, you know. You do all these *sort-of-extra things* to make sure that our family gets those basic rights that heterosexual couples get. You know what? I can see the importance, but then on the other hand, I sometimes think . . .
>
> CATHY: *I'm uncomfortable with the word marriage.* I don't know, I just—I'm uncomfortable with the word "marriage." But now that we have two children, and we're getting older, we think a lot more about what could happen and our rights, and something has to be done. I'm not sure I want the word marriage attached to us, but . . .
>
> VANESSA: But some sort of legal, you know, rights.
>
> CATHY: Yeah, we have to have our rights protected, so of course, *we're for that.*

VANESSA: It just seems like common sense, I mean, my goodness. Because you're heterosexual you get the corner on family protections and all that other stuff. It seems sort of *archaic* to me.

As was the case for a large proportion of the mothers we interviewed, having children was the catalyst for seeking out legal family protections.[11] In their musing about an "archaic" social system that privileges heterosexual families, Vanessa and Cathy raise an important point. They are "for" legal marriage if that is the only avenue for family rights and protections available to them. However, their needs for family protection also lead them to question the equity of a system in which some rights and protections are accessed solely through legal marriage.

Vanessa and Cathy's critique, like that of many of the mothers we interviewed, echoes that of feminist and queer leftist perspectives on same-sex marriage. As I have discussed, the liberal counterpoint to conservative constructions of citizenship frames marriage as the path of access to equal rights. Many of the legal issues lesbian mothers face *seem* to stem from the fact that same-sex marriage was illegal prior to 2015. At first glance, it seems that legalizing same-sex marriage would be the solution to this problem, and, indeed, it does extend some rights to a larger number of people. As feminist legal scholar Nancy Polikoff explains, "Advocating marriage for same-sex couples is a sensible way to champion equal civil rights for gay men and lesbians. Unfortunately, it is not a sensible approach toward achieving just outcomes for the wide range of family structures in which LGBT people, as well as many others, live. Those outcomes depend on eliminating the 'special rights' that only married couples receive and meeting the needs of a range of family forms" (2008, 84). This analysis reframes "special rights" as those that only straight married couples are given and challenges the systemic privileging of heterosexual families. Vanessa and Cathy's lived experience of second-class citizenship made visible for them the gaps in legal protection for mothers and children outside the legal definitions of legitimacy.

While little attention was paid in news discourse to these structural issues, many of the mothers we spoke with articulated perspectives on marriage as a patriarchal institution that echoed feminist and queer leftist critiques of same-sex marriage as a heteronormative assimilationist project.[12] These same tensions between assimilation and resistance have characterized academic research on LGBTQ families.[13] This view does not adequately address the ways the slippery tendrils of power invade our intimate familial spaces. As Vanessa and Cathy make clear, mothers have been able to live with contradictions in how they understood and experienced marriage, making clear that "lesbian mothers are never merely assimilationists or resistors" (Hequembourg 2007, 173).

The question of assimilation versus resistance is deeply intertwined in frameworks celebrating choice as equality. While the notion of resistance may be romantic, it is important to think critically about how deeply embroiled it is in power and in what ways the notion of resistance has been co-opted. Critiques of queer mothers coming from the left emphasize heteronormative, minivan-driving lesbian moms as assimilationist, selling out the radical potential of queer culture and sexuality.[14] Yet this argument, like those by conservatives about unwed mothers, also relies on the assumption that choice is free of social constraints. The core of the leftist critique is that lesbian moms made bad (consumer) choices—they secured mortgages, bought minivans, purchased sperm, and modeled their families on white suburban nuclear two-parent family ideals instead of embracing new familial models. While I may agree far more with this view than with conservative perspectives, I want to point out that both frameworks operate within the *choice-as-liberty-without-structural-constraints* framework. A critique of "choice" in sociopolitical debates about queer families must challenge the framework of assimilation versus resistance. We need to put those arguments into the broader context in which decisions about family-making are made. In a system not set up to recognize same-sex couples and the families they form, parents have to find ways of negotiating the limitations placed on them. No one can be free of power. Even while we protest its workings, we are imbricated in them. Even our resistance reinforces the scripts we push against: "Lesbian mothers are both enabled and constrained by the workings of power by which they are constituted" (Hequembourg 2007, 158). Accounting for these complex workings of power requires attention to race, gender, and class politics.

From a reproductive justice perspective, the more fundamental inequality—than not having the choice to legally wed—is that the rights of citizenship are tied to marriage at all. Legal scholar Melissa Murray argues that the lack of attention in the marriage equality debate to the ways social structure shapes "romantic and sexual decision-making" has grave consequences: "Constructing marriage as a choice that should be exercised if one is eligible renders invisible the constraints that make marriage a practical impossibility for the poor and working class, even if it is legally possible. And perversely, the economic misfortunes of this underclass are blamed on their 'choice' to forego marriage, when in fact their economic marginality may precede the decision to forego marriage" (2014, 430). Despite political claims to the contrary, marriage is unlikely to lift unwed mothers out of poverty.[15] Women are not experiencing poverty because they made bad choices, but, rather, because of systemic inequality. Marriage and adoption laws have differential effects on a broad range of people, not just lesbians. Paying attention to race, class, and gender, in addition to sexual orientation, makes evident the ways marriage functions as a legitimating arm of the state for mothers outside the nuclear family ideal.

Mainstream narratives of equality not only deny the salience of race, gender, and sexuality as forces of structural inequality, but in fact *rely upon* their exclusion to define "equality" through neoliberal emphasis on inclusion and choice. Lisa Duggan explains: "Neoliberalism, a later twentieth century incarnation of Liberalism, organizes material and political life *in terms of* race, gender, and sexuality as well as economic class and nationality, or ethnicity and religion. But the categories through which Liberalism (and thus also neoliberalism) classifies human activity and relationships *actively obscures* the connections among these organizing terms" (2003, 3). Social categories of identity organize access to social rights, privileges, and supports, while simultaneously denying the salience of race, gender, and sexuality. It is the disavowal of power relations animating these categories that allows "equality" to be narratively constructed as outside the influence of social context. This is not a new story.

Toni Morrison argues in *Playing in the Dark* that ideas of "Americanness" have historically been constructed "through and within a sometimes allegorical, sometimes metaphorical, but always choked representation of an African presence" (1992, 38). Her analysis illuminates the complex ways race functions as a covert presence in the US national narrative of progress and equality: "The rights of man, for example, an organizing principle upon which the nation was founded, was inevitably yoked to Africanism. Its history, its origin is permanently allied with another seductive concept: the hierarchy of race."(1992, 17). Morrison's analysis suggests that "American" conceptions of freedom and equality cannot be fully understood without attention to race, because the presence of African Americans has always existed as a representational counterpoint to social allegories of equality in the United States. In other words, constructions of American freedom and equality are only fully understood in the context of the history of slavery and systemic racial oppression. Extending this analysis into the realm of legal recognition, it would seem that considerations of equal protection and due process, as guaranteed by the Fourteenth Amendment, would similarly invoke, whether explicitly or covertly, the history of racial inequality as a precursor to full American citizenship. It is difficult to imagine the same-sex marriage debate not being constructed through public allegories of race and equality.

Conclusion

The denial of the continued existence of structural inequality in the United States was central to both liberal LGBTQ marriage activists and conservative activists and politicians in the years prior to 2015. Both sides embraced a view of government as neutral regarding race, gender, sexuality, disability, and religion. On this basis we can see the ways laws and policies can be imagined as outside the realm of influence of people's lived experiences: the story of a neutral state, free of limits or preferences, is necessary for narratives of individual liberty and equality to succeed. Yet, as Roberts makes clear, "private choices are shaped and facilitated by social institutions and government action" (1996, 388–89). The lived experience of citizenship of the mothers we spoke with provides a view of power inequalities and the gaps in family protection for the most economically vulnerable families in society. Assimilation versus resistance frameworks do not fully make sense in the context of intersectionality. Queer mothers of color are socially located in ways that make evident the contradictions often found between systems of sociocultural meaning available for understanding differences between women. What looks like conformity on a gender or sexuality front may be conceptualized as resistance on a racial-ethnic front, or vice versa. In the next chapter, I introduce a theoretical framework for exploring allegory at ethnographic, sociopolitical, and genealogical levels.

2

Reproductive Allegories

Family Trees and National Belonging

The family genealogy website I joined didn't let me list my wife, unless I listed myself as husband, or put one of us in the father category for our children. The quick fix leaves one of us represented as a pink box, the other as blue. No space for two moms here. I switched to another website that wasn't color-coded by gender, but the family tree template was fairly consistent across platforms. In the policy section addressing "non-traditional families" the site explains: "WikiTree doesn't require traditional family structures." Patriarchal heterosexual couplings are "just the default" setting, but adjustments can be made to represent same-sex couples: "It's slightly trickier with parents. It is possible on WikiTree for a child to have two male parents or two female parents. This may be appropriate for living people if the child is marked as *Non-Biological*. However, for non-living people, *genetic connections should be used* when they're known [emphasis original]."[1] These instructions suggest that genetics determines "truth" in this system of meaning. The site provides detailed instructions on how to mark a child as "*Non-Biological,*" when this is expected, and when it is required. Legitimacy is codified through biology; outsiders are marked. The family tree is an allegory about kinship, reproduction, and belonging, reaffirming that "traditional" families are connected biologically through heterosexual reproduction.

As an adoptee, I don't fit the genealogical template either. I only appear to fully belong because I refuse to label myself "*Non-biological.*" Adoption reveals the inconsistencies in social definitions of family legitimacy. Being adopted supposedly redeems me from the stigma of my illegitimate birth. Yet, at the same time, "DNA confirmed" is the gold standard of relationships in this genealogical web-space. I seem to be passing as real.

The website's template essentially functions as a script, shaping the way individuals and families perform kinship. I spent ages trying to figure out a way to represent having more than one set of parents. I try adding my half-biological siblings and sneaking my birth parents in through the back door, without success. *We are not legible here.* The website minces no words: "WikiTree only allows a person to have *one mother* and *one father*. This provides the basic structure for family trees. This means that with adoptions, step-children, etc., a choice needs to be made [emphasis original]."[2] The "choice" they urge users to make is between documenting parental relationships based in biology, or those based in affective relationships and lived experiences. Yet what of law and power? These instructions articulate social tensions about family and identity historically framed as nature versus nurture. Yet this framework ignores the role of social power in defining family legitimacy. "The basic structure for family trees" is reproduced every time a user enters a profile or views a family tree.

The emphasis on DNA in online genealogy websites both draws on and fosters a broadly accepted social narrative that biology determines "natural," and, thus, "real " family ties. Social narratives about family trees, heritability, likeness, and difference reinforce notions of family as biological, natural, and, thus, unchanging. The extension of this story, of course, enshrines heterosexual reproduction as natural. As feminist sociologist Laura Mamo explains: "Nature, or the 'facts of life,' is today biologized and geneticized. The conception narrative, which describes the origin of life, is webbed together with two other narratives: the kinship narrative, which explains the ties that make a family, and the genetic narrative, which explains individuals and their connections to the past and future" (2004, 192). Naturalized fictions of family and history are reproduced through the "common sense" tension between nature and nurture.

I was struck by the rigidity of the genealogy websites, as I tried to both research our families' past and document our present. Fictions of race, gender, class, sexuality, and family are embedded in the operating systems of free and commercial websites dedicated to family history research. Genealogy is literally a computer application program that provides a template for what counts as family. Participating requires negotiating with mainstream definitions of family legitimacy encoded in the application as biological and therefore natural. Engagement with these programs reproduces macrosocial definitions of family legitimacy at the individual and familial levels.

My discussion of adoption demonstrates that the definitions of family that structure the social practice of genealogy are more about recognizing socially legitimate family relationships than accurately portraying biological connections. Mamo argues: "Nothing within biology demands the nuclear family. It is a cultural and social system enforced by regulations and reinforced by legal discourse, medical practices, and cultural norms. Yet in the United States it is the nuclear family, bound by blood and legal arrangements of marriage and adoption, that represents social order, idealized kinship, and legitimate relations" (2007, 5). Family genealogy records the official story—legitimate marriages and births—and defines who gets left out or stigmatized. These rules are not random. They are deeply rooted in public law and policy. Stratified reproduction—"the arrangements by which some reproductive futures are valued while others are despised"—is useful for exploring how regulating legitimacy through family policy is connected to the reproduction of families that support the status quo (Ginsburg and Rapp 1995, 3). The techniques by which this inequality is accomplished and maintained are socially and historically specific, and it is important to critically consider both consistencies and contradictions in the ways legitimate kinship is defined in different eras and locations.

In the western patriarchal model, lineage is traced through legal matrimony. Children's status as legitimate citizens is determined through their mother's marriage to a man. Historically, legitimate lines of inheritance determine property transfer, class status, and social recognition, creating legal links between families and society. But what of the people who fall between the lines? Legitimacy is the axis upon which both social and legal recognition of family turns, which has profound consequences for families and persons deemed illegitimate. If my family is illegible in the online templates for kinship in the present, I have to wonder who was left out in the past.

What would a *genealogy of illegitimacy* look like? Not only would previously unrecognized kin become visible, but so too would the relations of power regulating these exclusions. This critical feminist genealogy fills in the blanks perpetrated by power inequalities at multiple intersecting locations of social meaning. What are the social functions of legitimate versions of family history? How are these stories naturalizing kinship reproduced at individual, familial, community, and structural levels? How has the concept of legitimacy structured political debates about same-sex marriage and adoption?

We cannot separate sociopolitical narratives from the lived experiences of families and individuals, or from the inequalities from which these stories divert attention. I read competing social narratives about queer kinship as allegories that articulate culturally and historically specific definitions of and expectations for family and citizenship in the United States. Members of all families have to make sense of their experiences through the contradictory definitions proffered by government, laws, policies, and media. According to critical race scholar Peggy Cooper Davis, "We lack a theoretical framework—a story of relationships among individuals, families, and the state—that makes sense of our conflicting beliefs about families and family values" (1997, 11). Personal stories interact with news media discourse about politics in complex and often contradictory ways. Narratives emerging from news and policy discussions inform the ways people learn to see the world. Yet they also function in relation to structural inequality and the laws enforcing it. I draw on narrative analysis in a broad range of disciplines, including cultural anthropology, critical race theory, women's and gender studies, sociology, and American studies. I construct a framework for exploring contemporary discourse about lesbian-headed families that emerges from interviews with mothers, news and policy dialogues, and the realm of reproductive and family law.[3] The stories issuing from these sites function in varying ways at different levels of society, and thus, require different modes of analysis.[4]

I explore allegories as links between individuals, families, media, and public law and policy—points of contact, measures of negotiation over social and political meaning. I engage a critical intersectional perspective that embraces tensions at the center of this issue. In the words of feminist scholar Vivian M. May, "As a critical orientation, intersectionality is forward-looking and historically focused. It asks that we imagine future possibilities and reconsider omissions, past and present, from a 'matrix' mindset: it also helps to expose historical silences and to understand oppression and privilege as lived experiences and processes situated in and shaped by material, political, and social conditions" (2015, 6). This analytical approach helps delineate the subtle and covert ways that power shapes family life, as well as the ways that families navigate inequality. The driving questions in this chapter concern how social definitions of legitimate families are reproduced at multiple levels of social meaning through the negotiation of narrative meanings of family. I argue that critical genealogical considerations of a broad population of people designated as "illegitimate"—in the past and the present—can be read as allegories about complex relationships between individuals, families, and nation. This approach makes visible the ways that white supremacy, patriarchy, compulsory heterosexuality, and economic inequality are reinscribed in social understandings of family, equality, and nation. I would like to suggest that an allegorical reading, grounded in a critical intersectional approach, provides a useful lens through which to discuss the deep complexities and contradictions between the stories coming from these different sites.

Ethnographic Allegories: Legitimacy and the Presumption of Parentage

> RAE: It is the duty of the state to protect everyone equally. And now even folks with money are not fully protected. Basic equality is not being afforded to people all over the country.

Rae is an African American mother of two biracial children, whom she coparents with her ex-husband, the father of her daughter, Hannah, and her ex-girlfriend, the other mother of her son, Jackson. At the time of our interview in 2008 the legal landscape of family law and policy in the United States regarding same-sex marriage and adoption was uneven and swiftly changing. Rae was a part-time student pursuing a master's degree in women's studies. She was also working part-time in the non-profit sector, parenting full-time, and practicing and performing with her band, the Honeybees, on a regular basis. Her personal charisma and easy smile make it obvious why she gravitates to performing and her band has a local following. In this section, I draw on Rae's stories to explore ethnographic allegory as a mode of analysis and to use that framework to illuminate relationships between family-making, social legibility, and inequality. I explore divisive political debates about same-sex families from Rae's perspective as a queer mother of color who is defined by the state as illegitimate.

Rae is socially located in a particularly vulnerable position in regards to parental rights. She and her ex-partner Jasmine—a white woman—conceived their son with the sperm of Jasmine's brother, who had no interest in being a legal or relational father. In the state of Iowa in 2003, when Jackson was born, unwed mothers were not allowed to enter the name of the father on the paperwork for birth certificates at the time of birth. Unmarried parents were required to file a separate set of forms declaring paternity in order to have the father's name listed, at which time an amended document would be issued. Without a second-parent adoption, there were no options for a second mother to be added. Thus, Rae is listed as Jackson's only parent on his birth certificate.

Their family structure makes clear the ways that politics, much more than biology, regulate parentage, and, consequently, access to social resources and protections. The contrast between Rae's two children's relationships to the state is instructive, illustrating that parental rights and responsibilities are determined by marriage, not biology. Her oldest daughter, Hannah, was born while Rae was married to a man, and her birth certificate establishes her "legitimacy" by listing both her parents. If Rae had used a sperm donor when she was legally married to a man, her husband would still automatically be listed as father on the birth certificate. Legal marriage determines parental rights for fathers in the United States under the doctrine of "presumption of parentage."

Same-sex marriage was not legal in Iowa in 2003, when Rae and Jasmine's son was born. Therefore, in the eyes of the law, he was born illegitimate to an unwed mother (though his two mothers were together at the time of his birth). As legal scholar Zanita E. Fenton explains:

> The presumption of legitimacy that inheres from the marriage of a child's parents, allows these children to automatically receive benefits, not readily available to non-marital children, including rights of inheritance, wrongful death damages for the death of the father, child support, United States citizenship, and many other government benefits. In addition, efforts to protect adopted children from the stigma of illegitimacy by sealing their birth records, continues the general stigma associated with birth status, both for these children and for those never adopted or "legitimized." (2014, 23)

Rae and Jasmine's son has two parents, yet Jasmine was unable to legally recognize her relationship with him without going through the expensive and invasive process of second-parent adoption. In Iowa, second-parent adoptions were legal, but so expensive they were financially out of reach for Rae and many others. As a result, Rae is his only legal parent, though his two mothers share custody.

Rae and Jasmine had the "choice" to protect their family relationships through second-parent adoption. However, they could not afford it, so it was not really a viable option. In a socially stratified capitalist society, having the option to purchase family protections is not the same as equality. Indeed, as critical race scholar Dorothy Roberts argues, US law and policy "protects all citizens' choices from the most direct and egregious abuses of government power, but it does nothing to dismantle social arrangements that make it impossible for some people to make a choice in the first place" (1997, 294). Roberts's important analysis of race and reproductive justice demonstrates that women of color and white women, and poor and middle-class women have historically been situated differently in relation to social institutions governing the range of choices available. As a queer mother of color, Rae is located outside the family protections offered heterosexual married parents. The intersection of her sexual orientation with her identity as a single African American mother limits Rae's access to family protection by publicly representing her as outside social definitions of legitimate family in multiple ways. As a single Black mother, she is more likely to experience discrimination in the labor market, which circumscribes her ability to legally protect her children.

Rae's family-making experiences make visible the ways that sexual orientation intersects with race, gender, and class through regulatory schema that circumscribe access to tangible family protections for nonmarried parents and their children. Her family is defined as illegitimate because she is not married. She cannot legally marry the mother of her child because they are not heterosexual. They cannot "legitimize" their son through second-parent adoption because they cannot financially afford the legal fees. This is stratified reproduction. No one should have to buy protections that are accorded by law to other citizens. This unequal distribution of rights and protections for children and parents is normalized and obscured by public policy narratives emphasizing the legitimate structure of "natural" and "traditional" families.

We can read her life—or anyone's—as allegorical through the ways social narratives inform her view of the world, as well as how her life story speaks beyond itself to articulate the contours of social power relations. Rae's interactions with law and policy can be read as a form of allegory in which we are able to trace "patterns of associations that point to additional meanings" (Clifford 100). There are connections between the stories she tells and those she receives from various sources, as her life stories are informed by the ways she is "narrated" in social interactions. She must engage with media representations that shape social understandings of single Black mothers, and with governmental definitions of motherhood and family. Her engagement with and resistance to social narratives defining queer mothers of color speak to the ways that families positioned as illegitimate—or *queer*—make meaning and navigate social worlds not designed to support them. I read her life story as allegorical, rather than "representative."

I draw on a tradition of person-centered ethnography, in which a central goal is to grasp the "insider" view, in order to explore how their lives are navigated and made meaningful in a complex world.[5] In drawing on this anthropological tradition, I explore how families headed by queer mothers make meanings from their experiences of negotiating a highly intricate world that often misrecognizes them. Yet it is also important to emphasize that there is no "representative" insider view of being a queer mom. "Allegory prompts us to say of any cultural description not 'this represents, or symbolizes, that' but rather, 'this is a (morally charged) *story* about that'" (Clifford 100). Ethnographic analysis does not rely on whether the research sample is representative or not; that language belongs to other academic frameworks. Rather, the emphasis here is deeply contextual. We learn about the intimate workings of power in everyday lives through the stories of mothers socially defined outside "normal" or "traditional" families.

Rae's experiences are shaped by her social locations as female, queer, middle class, and Black. Laws, policies, and social interactions regulate her life in varying and sometimes contradictory ways, and she draws on a range of cultural meaning systems to navigate various aspects of her identity. Exploring relationships between family-making stories, sociopolitical narratives about queer families, and family law and policy helps us map out the complexities of power relations as they shape family lives. Cultural representations come to us in the form of stories, and that is how we learn to reproduce social meaning. Reading allegorically is a way of linking individual stories to larger cultural and political narratives.

Sociopolitical Allegories: Bedtime Stories and Stratified Reproduction

In the 1990s a series of laws focused on family were passed that served to reproduce heterosexual white patriarchal middle-class families, and to dismantle some of the most socially vulnerable families in the United States. Political debates about family values identified same-sex marriage, welfare reform, immigration laws, and policies regulating adoption as key to "saving the family," and thus, the future of civilization. The stories used to justify governmental disinvestment in families make visible the ways that *everyone* outside the nuclear family ideal is labeled deviant, yet in different ways. Narrative is crucial to this policing. In this section I explore two distinct ways that allegories function in the sociopolitical realm. I consider how the deployment of sociopolitical allegories about mothers and children of different races, ethnicities, classes, sexualities, and disabilities were used to justify the passage of punitive social policies designed to combat "illegitimacy." I also explore how these same stories shaped the lived experiences of families defined outside the white, heteronormative, middle-class, nuclear family ideal.

The passage of DOMA lends structural weight to discussions of two-mom and two-dad families as threats to the nation, and informs the ways LGBTQ families interact with governmental institutions. Being excluded—from coverage, from definitions of family—teaches parents and children where, whether, and how we belong in society. Lerman and Weaver remind us that personal understandings of citizenship are constructed through interactions with the state: "At the same time that they glean lessons about the nature of government, interactions with the state influence individuals' perceptions of their own political standing, membership, and efficacy. Institutions allow us to observe how the state treats and responds to people 'like us'" (2014, 12). We learn about our own status as citizens by assessing stories about the way the state treats other families. The mothers we spoke with were not only highly attuned to the social and political contexts in which they lived, but were vigilant about how their families were treated, socially read, legally recognized, and publicly narrated—in other words, about their legibility.

Rae is regularly inundated with social messages that tell her that people "like us" are deviant second-class citizens. Not being seen as who you feel yourself to be, not having your family legible to others, can be painful. It causes stress, anxiety, and anger. When the state labels your family illegitimate, and public media is jammed with conservative tales about the dangers of queer families and the bad economic and reproductive choices mothers of color supposedly make, you have to find ways of surviving, communities where you feel at home, and avenues through which to resist. Children in particular need to learn how to critique, counter, and redefine negative social messages they will likely hear about families like their own.[6] The mothers we interviewed paid close attention to media narratives about same-sex couples with children in order to gauge how their families might be treated. In a sense, they employ a practice of reading allegorically to assess their own sense of belonging in the nation.

Allegories are about relationships between small stories and big stories—personal narratives, social fables, historical tales, legal fictions. As Loseke reminds us, "Socially circulating formula stories are continually created, modified, challenged, and discarded. Some stories, such as the 'Standard North American Family' with its categorical identities of husband/wife, mother/father, son/daughter, and so forth . . . or 'citizenship' with its identities of citizen/noncitizen . . . were authored long ago and observers examine how such stories are continually reproduced through the work of social institutions and practical reasoning in daily life" (2007, 664). Family narratives do not simply mirror public representation of families, nor is the reverse true in any straightforward sense. Families function in negotiation with social narratives about kinship and citizenship, as well as through concrete interactions with the laws and policies shaping their access to social resources and protections.

Mothers responded to the negative messages about their families by purposefully introducing books and media about families like their own, by creating communities of supportive friends and family, and by attending events like Pride and Family Week. In our interview in 2005, Lisa and Allison, a white lesbian couple living in San Jose, California, discussed children's books:

ALLISON: When we did the stepparent adoption we went out to lunch with my sister and another couple that had been through adoption too. And my sister bought us a bunch of books. And she had like gone on Amazon and typed in—

LISA: Which apparently has these really crazy reviewers who will go in and write reviews of these children's books—you know, they're like board books for babies with "gay" characters in them. And people will write these reviews about how *horrific* and *culture-destroying* these books are. And then Jillian gives us a bunch of these books, and we're looking and they're sort of nice, but we're like, these are not like insanely or overtly gay.

ALLISON: It's not *Heather Has Two Mommies*. You know, it's just "every day, everywhere, babies are walked" and in the picture there are all kinds of different couples. But I just think it's really cool how . . .

[We all laugh.]

SANDI: How horrific!

ALLISON: I know! Weakening straight parents, let me tell ya [said sarcastically].

[Baby Eleanor laughs]

LISA: Is that funny, Eleanor?

ALLISON: I just think it's really cool that we've been given a lot of different books. I think that's really cool—

LISA: —that those books exist—

ALLISON: —and that you can get them. They're not just from some weird distributor—

LISA: —some woman that's just hand-stamping them in her own basement.

As this discussion hints, *Heather Has Two Mommies*, a 1989 children's book that tells the story of a white toddler with two white mothers, has been the subject of controversy since its publication. In conservative political discussions *Heather Has Two Mommies* was offered as proof of the breakdown of the family and a portent of the downfall of Western civilization, and it figured prominently in congressional debates in the 1990s about the passage of DOMA.

The series of social controversies over the presence of the book in libraries and public schools in the 1990s elevated it to a symbol of the contested concepts of "family values" and "legitimacy" on both sides of the argument. The mothers engaged in the above dialogue use sarcasm to diffuse the sting of public commentary about the "culture-destroying" effects of queer families. The quips respond to what, in their mind, are ridiculous views, but their comments also implicate structural power. The humor in the last few lines about the availability of the book is grounded in an understanding of the politics of knowledge production, representation, and power relations. "[Alison:]They're not just from some weird distributor—[Lisa:]—some woman that's just hand-stamping them in her own basement." Representation and public visibility of lesbian- and gay-headed families is politicized, and Lisa and Allison's comments reflect an understanding that the currency of political arguments are public stories and representations.

In public narratives that emerged from conservative legislators and pundits about same-sex marriage, the children's book *Heather Has Two Mommies* was offered as evidence of the dangers of homosexuality for the future of the nation. Representative Melton D. Hancock, of the Seventh District of Missouri linked family legitimacy with public media, socialization, and education in his congressional amendment to the Improving America's School Act of 1994: "Some Members may ask why this amendment is necessary at all. Many may not be aware of what sort of prohomosexual propaganda is actually infiltrating our public schools. Believe it or not, right now in community after community, our children are being exposed to the homosexual lifestyle as early as elementary school. That lifestyle is presented in an approving manner and as a legitimate alternative lifestyle. This clearly defies the values of the overwhelming majority of parents and taxpayers throughout America" (*Congressional Record* March 24, 1994, 1542). The representative is appalled that the homosexual "lifestyle" is presented to children as "legitimate." These are not the "values" of most Americans, he argues. He continues: "In New York City, even elementary schools are exposed to prohomosexual propaganda, including two books entitled, 'Heather's Two Mommies,' [*sic*] and 'Daddy's Roommate.' This is a clear effort to target our young people" (*Congressional Record* March 24, 1994, 1542). Conservatives excoriate this bedtime story as evidence of the moral decline of the United States and the insidious "gay agenda," citing it repeatedly in congressional testimonies. The New York City School Board includes *Heather Has Two Mommies* in an optional reading list promoting cultural sensitivity and awareness of diversity in their elementary school curriculum.[7] Queer parents often see reading *Heather Has Two Mommies* as positive for their children's sense of belonging in society. One of the striking features of this allegory is that it is shared *and* contested. *Heather Has Two Mommies* is the common narrative, yet it holds drastically different meanings for different people.

Each of these conflicting perspectives enacts a sociopolitical allegory that links the socialization of children with the future of the nation. Historian Robin Bernstein asks how stories about children can be so flexible that they can be used to support opposing political agendas: "How did childhood acquire so much affective weight that the exhortation to 'protect the children' seems to add persuasive power to almost any argument? How did the idea of 'childhood innocence' become a crucial but naturalized element of contests over race and rights?" (2001, 2). Much of this debate over family values was about competing visions for the nation's future, and these projections were deeply racialized.

The debate over DOMA was part of a larger policy agenda concerned with the politics of reproduction and family. In the 1990s public discourse was saturated with rhetoric citing "family breakdown" as the cause of contemporary social ills. The details of said breakdown were different, depending on the population under consideration, but converged around the idea of the irresponsible childbearing and rearing by mothers in a range of social locations. Unmarried mothers—whether women receiving AFDC benefits, undocumented immigrant-mothers of children who were US citizens, or queers—were the targets of both conservative and centrist political ire. Reproductive justice scholar Laura Briggs explains: "In the welfare reform debate, conservatives painted families that needed public benefits as Black, Latinx, immigrant, or Native. The more successful they were in demonizing people of color and welfare, the less public support there was for anyone's household, even if it was middle-class and white" (2017, 11). Racial narratives were woven into the discourse at the most basic level. Policy proposals focused on regulating the reproductive capacities of women deemed "unfit" as mothers, because they are not in legally sanctioned marital relationships with "productive citizens" (i.e., legally employed men). Political discussions about unfit mothers drew on a deep history of racist political representations of women of color. As philosopher Robert Gooding-Williams argues, "But over and beyond contesting false characterizations, a critique of racial ideology should also explore the ways in which explanations and other representations of black bodies function as forms of sociopolitical imagination. To be more precise, it should investigate the ways that these representations present themselves as allegories of social organization and political community" (2013, 17). Gooding-Williams's analysis insists on considering the social function of racialized narratives. In this political debate legitimacy was figured as white, straight, and middle-class. Mothers of color came to signal illegitimacy and bad mothering without their race being explicitly named.

The concept of illegitimate family and citizenship links these arenas of policy. In public discussions of poverty in the United States in the 1990s, illegitimacy gained consensus among conservatives and centrists alike as the primary cause of social chaos and economic decline, as evidenced by crime, poverty, teen pregnancy, gang violence, and drug abuse.[8] This was most often represented as a primarily black and brown pattern that had begun to spread to white families. In the United States, as reproductive justice historian Rickie Solinger writes,

> Official discussions about reproductive politics have rarely been women-centered. More often than not, debate and discussion about reproductive politics—*where the power to manage women's reproductive capacity should reside*—have been part of discussions about *how to solve certain large social problems facing the country.* These social or economic or political problems have changed over time. And the fertility of different groups of women has been associated with solutions to different problems. But across time, the social-problem approach to female fertility has prevailed [emphasis original]. (2005, 4)

The most pervasive arguments about the social problems of the 1990s located the source in the bad choices of unmarried women. Their failures were described as dependency on the state, sexual deviance, and their poor socialization of children. Once illegitimacy was agreed upon as the central social problem driving all other social issues, policy responses then focused on regulating the reproductive behavior of "illegitimate" mothers and children, diverting attention from systemic critiques of US poverty and reproductive policies.

Media narratives and imagery—in the news, as well as in entertainment—are crucial to hiding power relations. As Bonnie Thornton Dill, Maxine Baca Zinn, and I have written in regards to the welfare reform, immigration, and family values rhetoric of the 1990s, "Narrative analyses of policy argue for the importance of recognizing that public policy dialogues are, indeed, *public* discussions situated in complex discursive, legislative, and sociopolitical histories. Legislative agendas do not exist in isolation from popular culture and public opinion, and, in our view, it is necessary to explore the relationships between shifts in public policy and widespread media narratives in order to fully understand the relations of power at work in such social shifts [emphasis original]"(1999, 264). Ideological stories suggest that heteronormative nuclear families, headed by patriarchal fathers and dutifully feminine mothers, are natural and normal and have been the traditional family form since the beginning of time. The research of feminist scholars makes the fallacy of this construction of the past glaringly obvious. In fact, the nuclear family ideal as we currently understand it is a relatively recent historical development.[9] What conservatives tout as "traditional" is more accurately grounded in the post–World War II family ideal represented in 1950s television— middle-class, white, and straight as a picket fence. In family values debates, the past, present, and future of the nation are all contested.

While aiming to rid the larger public of the social problems supposedly resulting from illegitimacy, in various manifestations, the multiple forms of legislation targeted the reproductive behavior of women outside the bounds of heterosexual legal marriage and citizenship. DOMA prohibited same-sex marriage. Aid to Families with Dependent Children (AFDC), the federal entitlement program, was dismantled and replaced by block grants provided to each state, along with a host of limitations, including a five-year lifetime limit on eligibility for benefits, obligatory workfare, and mandatory paternity identification. Changes in immigration laws increased border patrols, surveillance, and penalties for undocumented immigrants caught inside US borders, and also deepened restrictions on employment, benefits, and assistance for legal immigrants. Sociopolitical allegories function as a means of justifying punitive social policies designed to regulate women's reproductive behavior at the level of media and policy discussion. These massive legal changes made clear that some mothers and children were valued over others. The agreement attained among conservatives, centrists, and liberals that illegitimacy was the root of all social problems would prove profoundly important to how the same-sex marriage debate would play out. I will discuss the policy debate over illegitimacy in more depth in chapter 4.

These narratives also inform individual and familial interactions with social institutions. This, of course, shapes how people live their lives and how we learn to see ourselves and others. Rae tells a story about interacting with the social welfare system when she was pregnant that exemplifies the ways that public narratives about race, gender, class, sexuality, and motherhood converge to inform the lived experience of citizenship. She was several months pregnant in 2003, when she changed jobs. Her new employer required a three-month waiting period before her health insurance would be activated. She applied for Medicaid in order to maintain prenatal care throughout her entire pregnancy—a claim on her standing as a US citizen.

> RAE: You had to wait sixty or ninety days, and so in the short term I had to get Title 19, Medicaid, whatever it was, just to supplement, whatever, until my insurance kicked in. So here I am about to give birth and I have to go sign up for state aid medical. And the guy, bless his heart, was as cool as he could possibly be, but again, I wasn't going to lie. "I know who the *biological sperm donor* is, but *this baby doesn't have a father.*" Like you have to fill out all the paperwork. I'm like, "He's got another Mom, and I don't really know how to do your paperwork. And I'm not being difficult. I'm just being honest. I'm not gonna lie. I'm also not gonna name someone who says 'I don't want to be a dad. You know, I'm just giving you this stuff 'cause I know it will work.' You know." So the guys says to me, he's like, "You know what? That's cool." He's like, "Okay, but if your benefits or whatever—if you're ever audited . . ." Or whatever it is they do to see if you really should be getting benefits— "*You're gonna have to come up with something.*" He says, "*And the best thing I can tell ya is to say that you*

were really wasted one night and you had sex with multiple men and
you don't even remember who they are. And you got pregnant." And so
when he said that I did . . . I was just kind of like . . . really?

This governmental employee narrates her identity as a mother and a
citizen in relation to the state through hackneyed narratives about economically irresponsible Black women having one-night-stands with
multiple men.

Politics is bartered in stories. The Medicaid man needs a story that
fits into the state's box. Politicians need a tale that justifies destroying the
social safety net for mothers and children in poverty. Rae tried to tell her
story, but it didn't fit the narrative structure written by the state. There
was no space for the recognition of a Black lesbian mother. "Sperm
donor" was not part of the lexicon of the social welfare system. There
was no room for cognizance of multiple family forms: mothers were
only legible in relation to fathers. This story not only saturates widely
disseminated sociopolitical narratives, but it is activated and enforced
through welfare policies passed in the 1990s that require paternity information on applications for public assistance.

Reading this as a sociopolitical allegory entails an exploration of the
social functions of the story. Power is the absent character in this script.
How does this effacement of power function as a story blaming individual mothers for larger social problems? What makes this narrative
effective in justifying punitive social policies? In what ways is this story
reproduced again and again, in different sites, in various voices, through
a range of media?

These very old stories are entrenched in and through social policy,
media representations, and constructions of history, and they function
here through Higginbotham's notion of a metalanguage. Rae's story
shows us how race narrates social relations while denying its very existence. The Medicaid man did not have to mention race because it was
already embedded in sociopolitical allegories about Black women's irresponsible sexual decisions. Structural inequality based on intersections
of race, gender, sexuality, and class is reproduced and maintained while
simultaneously denying the social relevance of these categorizations.
Sociopolitical narratives do the work of racialization. As we see in Rae's
story, these ideologies are reproduced and performed in surprisingly sly

ways. Public narratives about women of color as sexually licentious have been a remarkably consistent storyline in the justification of reproductive control for the "betterment" of the nation.[10]

Genealogical Allegories: Unearthing Buried Roots

Conservative politicians at the turn of the twenty-first century spun narratives linking gender, race, sexual deviance, poverty, and illegitimacy as the new threat to the American family, and, by extension, society. Mothers and children outside the patriarchal heteronormative ideal—lesbians, women of color, immigrants, women experiencing poverty—were cast as dangerous for traditional family morality. Yet turning a critical eye on constructions of history makes clear that marriage and legitimacy have always regulated family and citizenship through exclusion. The "families have always been this way" narrative depends on the denial of anyone outside the boundaries of family legitimacy.

I interviewed Yvonne and Ronnie at Albuquerque Pride in 2007. They had driven almost four hours from the Navajo reservation in Tsaile, Arizona, in order to interact with families like theirs. It was particularly important to them that their five-year-old son be able to see other families with two moms and two dads, as he was the only child of same-sex parents where they lived. Ronnie locates their family in a "two spirit" history:

RONNIE: In Navajo tradition and culture we have twelve worlds. We've already gone past one—the first, the second, the third, and the fourth world. We're presently living in the fifth world. During the third world the sexes separated; it's called the *separation of the sexes*. Females went their own way and the men went their own way. Because there was a dispute upon how like women said they could do men's things and how men said that they could do female things. During that time *homosexuality existed*, because women needed their needs and men needed their needs. So, I guess you could say the hetero men slept with the two-spirit males and the females slept with the females that were two-spirited. In our culture it's not really called two-spirits. It's a—*we were called the Nadleehi*—basically homosexuality, because we carried the characteristics of male and female, for male

FIGURE 2.1. Yvonne and Ronnie, Albuquerque Pride. Photo credit: Sandra Patton-Imani.

and female, they *carried both characteristics.* And by the end of the third world, the Nadleehi, the homosexuals got together, had a little meeting, and then brought the—brought the male and female back together to live in a harmonious world, to continue on to the fourth. And hence, now we're in the fifth world based on what had happened in the past in the third world.

Ronnie presents as butch, and she places herself, through the telling of this story, in this Nadleehi history. Like many contemporary Indigenous queers, she draws on the Navajo origin story to locate herself and her family in a tradition much older than the United States. As she emphasizes, *"We* were called Nadleehi."

Stories of "two-spirit" people among North American tribes have been continually erased from mainstream history. Complex relations of domination supporting patriarchal white supremacy have whitewashed, if not buried, Nadleehi history (Denetdale 2009). In this origin narrative, gender, queerness, and Navajo tradition are inextricable and cannot be fully understood without attention to the social, political, and legal contexts in which these queer cultural practices were (and are) expunged. This erasure is fueled by settler colonialism and its assimilationist imperative. Cultural studies scholar Julia Watson emphasizes the disjuncture between Western genealogy and the family structures of Indigenous, enslaved, and colonized people in the United States: "If we turn to accounts of how to map genealogy for historical 'others,' it becomes clear that its practices have been formed around the norma- tive WASP subjects who first invaded and ordered America" (1996, 308). Genealogical templates for "legitimate" Eurocentric family trees cannot accommodate the multiplicity of sex-gender identities in the histories of North American Indigenous tribes, nor traditional matrilineal family structure.

Online family tree programs operationalize patriarchal family ideol- ogy, forcing exclusions by only offering narrow options. Not only are the categories for entry rigid, but the default settings—the social and cul- tural assumptions guiding this construction of family—are colorblind, heterosexual, and cisgender. Neither Yvonne and Ronnie, nor their Nadleehi ancestors, fit this template for family legitimacy. Each familial entry requires that gender be specified, by checking the male or female box; entries only allow space for one father and one mother. By collaps- ing gender and sex the program naturalizes patriarchal gender expecta- tions for men and women, foreclosing kin whose identities cannot be contained within these polarized categories. The inflexible options func- tion as a gatekeeping mechanism, enforcing ideological constructions of heteronormative gender identities as "common sense." Engaging with these programs continually reconstructs and maintains US patriarchal definitions of family in individual genealogical records.

Historian Jennifer Nez Denetdale's important research links this con- struction of "traditional values" with the erasure of Navajo (Diné) his- tory and culture, and the continued effects of colonization. She writes, "The conflation of Navajo traditional values with mainstream American values gives credence to the multicultural narrative that America has created about itself and renders invisible the links between the past and the present, wherein Native peoples still live with the consequences of dispossession and disenfranchisement" (2008, 289). In other words, a redefinition of Navajo history and tradition as synonymous with "main- stream American values" obscures our view of a history of policy and law that compels assimilation. Family has been a primary site of that project, as evidenced by a long and complex history of child removal from Native families to government-run boarding schools or white adoptive parents, in which socialization to American values was a central goal.[11]

I read the social practice of genealogy as an operationalizing narrative enforcing normative constructions of legitimate families by shaping individual documentation of family to fit its template. These genealogical frameworks correspond to social and legal definitions of legitimate kinship. The structure of the online family tree programs literally enforces a normative public family story, and this is useful for thinking about the complexities of interaction between families, social and political narratives about families, and laws and policies regulating legitimacy and access to social rights and protections.

Assimilation projects take many forms. Family tree applications function to naturalize historically and socially specific constructions of family (Eurocentric and patriarchal), while narrating them as universal. This enforcement of power inequalities is accomplished in complex ways, many of which function invisibly. The logistical boundaries of various computer applications available for exploring and documenting family history are regulated by the computer operating systems in which they function. New media scholar Tara McPherson's analysis of these systems shows how the seemingly culture-free realm of codes and computations is shaped and constructed in historically and socially specific ways: "The development of computer operating systems at midcentury installed an extreme logic of modularity that 'black-boxed' knowledge in a manner quite similar to emerging logics of racial visibility and racism. An operating system like unix (an OS that drives most of our computation, directly or indirectly) works by removing context and decreasing complexity" (2014, 181). The ideology of colorblindness is deeply encoded in the logics of knowledge production guiding our everyday understandings of family history in the post–World War II era. The logic of colorblindness as a sociolegal system is that race is "merely" a biological category with no inherent meaning, and, so, any attention to racial difference is spurious.

Native American Studies scholar Joanne Barker highlights the tensions produced by racialized terms of recognition. She writes, "The rub, as it were, for Native peoples is that they are only recognized as Native within the legal terms and social conditions of racialized discourses that serve the national interests of the United States in maintaining colonial and imperial relations with Native peoples" (2011, 6). "Blood quantum" terms of tribal recognition engage biologically based definitions of belonging that reinforce colonial US representations of family, race, tradition, and legitimacy as natural. Online family tree programs actually and allegorically function as assimilationist strategies, as tools of settler colonialism. Those outside the "black-boxed" knowledge of the computer and social operating systems—like those outside blood quantum definitions in the law—are invisible.

The absence of attention to context or complexity in the operating system unix is mirrored in the ideologies of colorblindness undergirding the US legal and ideological system in the post–World War II era. Dorothy Roberts explains how the logic of legal colorblindness depends upon the absence of attention to social context and power relations. While her work focuses on African Americans, her analysis of the ways that people of color are defined through rigid, ahistorical, and homogenous definitions of race are useful for thinking critically about the social locations of all peoples defined as "nonwhite": "This color-blind approach to equality disregards preexisting discriminatory structures that disproportionately harm blacks even in the absence of official discriminatory motive and that may require race conscious remedies. Color blindness permits racial subordination to continue by leaving intact institutions created by centuries of official and private oppression. Viewing all government recognition of race as equally pernicious manifests an incredible blindness to current arrangements of power" (1996, 366). The exclusions of this system of knowledge production are mirrored in family legitimacy as a social operating system. The "blindness" or evasiveness of this ideology is its purposeful denial of power as a force shaping families differently based on their social location in relation to white heterosexual middle-class family ideals.

The categories of the online family tree programs structure identity and family through clear lines of white patriarchal heredity. Unless I specify racial identity in the "notes" section for a person's entry in these applications, the default assumption is white. My own family history illustrates the narrative reproduction of whiteness. The process of racializing my family genealogy as white depends, first, on the omission of slavery in our oral family history, and, second, on the legal and social fictions of genealogical legitimacy that erase enslaved ancestors from the genealogical record. Laws regulating marriage, adoption, inheritance, antimiscegenation, labor, and property transfer support social views of legitimate family relationships as natural, traditional, and unchanging. This construction of whiteness obscures awareness that social categories of identity and family are shaped by power relations that shift over time, to accommodate the needs of the state. Constructions of the ideal white patriarchal family are the hinge upon which the outsiderness of "others" is defined; therefore, this public narrative of whiteness as purity must be critically explored (Dill 1988).

My family, it seems, has been passing as "white" for generations.[12] We thought we had always been Northerners, until I learned that my great-great-grandfather and his brother were the only members of their prominent Southern slaveholding family to enlist in the Union military during the Civil War. When they left the South for good, they left those family stories behind. This discovery links me to a meticulously documented lineage available on the WikiTree genealogy website, where I find histories including kings and queens, lords and ladies, and founding fathers. Along with knowledge of these prominent historical figures comes a disturbing history of enslavement, settler colonialism, and oppression that some of my ancestors were apparently eager to rebel against. What is my connection to this history? As an adoptee, I already have a troubled relationship to the very notion of genealogy—not belonging fully to either my adoptive or birth family histories.

Indeed, I have felt a sense of dislocation from family history since I was given a family tree assignment in elementary school. I remember feeling *outed* as an adoptee by the requirement, and deeply disturbed by the irreconcilable dilemma in which I was caught. I knew that the questions behind this assignment were about my biological ancestors, but, as an adoptee with sealed birth records, I felt trapped by the logic of the family tree story. All I knew about my birth parents at that point was that they were unmarried teenagers. If I embraced the social narrative of genetics, my biology should tell the story of my identity, leaving me with absence, disappearance, and sealed records. This tension is often a palpable impediment to a sense of belonging in family, society, and history, and, in fact, is the impetus for many adoptees to search for their origins (Yngvesson 2005, 2010). I could reconcile my parents, siblings, grandparents, aunts, uncles, and cousins as family because we loved each other, but as a kid I struggled with how to justify claiming the ancestors of my adoptive family as my own. I didn't know them, so how could they be shaping who I am? I was surrounded by social narratives celebrating biology and genetics as real family connections. What did that mean for me?

The metaphor that moves me toward reconciling these tensions is that of a grafted tree. Once the young branch of an apple tree is grafted onto a peach tree, it is nurtured by the roots of the peach tree as it grows. This image provides a way for me to imagine my life and identity as having been structured by both my birth and adoptive families. "Blood" only gains meaning through stories. I do not carry the bloodline or genetic legacy of my adoptive family encoded in my body. Yet my adoptive family's care, socialization, cultural meaning systems, and stories have shaped the growth of my bones and the substance of my flesh. I have some agency in this process when I move beyond rigid understandings of genetic heritability and focus on cultural socialization. I have a place to stand in these larger narratives about family, nation, and belonging.

My identification leans toward the insider-outsider kin in this grafted tree. In the interstitial spaces between stories of white pedigrees, I find my multiracial ancestors. I call her Great-Aunt Julia, as way of reclaiming her as kin, in resistance to the newly discovered horrors of enslavement I find in my family tree. One of my Southern great-grandfathers, seven generations back, "conveyed by deed of trust" three enslaved girls: "Sally and Charlotte two negro girls . . . and Julia a mulatto girl" to his son-in-law, for "the use and benefit of his daughter" on December 24, 1813.[13] Christmas gifts to his daughter? Was "Julia a mulatto girl," his daughter, too? Did he send her away to remove the reminder, for his wife, that he increased their wealth by raping and impregnating enslaved women? Virginia law dictated that the race of the child follow the race of the mother. The children Massa fathered with the women he enslaved were legally Black and enslaved like their mothers. Dorothy Roberts explains: "Racism created for white slaveowners the possibility of unrestrained reproductive control. The social order established by powerful white men was founded on two inseparable ingredients: the dehumanization of Africans on the basis of race, and the control of women's sexuality and reproduction. The American legal system is rooted in this monstrous combination of racial and gender domination. One of America's first laws concerned the status of children born to slave mothers and fathered by white men: a 1662 Virginia statute made these children slaves" (1997, 23). Who was Julia's mother? Under what circumstances did a white man impregnate this unnamed enslaved Black woman? How did he justify his barbaric behavior? Did he tell himself she wanted it? Did he know her name? Or did he just think of her as "Jezebel"?[14]

As I discussed in the previous section, narratives of Black women's deviant sexuality have been a consistent feature in public discussions of race, gender, class, sexuality, and family throughout the history of the United States. The circumstances of oppression these stories justify and obscure have shifted over time and place. Yet stories of women of color as sexually licentious manipulators have remained an insidious leitmotif articulating relationships between the state and mothers of color.[15] This narrative stream operates to support the status quo at multiple levels of society in profoundly complex ways. Political scientist Kimala Price discusses the differences in how intersectionality functions at individual, structural, and political levels, explaining that "structural intersectionality addresses the effects of oppression, such as racism, sexism, classism, heterosexism, trans oppression, and ableism, on the people's lives" (2018, 595). The suppression of the lives of Julia, her mother, and all those she viewed as kin from legitimate genealogies of family and national history demonstrates the sedimentation of structural oppression achieved through the regulation of intimate relationships. It clearly demonstrates that legitimacy, not biology, determined "real" kinship relations in the antebellum era. These absences in my family tree show us the ways that white supremacy, reproduction, gender, patriarchy, and capitalism shape how events and lives of the past become part of what we think of as history.

Structural inequality is constructed, debated, and enforced through the deployment of sociopolitical allegories. As Price explains, "Political intersectionality concerns the tactics employed by political actors to achieve their political goals and how those tactics may include or exclude groups of people within a movement or other collectivity" (2018, 595). Belonging is narrated through laws, policy debates, political fables, institutional practices, familial traditions, and social interactions. If ethnographic allegory provides a link from individual life stories to larger sociopolitical narratives and public laws, then we might think of genealogical allegory as working in the opposite direction. If we begin with broadly available sociopolitical allegories, we must make visible the scaffolding of social law they support and critically explore the ways that these complex regulations of family operate through legal fictions of exclusion that are reproduced both subtly and overtly in everyday life. In her award-winning book *The Hemingses of Monticello*, historian Annette Gordon-Reed discusses family legitimacy under slavery:

> The fictions and presumptions about bastardy and marriage served definite purposes in a legal system seeking easy ways to determine who was eligible to inherit property, who had the right to a child's labor, and who could be held liable for support of a child. Efficient as they may have been these fictions yielded answers that were not always truthful and certainly not always moral. Although they were tailor-made for the needs of the law, and not so perfect a fit for historical or biological conclusions, there is little doubt that they have come to represent what people take to be actual reality. They hover in the consciousness even when outside indicators suggest they should not be relied upon. (2008, 83)

Fictions and erasures of kin function in relation to laws defining family members beyond the pale as illegitimate. Constructions of whiteness were, and are, central to social definitions of legitimate family and citizenship in the United States.

Racial distinctions functioned to define close biological family members as *fictively not-kin*. In this social system Julia, a young girl, was given as property—"conveyed by deed of trust"—by the man who was likely her biological father, to a new mistress, who was probably her half-sister. Fictions of kinship and race designed to support the system of slavery precluded official acknowledgement of these relationships as anything other than owner and property. Who was Julia's family? Her white father and sister would not have acknowledged their filial relationships. What happened to her after she was taken from the family she had known? One of the most devastating horrors of enslavement was the separation of families, and the constant threat of loss. Who cared for her when she was separated from her mother? Who became Julia's kin? Sally and Charlotte, the two "negro girls" who were also "given" as property on

Christmas Eve, were likely counted among her family. Did Julia have children? Who fathered them? Who cared for them when she could not? How did she teach them to survive the horrors of enslavement?

Historians of slavery emphasize a tradition of collective childrearing that developed among enslaved families as a survival strategy in the destructive social system in which they were legally defined as property rather than full human beings. Extralegal cultural practices such as "jumping the broom," informal adoption, and a history of women mothering and caring for children to whom they had no biological connection provided avenues through which to perform family in meaningful and resistant ways that contributed to their physical, spiritual, and emotional survival under horrific circumstances.[16] Kinship among enslaved people was not strictly experienced through biological heritability, nor legal definitions of legitimate family.

We recognize a history of "other-mothering" among women of color, but why would we assume all these women were heterosexual?[17] Fictions of white heteronormativity typically foreclose considerations of ancestors as queer. We cannot impose contemporary categories of homosexuality onto people of the past, but neither can we assume that heterosexuality, as we currently understand it, was the exclusive norm. In his study of Black queer culture in the Southern United States, ethnographer Matt Richardson pushes the boundaries of "legitimate" history by making visible genealogies of oppression that have contributed to erasures of queer people of color:

> The Black queer ancestor is an unimaginable figure in mainstream diasporic memory. That she does not exist is a fiction of domination, an effect of trauma that has made her illegible even in alternative archives. To speak of her, one has to be creative and seize the means of archival production while pointing to her absence in written history and in memory. Black lesbian writing, then, is a practice of historical commentary, a trespass against demands of evidence, finding recourse and voice through the creation of imaginative counternarratives and embodied practices. (2013, 14)

Domination wrote history, and struggles over who and what were excluded continue to rewrite it. What if some of the "othermothers" who raised so many nonbio children were queer? Julia may have found comfort in the arms of another woman; we have no way of knowing the intimate details of her life. Whether "queer" or not—in the sense we understand it today—Julia likely experienced care from at least two mothers, and likely mothered many children, along with othermothers, whose family ties were relational, if not legally recognized. Engaging a definition of queer as a stance of critical resistance, I read her *queerly* as a family member defined outside the boundaries of genealogical legitimacy in the era in which she lived. Julia is included in a grafted family tree, as are the power relations that exclude her from the legitimate lineage.

My family tree exploration became a critical endeavor—personally and academically—revealing the social reproduction of whiteness, Blackness, gender, sexuality, queerness, and legitimacy. I didn't find Great-Aunt Julia in the legitimate family tree, but in the Fairfax County Virginia property transfer records. She only becomes legible as family when I move beyond the ideological template of genealogical legitimacy. I have to literally refocus my lens from birth certificates and census lists to property transfer records. She only becomes discernable, as family, when power relations quietly regulating the system are made visible. I reclaim her and the unnamed ancestors left out of the legitimate lineage, to which I, as a queer adoptee, also do not fully belong.

Conclusion: Resistant Narratives of Family and Nation

Allegories about family trees, with images of roots and branches and plots about apples not falling too far, reinforce notions of family as natural and unchangeable over time and across cultures. We learn to see families through Fibonacci-like patterns—templates for legitimate citizenship balanced with exponential pairings of straight, same-race, gender-specific opposites. Unless you prune them to conform, trees don't actually have that rigid structure. Branches are tangled and unpredictable—sprouts pop, leaves fall. Roots are buried so deep the foundation of the tree cannot be seen. We cannot call trees *or* families "natural" in any pure sense. Both are pruned and regulated by their interactions with the parts of the world in which their roots take hold. Not all land is hospitable to all kinds of trees. As Toni Morrison reminds us in *The Bluest Eye*, some "soil is bad for certain kinds of flowers. Certain seeds it will not nurture, certain fruit it will not bear, and when the land kills of its own volition, we acquiesce and say the victim had no right to live" (1970, 206). Some trees thrive in federally protected forests while others are logged and plundered for their resources. Context matters.

The metaphor of a grafted tree is useful for thinking critically about the systemic level of familial and national belonging. This allegory about kinship implicates power. Whose hand splices the branches and ties them together? Whose social vision shapes the planting and care of the orchard? Who waters and cares for fragile young shoots? Trees and families grow and are sustained in relation to the nurture they receive, but they are also maintained by the power relations shaping the care and resources provided. Who owns the land and how is it valued? Grafted trees are a useful allegory for thinking about the complex ways that nature, nurture, and power interact to shape social understandings of contemporary families. This template moves beyond simplistic either/ or questions about nature versus nurture, recognizing that biology, culture, and power interact to shape all family trees. A critical genealogical exploration makes evident the contingencies of what we take for granted as natural and normal in constructions of identity and family.

In the next chapter I turn to the origin stories and family-making narratives of the mothers we interviewed. I consider in particular narratives of interaction with the fertility industry and the adoption system. I explore the ways that mothering experiences are differentially stratified in relation to the state, depending on intersections between and among socioeconomic status, geographic location, and race and ethnicity. Engaging a critical intersectional analysis, I delve into the complexities of stratification between queer and heterosexual mothers, as well as among lesbians in different social locations.

3

Making Family

Origin Narratives and Stratified Reproduction

"Sophie likes to say she has five mothers," explains Mischa, one the moms of the then-eight-year-old that we interviewed in 2008 in Iowa City. "And one birth father," Sophie adds with a shy smile. As I have discussed, Sophie was adopted as an infant from Cambodia in 1999 by Kimberly—represented as a single white mother—and has lived in Iowa ever since. Her birth parents' rights were formally severed and she was reclassified as a legal orphan under US immigration law in order to become eligible for adoption.[1] Along with her brother Theo, she alternates each week between the two houses of her four white mothers.

While Sophie's family stories are by no means representative of queer families in the United States, I begin with them because they speak to a broad range of concerns. Sophie's family tree, like that of many children in the United States, is far more complicated than media narratives about families, or the available legal options for recognizing family relationships, would suggest. In the eyes of the law Sophie has two parents—both mothers—but her lived experience, like that of most humans, is more complex.

Children conceived through assisted reproduction—by straight and queer parents—can also, depending upon the medical and legal situations, have an array of parents, including egg donor, sperm donor, gestational mother, legal mother, and legal second parent (whether through the presumption of parentage or through second-parent adoption). Families constructed through assisted reproduction are certainly not immune to the vagaries of adult relationships and breakups, and new relationships can add stepparents to the roster.

Traditional family tree templates, as I have discussed, cannot accommodate the complexities of queer or adoptive families, nor do they accurately account for the ways that all families are shaped by the sociopolitical contexts in which adults come together, children arrive, and families are recognized. A genealogy of Sophie's family includes the family members she knows and loves, as well as her unknown Cambodian birth parents and their ancestors—her families by birth, law, and affiliation. This framework is useful for thinking about the ways that all families are shaped by power, often subtly and beneath our awareness. I would like to suggest that considerations of these family-making narratives at the level of lived experience makes evident that reproduction is stratified both between LGBTQ mothers and presumably straight mothers, and between queer moms in different social and geographic locations. The stories of these mothers articulate the contours of structural inequality at the level of lived experience and the complex ways in which it is enforced.

Whatever the circumstances of family-making, each of the mothers we interviewed participated in a system of stratified reproduction. Some of the mothers gave birth to children while in relationships with men. As their lives changed and their families expanded, their definitions of family shifted. Some of these families, like Sophie's, also morphed through breakups, divorces, and new relationships. Most of the mothers we interviewed formed families either through assisted reproduction or adoption. I focus this chapter primarily on these two paths to parenthood.

Nature Nurture Power

LISA: And we always joke that I'm the nature and she's the nurture, so anything that's wrong with Eleanor twenty years from now we can say is—

ALLISON: Down to both of us.

LISA: Down to both of us, evenly.

Adoption and assisted reproduction may seem, at first glance, to support opposing definitions of family in a social framework organizing kinship through narratives emphasizing nature versus nurture. Assisted reproduction is narrated as a miracle of science facilitating the genetic reproduction of offspring, while adoption narratives emphasize culture and care as the basis for defining family, yet both are organized by the notion of heredity. Exploring these family-making stories in social and historical context shows that both practices are strongly shaped by widely embraced social understandings of the white patriarchal nuclear family as a seemingly natural entity that has existed in all places across all time periods. Both social practices function as ways of reproducing this family ideal, while simultaneously denying the presence of power relations in either process through an emphasis on family-making through "choice." Queer parents participate, as do all parents, in relations of both inequality and privilege in their negotiations with the state over family protection and citizenship.

Stratified reproduction can be seen in stories of queer families constructed through US and transnational adoption practices, as well as the social practices of donor insemination and other medically supervised fertility treatments. As sociologist Laura Mamo's ethnographic research with lesbians using assisted reproduction makes clear, the medical-business practice of what she refers to as "Fertility, Inc." is deeply stratified by intersections of income, race, gender, and sexuality: "The cultural representations and material practices of infertility correspond with the stratification of reproduction across the twentieth century: wealthy (white) women receive support in order to reproduce and are able to access infertility services, while poor women and women of color do not receive such support" (2004, 32). Like adoption, the fertility industry functions as means through which to reproduce white heteronormative nuclear families. Both practices enact and enforce social definitions of fit and unfit parenthood that stratify access to legitimacy and social recognition, and, consequently, social resources.

Assisted reproduction and adoption both emphasize the importance of heritability organized through tensions between nature and nurture. This often translates to ideas about "real" versus "fictive" kin. In her classic 1991 ethnography, *Families We Choose*, anthropologist Kath Weston overturns this widely accepted dichotomy in her discussion of LGBTQ families: "The concept of fictive kin lost credibility with the advent of symbolic anthropology and the realization that all kinship is in some sense fictional—that is, meaningfully constituted rather than 'out there' in a positivist sense. Viewed in this light, genes and blood appear as symbols implicated in one culturally specific way of demarcating and calculating relationships" (1991, 105). *All* kinship relations are fictive. Genes and blood are *symbols*. The significance of this insight goes well beyond the recognition that nonbiological family relationships—what anthropologists historically called "fictive kin"—are often experienced as real by the people involved. While this is vitally important, so is the accompanying insight that even biological family relationships are fictive. We learn to think of family as natural, yet the ways people create and sustain kinship in particular social and historical contexts are always shaped by specific cultural, economic, and legal systems. Narratives of real and natural families have historically functioned as ideological scaffolding undergirding efforts to justify oppression against people whose gender, sexuality, race, ethnicity, class status, or disability deviate from patriarchal family ideals. Allegories of grafted trees make visible the ways that all families are shaped through their interaction with social institutions, laws, and policies regulating family-making. Grafting accounts for connections not originally conceived biologically, yet nurtured through the roots like all the other branches. All of Sophie's mothers are included in this story about kinship.

Assisted Reproduction: "I'd Love to Say Turkey Baster— Little Syringe"

KATIE: I think, like most couples who are in love and in committed relationships, we, too, started talking about early on wanting to have children, and finding out how the other felt about having children. And it was pretty clear right away that we both very much wanted to have [pause] *a* child. We didn't go beyond that. And so that was a given, and then we wanted to be together for a period of time before we pursued that. And that was, I don't know, a year, year and a half and then we proceeded to look into the options for making that happen.

Katie and Gwen are a white middle-class lesbian couple that live in Minneapolis, Minnesota. Some of the stories of pregnancy I share here, like theirs, emphasize the similarities in family-making among all kinds of people in a heteronormative society. Other mothers we interviewed were more deliberate in their resistance to mainstream expectations for family-making. Whether they identified with or resisted normative definitions of kinship, in forming their families these mothers had to engage with social institutions, laws, and policies regulating family relationships.

Family-making requires a different level of intervention and effort for people unable to conceive via sexual intercourse. Whether straight or queer, engaging with the fertility industry requires immersion in a family-making process organized through social and structural templates for family legitimacy. Each step of the process involves negotiation with public narratives embodied in interactions, representations, and policies. These regulatory practices are deployed covertly through the seemingly natural social categories of gender, sexuality, and race. The fertility industry is part of a capitalist marketplace in which all phases of the process are commodified, and, hence, access is deeply stratified by income and class location.

On one hand, reproductive medicine has created new possibilities for family-making by separating sex from conception, creating new patterns through which to define family. On the other hand, these options have the capacity to further entrench social expectations for reproducing heteronormative ideal families, or those as close to that as possible. Mamo argues, "Lesbian reproduction does not represent liberation from gender norms and the sexual and reproductive order, nor does it merely reinforce that order. Further, reproduction has always been and will continue to be stratified as groups are differentially supported and constrained in exercising their reproductive rights" (Collins 1999; Mamo 2007, 57). Gwen and Katie were fortunate enough to have health insurance that covered fertility treatments. This was not the case for many of the mothers we interviewed, and, thus, many of them pursued a DIY version of alternative insemination. Not everyone has access to the same range of options. Neither are families created in isolation. The decisions each couple makes occur within a particular set of social constraints and economic limitations that are linked to their complex and shifting locations in a stratified social order based on race, gender, class, sexuality, and geographic location.

Among the mothers we interviewed, each couple's ideas and definitions of family and kinship also influenced the decisions they made regarding assisted reproduction, which was particularly evident in discussions about which mother would seek to get pregnant. For example, the few adoptees articulated perspectives on heritability and biology that they linked to their experiences as adoptees. Each of the adoptee-mothers felt a strong need to be the mom that gets pregnant, though this was not simply explained by the desire for genetic connection. Other couples we spoke with had a range of responses to the question of who would carry their future child. A few of the mothers were clear about not wanting to get pregnant. Dana was unequivocal: "I wasn't giving birth." Lisa said she had never imagined herself as a mother, even prior to her own understanding of herself as queer. It was when she discovered she was a lesbian that motherhood became a real possibility for her because there was another woman to give birth. As Allison said, "The idea that I could be a mom and not have to actually give birth—[chuckle] I thought that was a great idea." Some of the couples had an understanding that if one of them did not get pregnant the other would try. Heather and Sara, a white couple who live in Los Cruces, New Mexico, laughed hard as Heather declared her profound relief that Sara had easily become pregnant. She said that watching Sara go through the pregnancy had strongly confirmed that feeling.

The two primary strategies for insemination used by these moms were assisted reproduction through medical intervention (including donor insemination, in vitro fertilization, fertility medicines), and the DIY method. Financial limitations were fundamental barriers to medically assisted reproduction for many couples. Paying out-of-pocket for such medical treatment is extremely expensive, and insurance coverage of fertility treatments is inconsistent across insurance providers. There are also differences depending on geographic location. Carol and Cheryl, whose fertility treatments resulted in triplets, explain the benefits of living in Massachusetts: "It's mandatory coverage for fertility. That's why you see so many multiples in Massachusetts. In general, not just of same-sex parents." This is the case in only a handful of US states. In the face of such limitations, people were strategic in their use of fertility medicines. Valory, a single Japanese (Okinawan) American mother who lives in Los Angeles, California, had health insurance that covered her fertility treatments, but, as she explained, "I know some people who don't—who don't have insurance and so they're like taking the Clomid cause they want to up their chances, since they're paying out-of-pocket." (Clomid is a fertility-enhancing medication taken in pill form that stimulates the production of ova so that more eggs are released at ovulation, increasing the chances for conception.)

DIY inseminations were important to some people because they wanted conception to be personal and intimate, not mediated through doctors, nurses, tests, and sterile instruments. Jen and Chris, a white middle-class couple living in Des Moines, Iowa, were adamant about avoiding the fertility industry. Jen explained, "We didn't involve any medical practitioners." While some of the mothers discussed a feminist approach to childbirth as part of their motivation for at-home insemination, even that was affected by the realities of insurance and the high cost of fertility treatments.

> ALLISON: Several years ago, we were at the Michigan Womyn's Music
> Festival and we went to a workshop—you know they have workshops
> there. And we went to this workshop on insemination.
> LISA: Or, yeah, lesbian conception or something.
> ALLISON: And, you know, you sit in the woods in a circle and you
> know. . . . Different people are talking about their different stories. So
> just listening to what other people in the world are experiencing. It's
> kind of amazing. And people who felt kinda like they wanted their
> insurance to cover fertility stuff. But the insurance wouldn't cover it
> until they had had you know unsuccessful attempts to get pregnant
> for six months. And they wouldn't consider lying about it. And we
> were like shoot, like just tell 'em . . .
> SANDI: [Joking] We've been trying and trying . . .
> LISA: I know—we don't know what's wrong! [laughter]

Along with their decision to avoid medical intervention also came, for a number of mothers, the desire for a known donor.

Shelley and Naomi, a middle-class white couple with two children who live in Taos, New Mexico, also felt strongly about excluding medical practitioners from their process, and about using a known donor. They did not have a donor in mind, but they were clear that they wanted someone to volunteer, rather than be asked. When no one initially volunteered, they purchased sperm from a sperm bank and inseminated at home.

NAOMI: Because word got out that we were trying, some friends said, "Oh, are you pregnant?" "No, we just tried today, but we'll let you know." And she said—you know, it was a married couple—the wife said, "Well, if you're not pregnant we'll give you sperm." And Shelley went, "Oh, wow."

This man became the donor for their first child, Eden. Sadly, he passed away shortly after their daughter's birth. A similar sort of serendipity seemed at work when they were ready to have their second child:

NAOMI: Both times it was the woman partner who had the idea.
SHELLEY: *She owns the sperm.* She really, she is the owner of that sperm. And if it doesn't come from the wife or the female partner or whatever it is, you're not gonna get any of that sperm.
NAOMI: Some of my very best friends who have husbands were like, "Don't come sniffin' at my door."
SHELLEY: Right. That's exactly what they did.

Shelley and Naomi made sense of these fortuitous genetic donations through their spiritual understanding of the world—somewhat new age, partially Eastern, and very much fluid and connected to the earth—which was supported and informed by the community in which they live. Shelly shared a story she called "chasing the Zen sperm."

SHELLEY: Right before the second insemination I was like, no, I'm not. . . . I don't want to do it, and called everything off. And the next morning I was like, "Oh, my god. What if I'm wrong? Do I really want to carry this kind of decision up against the universe, where everything has fallen into place and now I've decided no?!" And so I went home and said, "Okay, I've changed my mind. I don't want that kind of responsibility in a decision." And she said, "Well, Bruce is gone." And we literally packed the car in one hour.
NAOMI: I had fertile mucus. I had two lines on the ovulation stick. And he was in Colorado.
SHELLEY: Going to a Zen retreat.
NAOMI: No one had a way to get ahold of him, and Michelle, his wife, didn't even know what town he was going to. It was this obscure retreat center.

Shelley and Naomi hit the road and intercepted him on his way:

NAOMI: I was calling this monk in Boulder who was looking up different retreats that started with an L, cause that's all Michelle knew, that it started with an L, that the town started with an L. And finally, right when he was like, "Maybe it's this one," Bruce had gotten off the highway, uncharacteristically turned on his cell phone and called Michelle. And it all happened. We met at Subway. We got a crazy motel room in a place called Castle Rock. It was like a $30 motel room with the TV on the ceiling, and basically . . .

SHELLEY: Lacking a quarter vibrating bed—that's all it was lacking.

NAOMI: He did his thing and, you know, said a quick goodbye, handed it over and left so he wouldn't miss the beginning of his retreat. And Shelley inseminated me on the bed, with Eden watching cartoons. I'm like half-breastfeeding and trying to pull the speculum out.

SHELLEY: But I couldn't see. I had to go get my reading glasses, so I was like, "Wait a minute!"

NAOMI: It was so crazy. It was such a crazy scene. It was so crazy that we knew that if the spirit had a sense of humor that the child would choose to come right at that moment, because it would be such a good story.

The way they formed their family was grounded in their spiritually expansive understanding of family and community. As they describe:

SHELLEY: But when we left the seedy hotel room we looked up and it was almost the exact same sky as when Eden was conceived, where there were lots and lots of clouds, and it was gonna rain, or had already rained. And there was a *rainbow* going through a cloud—

NAOMI: —*straight down from the sky into another cloud.* In a line instead of any kind of arch. And it was the same exact rainbow as when Eden had been conceived. So I was driving and I grabbed her. And we knew. We knew it was done.

And, indeed, on this night their son Ezra was conceived.

Another strategy in known-donor decisions was to ask a male family member of the nongestational mother to contribute sperm. Debby and

FIGURE 3.1. Debby and Liz, Family Pride Week, Provincetown, Massachusetts. Photo credit: Sandra Patton-Imani.

Liz, an interracial (African American and white) middle-class couple who live in Brooklyn, New York, used the sperm of Liz's brother to get Debby pregnant. Thus, each of the mothers has a genetic connection to their son. This connection with the donor was important to both of them, but even more so for Debby, as an adoptee: "I kind of wanted, whatever we decided to do, to be able to tell our son who his father was if he asked." This was grounded in her experience of not knowing her birth parents. The most widely articulated reason for using an at-home method was financial, which was also a primary factor for Debby and Liz.

> DEBBY: We looked at sperm banks and stuff like that and we decided we couldn't afford to do it like that. So that's part of the reason we chose the way we wanted to do it. We ended up doing it ourselves, at home.

Rae and Jasmine also recruited a family member as donor. They emphasized the necessity of avoiding the medical approach because they could not afford it:

RAE: It was the eldest of her younger brothers. And so we got very
lucky because I'm really fertile. And also because we did it at home
for like ten bucks.

Sue and Adrienne, an interracial couple (white and African American)
that live in Iowa City, also sought out a donor from Adrienne's family. A
cousin of hers agreed and worked with them over several months, but
none of the inseminations resulted in pregnancy. He lived out of state
and the logistics proved too difficult for them to continue, so the couple
moved on to the world of sperm banks.

SUE: Total turkey baster. Total home temp. Total home temp. And you
know, I'd love to say turkey baster—little syringe. Okay, let's be truth-
ful here people!

It was perhaps in the arena of donor selection that experiences were
most blatantly framed by the language of consumer choice. Many of
the mothers joked about the means through which sperm donors were
advertised:

KATIE: They provided us with a *choice*. Well, maybe you can describe
it better than I am describing it. *Shopper's guide* isn't probably a—
certainly isn't a politically correct term—but it was almost like—
GWEN: It was a catalog is what it was.
KATIE: It was a *catalog of sperm donors*.
GWEN: All of the donors in the catalog have an excellent medical history, so that is an important thing, the number-one thing. And the
second is to try and get a donor that complemented my background
as well as the mother who's already got a lot more input than I. So,
we tried to find a donor that matched my background in terms of
nationality, etc. And the rest is history.

This emphasis on reproducing the "as if" model of family construction—
largely borrowed from de facto matching policies historically regulating
child placement decisions in the post–World War II era of US adoption—
was articulated by most of the mothers we spoke with that used donor
sperm. The primary exception was in cases in which mothers chose

known donors, often close friends or family. Social understandings of heredity—some grounded in science, others rooted in eugenics—shape this aspect of family-making. Anthropologist Diane Tober refers to "the complex interactions between technology, culture, sexuality, and lay interpretations of genetics" as "folk genetic beliefs" that "influence how people select donors and lead to a type of 'grassroots eugenics'— selecting for perceived desired traits" (2019, 5). Folk genetic beliefs contributed to the ways that couples choose donors, but, perhaps more significantly, these hereditarian narratives were built into the structure of the fertility industry through less overt policies, such as screening protocols for donors.

As Gwen mentioned above, health was the most commonly articulated concern in choosing donors, and the fertility industry has made a tidy profit on ensuring the medical health of its donors and the viability of their sperm through medical testing and donor screening policies. Prospective parents draw on such public narratives about heredity to choose donors based on traits they expect will produce children that look "as if" they were genetically related. As Kelly said," "You know we picked the donor so it would be somebody that looked like Sam. This was the most commonly articulated strategy among the mothers that used unknown donor sperm. For a fee, sperm banks provide more detailed information about potential donors. Some places make available childhood photos and hand-written descriptions. Enacting these assumptions about heredity reproduces families according to social understandings of the ways that genetics informs identity. It also functions, in practice, as a strategy for reducing social commentary from strangers on their families. Passing—or, at least, not flagging one's difference—is often seen as a benefit to a child's sense of self in a homophobic society.[2]

People also made purposeful decisions in an attempt to control for what they perceived as their own deficits. The overwhelmingly most highly favored trait was tallness, and many mothers noted their own short stature when considering the possibility of having boys. Another strategy was to choose the "best" donor they could find, according to what they believed would give their children the best chances in life. Valory shares her discomfort at the donor-choosing process:

VALORY: It was a little weird. It felt very *eugenicist*. But you know, it's
   kind of the way it's set up.
SANDI: Hmm. Say more about that. We found the same thing.
VALORY: It's odd, and just sort of seeing my friends' kids—I mean,
   they're the blondest, you know, kids you'll see—most of the kids of
   the lesbians I know.

She clarified that she was talking about white couples, and that the interracial couples and couples of color she knows primarily chose donors
that racially matched the nonbiological mom.

VALORY: Like people would shop for *PhD sperm*, or whatever. You
   know, I'm not too bad in the brains department so I'm sure the
   kid will be, hopefully, okay. It just gets a little strange. And I think
   some of the materials refer to women trying to find the guy that
   they would have dated. Like, the voice-over—I went to a bank
   where you could listen to, or buy a long voice recording or buy
   pictures. It seemed that *everything was monetized*. And you know,
   the long medical history and stuff. I got the audiotape or the CD,
   and it was like—they had like romantic music in the background.
   And it was sorta like questions that they were answering like if
   you were dating someone, like: "What do you like to do on a date?
   What do you like to do in your spare time? Oh, I like walking on
   the beach." It was just like, "Oh, my god." It's really funny. So that
   was interesting.

Mothers' views of their children's "best" possibilities are informed by
social understandings of ideal masculinity and personhood in a capitalist society.

Adrienne, a lawyer and an African American mom of twins, wanted
to cover all bases, and sought donors with a "graduate degree and high
SAT scores." This desire was difficult to reconcile with what her partner, Sue, explained was their other primary consideration, which was
finding a donor of color: "As Adrienne said, bring a little beige into the
family." This was in line with the majority of mothers, who constructed
their families through an "as if" model, matching races, ethnicities, and

physical characteristics of the non–birth mother in order to make a family that reflected the identities of both parents.

Melanie and I followed this same trajectory in our own family-making, selecting an African American donor whose description of self seemed similar to Melanie. It felt like common sense to follow this logic. At the same time, we experienced a great deal of discomfort as we read through endless donor descriptions. As an adoptee, I have to question how much of human identity development is about genetics and how much is about socialization and culture. The most dominant assumptions of folk genetics suggest that genetics are key to who we are, which often translates to overly simplistic assumptions about heredity and what can be controlled for. Our running joke throughout the process was about how we could breed for calm children; and the joke now is that it definitely did not work.

In what ways does eugenics haunt these choices? While US eugenic population control policies were not openly practiced after the horrors of World War II, the hereditarian assumptions undergirding this attempt at improving the population continue to shape popular belief and public policy.[3] As I have discussed, class is the primary regulator of which women are able to reproduce through medically assisted fertility treatment. All of the mothers that used fertility doctors were middle class; they either had jobs with medical insurance that covered fertility treatments, or they had the financial means to afford this extremely expensive option. The eugenic selection of men to reproduce these families is even more blatant and direct. Screening processes for sperm donors typically require donors have at least one advanced degree. Only some accept undergraduate students, and fewer still accept high school graduates. Adrienne and Sue were unable to find an African American donor who met their health and education requirements. They eased their expectations for advanced degrees, but still encountered difficulty finding Black donors with the level of family health they felt was necessary. They choose a Native American donor—to reflect another aspect of Adrienne's heritage—whose health status appeared to be excellent. They noted the bitter irony that their daughter inherited a severe genetic developmental disorder that is carried through paternal DNA.[4]

Vanessa and Cathy's oldest daughter was conceived with a known donor; that he was white was much less important to them than the fact that they had been friends for many years. When they decided to have a second child he no longer lived in New Mexico and the logistics were too difficult. Cathy was again the gestational mother, and they decided to choose an African American donor for their second child, to bring "some of Vanessa's heritage" into the family.

SANDI: Was it hard to find a Black donor?
BOTH: Yes. Very hard.
VANESSA: Very difficult.
CATHY: And they explained it has to do with their genetics some of the time. Well, first of all, a lot of African American men just don't come out to do it.
VANESSA: It's just something that's not in their culture. And those that do, get disqualified for their family medical history.
CATHY: So it's hard.

In struggling to understand the reason for the low number of donors of color available, Vanessa and Cathy vacillate between cultural and biological explanations. Power is not considered. The question of the health of donors of color makes more sense when we consider the public health issues associated with social inequality. What is interpreted as hereditary—for example, heart problems or diabetes—may very well be the bodily effects of systemic oppression.[5] Public narratives about heredity are pervasive, while systemic explanations for poverty and poor health outcomes are largely absent from public dialogues about inequality. What is explained as a lack of interest because it is not part of African American culture can be more accurately accounted for by socioeconomic inequality and stratified access to education.

Even white middle-class couples noticed the stratification in availability and cost of donor sperm. As Heather said, "Wow, we're kinda lucky we're looking for someone who's got the European background, and you know, the hazel eyes, and the (blond) hair, you know, because those were in abundance." Brenda and Jody, a white couple living in Iowa City, were shocked to see that the sperm of donors with advanced degrees was more expensive than that of donors with a bachelor's degree.

Yet these were only the most blatant means of winnowing out donors by intersections of race and class. The larger structural force here—and, thus, the least visible in a system of racial meaning structured through colorblindness—is that there is a low market demand for nonwhite sperm. The ideal family is genetically reproduced in subtle, race-evasive ways that function to divert attention from the structural inequalities that put men of color in social locations that reproduce inequality. Power relations are typically left out of stories about the social reproduction of family.

Vanessa and Cathy continue their discussion of the factors they considered:

> VANESSA: We found a total of three or four (Black donors). And then it was important that it at least be donor-release.
> CATHY: Yeah, it had to be identity-release.
> VANESSA: Identity-release. So at some point if the—you know, if Regan wanted to, she could you know, contact, or at least know who her biological father is.
> CATHY: When she's eighteen.
> VANESSA: Which also narrowed the field even further.

Their view, like that of Debby and Liz, was shared by a large number of mothers we interviewed. This definition of family is inclusive of both bio and nonbio relationships, and families embraced this logic in varying degrees. Other families were more resistant to including sperm donors as family members.

> HEATHER: And I'm like, "Well, it's *not a father*. It's a *sperm donor*." Right? And he will not have a father in that sense, you know? And we opted for a closed donor because we didn't—because we want to make sure that the understanding is that *this is what family is*, you know, that family isn't necessarily the blood that runs through your genes. That it's about love and commitment and it's about support and the everydayness.

Both perspectives embody elements of resistance and assimilation. In a sense, that is what the process of navigating family-making is in a complex, power-differential society.

Adoption: "It's Kind of Precarious for Us"

Sophie's family begins to look less unusual as we explore the stories of the families we interviewed. While the specificities of her origin story differ from those I have discussed above, the commonalities in regards to reproductive stratification are instructive. Like assisted reproduction, adoption functions as the literal social reproduction of legitimate heteronormative families, yet these structural factors shaping family-making only tell part of the story. Whether or not the state recognizes the legitimacy of their relationships, these families are rewriting and representing personal and public narratives about contemporary families in the United States.

Sharon, who is African American, and her partner, Luisa, who is Latina, participated in a women-of-color roundtable during Family Week in Provincetown, Massachusetts, in 2007. They discuss their experiences as queer mothers of color adopting their African American infant son:

SHARON: It's not a natural fit—which I don't think exists—in terms of a community. I mean, I've always felt like we've been on kind of the *outskirts* of any kind of *mainstream gay enrollment*. I just feel like we've had to create so many spaces for ourselves because we can't find it. So, with this adoption process, it's just a really interesting thing to go through as a family with two heads of household who are of color. Most people mistake Luisa for white. I don't know. It's kind of *precarious* for us.

LUISA: I think also, that said, we were thinking about adoption as a process and how it's a—it's almost something that's given to *privileged families*, and most of those in terms of race, class, and gender. . . . Being two women who are heads of household we're the lowest on the totem pole economically. We are not going to make as much as our counterparts who are white women or even men of color. So we are really privileged to be able to pull together the resources, raise the money to adopt, and create a community of people that accept and love this child.

SHARON: So even within adoption circles we're, like, atypical because we didn't have the funds readily available. We had to do fundrais-

ers. We had to have community parties. We had to, you know, wait
and save for two years to get him. It's just really different. I think
we're in kind of a unique position. I like it, but I also miss finding
community.

Sharon and Luisa articulate here both cultural and structural barriers to family-making. Not only has their social location as lesbians of
color shaped their access to adoption, but it has also been difficult for
them to find a sense of meaningful community among "mainstream gay
enrollment."

Sharon and Luisa are correct in their assessment of their location
in the structure of privilege that organizes adoption. The US adoption
market has historically functioned in response to the desires of middle-
class, straight, married white couples.[6] Their needs are most readily ca-
tered to.[7] The best interests of children have historically been subsumed
beneath the demands of the market. Sociologist Elizabeth Raleigh's research demonstrates that the US private adoption market is organized
into upper- and lower-tier parents and children. As the research of sociologist Dawn Day documents, the US child welfare system (the public
market) also has a long history of discriminating against prospective
African American parents in both subtle and blatant ways (Day 1979).
Race, marital status, sexual orientation, and socioeconomic status have
fundamentally shaped the history of adoption in the United States. As
Raleigh explains, "The end result was that a stratified marketplace was
created, where the most deserving parents got the most adoptable children" (2018, 102). Second-tier parents get second-tier children, and these
tiers are structured by how closely prospective parents conform to institutional narratives of ideal families.

Adoption is one of the social practices in which race, class, and gender issues intersect with sexuality to create an intensification of discrimination for queer people of color. In their stories, lesbian adoptive
mothers recall interactions with various forms of local, state, national,
and transnational power. Transnational adoption adds layers of bu-
reaucracy, greater financial demands, and nation-specific requirements
regarding adoptive parents. For example, Korea requires, among other
things, that adoptive parents be (heterosexually) married, meet weight
requirements and income levels, and be clear of an array of medical is-

sues that may disqualify many prospective adopters. On the other hand, adoptions from Guatemala by single mothers were very common in this era, facilitating the adoption process for many queer moms, provided (in most instances) they were willing to pass as straight single women. Briggs explains: "The wide-open neoliberal markets of Guatemala were one of the few places that did not have bars to gay and lesbian adoptive parents" (2012, 241–42).

Cal and Mo are a white lesbian couple with three children, who live in Albuquerque, New Mexico. Mo gave birth through insemination to their oldest daughter, and Cal became her legal second parent through adoption. Several years later they began the process of adopting a child from Guatemala.

> CAL: The Guatemalan government noticed on our social work paper-
> work that there were two women living in the household and they
> stopped the adoption.

Cal and Mo rallied support from the US government at every level they could, and the process was reignited, with greater caution in the preparation of application materials.

> MO: A single woman adoption—so Cal was the legal parent for
> Atusena, and I was the legal parent for Alejandro. And then when
> we got back to New Mexico we had to do a whole other adoption
> process.

In addition to the two transnational adoptions, they also had to pay for and navigate the legal process of second-parent adoption for each of their three children. They considered themselves fortunate that New Mexico law does not prohibit second-parent adoption. They were also able to afford this series of expensive adoptions, unlike many of the other mothers with whom we spoke.

The home study, a requirement to becoming adoptive parents in the United States, is an aspect of the process that requires finesse. In this era the specifics of this process varied dramatically by region. In some states, adoption by LGBTQ people was illegal, and in others it was "not strictly prohibited." In such situations, adopters were forced to perform as single straight women. Kimberly and Mischa faced a similar legal situation in Iowa.

> KIMBERLY: So she [the social worker] did it [the home study] for us as a couple, but wrote it for me as an individual.
>
> MISCHA: None of our adoptions have happened as a couple. Primarily I think it's because foreign adoptions or international adoptions, a lot of paperwork goes through INS, and it's still not allowed by INS. You know if you—even today—if you go to the library to check out the international adoption books, they have a *list*—the INS has a list of people who aren't allowed to adopt. And it includes—I don't know— *psychopaths* and *sex offenders* and. . . . And *we are on the same list*.
>
> SANDI: Psychopaths and lesbians!
>
> MISCHA: Homosexuals are in there.

The ways that queer couples have pushed the historical boundaries of adoption law and expanded the range of children and adults served by the child welfare system has been a process of redefining family that involved seeking balance between resistance and assimilation.

> MISCHA: Do you want to adopt a child or do you want to make history? 'Cause that was the choice at that time. And you know, it was the adoption of the child. And so it was written—again, the [the social worker] was well aware of the situation—but it was written in a way that the other person was a "roommate." There are a lot of roommate situations goin' on!

Passing as straight single women was strategically necessary at different levels of engagement in the adoption process. This performance of assimilation was more complex than it might first appear. Rather than represent homonormativity overtaking queer resistance to mainstream social expectations, this performance cannily utilized social expectations for gender identity and mothering in order to successfully navigate a system designed to reproduce heteronormative nuclear families. The subterfuge they felt was necessary makes evident that queer women's experiences are limited in ways that those of straight women—single or married—are not.[8]

The most prominent and widely embraced public story in the contemporary United States about transnational adoption is the orphan-salvation myth. This deeply raced, gendered, and classed origin tale encourages prospective parents to "save" the children of poor brown women from developing countries through the creation of adoptive families.[9] Whether this narrative matches a family's actual origin story or not, their lived experiences are shaped by such pervasive fictions. The contrasts between this mythic tale and the politics of reproduction for mothers in impoverished countries point toward stories of devastating poverty, oppression, and coercion that undercut this sociopolitical allegory.

In fact, in 2001, two years after Sophie was adopted, the United States, along with several other Western countries, suspended adoptions from Cambodia due to widespread child trafficking and corruption. As far as her family is aware, Sophie was legally relinquished to an orphanage by her father because of extreme poverty. Nevertheless, the stark inequalities of global poverty are the foundational conditions facilitating *both* the illegal and legal trafficking of children from poor families in developing countries to middle-class families in Western countries.

> KIMBERLY: We know a little bit about their birth parents. We were lucky enough when we adopted Sophie to get a picture with her and her dad. He had walked many miles to bring her to the orphanage. Her mom had gotten quite ill when she delivered her, and she didn't have any breast milk. And they were not in a position to buy formula. And so Sophie was living on sugar water for her first four weeks. And got really healthy then once she went to the orphanage, which we are lucky about. So, she was four weeks old when her dad brought her in and we have a picture.

The fairy-tale adoption stories feel flimsy when compared to the actualities of poverty that drive most relinquishments and removals. She was not really an "orphan" in the way the term is most commonly used. Yet her identity and sense of belonging in the world are navigated through, with, and against the laws, public narratives, and social circumstances that shaped and regulated the decisions each of her parents were able to make.

Cal and Mo assume their children were voluntarily relinquished by their birth mothers, but they have no way of knowing for sure. Guatemalan adoptions were halted by the government in 2007 because of widespread child trafficking. As National Public Radio has reported: "Guatemala's international anti-corruption commission, set up with the United Nations, documented over 3,000 cases of irregular adoptions before international pressure led Guatemala to put a halt to them in 2007."[10] Allegations of kidnapping and child trafficking were widespread, and a system of forging documentation to facilitate lucrative adoptions to the United States makes it impossible for parents of children adopted from Guatemala to know the circumstances under which those children were separated from their mothers. In fact, as historian Karen Dubinsky's research demonstrates, tensions between explanations of "international kidnap" and "humanitarian rescue" have characterized mainstream and scholarly understandings of adoption from Guatemala (2010, 3). Her work emphasizes the importance of moving beyond this "false dichotomy" to recognize the complexities and contradictions built into the process. These intricacies are part of Atusena and Alejandro's grafted family tree.

Kimberly and Mischa traveled to each of their children's home countries so they could learn as much about their origins as possible. They traveled to Haiti to pick up their youngest child, Jonas, in 2003.

MISCHA: With Jonas we were actually lucky enough to spend a good part of a day with his—
KIMBERLY: We met his mom and one of his sisters, who was about Sophie's age. And that was—
MISCHA: That was amazing.
KIMBERLY: That was great. It was very sad, but it felt wonderful to be able to meet her and have that connection. You know, to be able to take a picture of her holding Jonas. And to take a picture of his sister.

It is no wonder that media representations of transnational adoption typically leave out the circumstances preventing birth parents from being able to care for their children. These are not random circumstances, but, rather, the effects of transnational economic policies. Kim continues with Jonas's origin story:

KIMBERLY: So, he was from a big family, and his mother was extremely poor. The woman who directed the orphanage just kinda shook her head and she said, "I don't know how any of these people are living."

Jonas's birth mother was employed sweeping streets in a governmental work program. The orphanage director explained that the program was so badly run the women were rarely paid for the work they did. Even when she did get paid, it was not enough to afford food, housing, and education for her children.

KIMBERLY: So, clearly, it was poverty that was the root of his adoption. And she left him. But he went into the orphanage when he was just seven days old. She visited him once a month while he was waiting for us to adopt him.

I have spent many years, as an adoptee and as a researcher, listening to adoptive parents discuss their children's origins. This is among the most open-minded and empathetic responses I have heard. I cannot tell you how many times I have listened to middle-class white parents—both straight and queer—talk about a "benefit" of transnational adoption being that you do not have the worry that birth parents will show up at your door sometime in the future.[11] I have sat in too many rooms with too many adoptive parents who expressed anger or argued with me when I pointed out that poverty is the primary factor in children becoming available for adoption throughout the world. Many people are invested in mainstream media accounts of adoption as the salvation of children without parents, not children whose parents are too poor to raise them.[12] Feminist scholar Leifa Mayers discusses the social function of policy narratives about "vulnerable" children: "In state discourses of the child's adoption into the family or nation, persistent focus on the (orphan) child's vulnerability detracts attention from the maldistribution of poverty, labor exploitation, and violence by which the production of vulnerability becomes routinized. The futurity of the rescuing couple and nation, in turn, is imagined through the child's cultural ascendance" (2016, 74). The birth mothers of Sophie, Jonas, Theo, Sheridan, Atusena, and Alejandro come to represent the absence of care, the disregard for rights, and the transnational movement of "adoptable" infants from mothers who are experiencing poverty so extreme they are unable to raise their children. If Jonas's mother had a job that paid a living wage, she could support all her children. Sociopolitical narratives about birth mothers celebrate the selfless choices they made to provide a better life for their children; it is is clear, however, from these stories that systemic poverty regulates their lives. These tensions are difficult to reconcile. Mischa and Kimberly acknowledge the circumstances that keep Sophie's and Jonas's mothers from being able to raise them, but they are constrained by the system in which they operate. They cannot change the circumstances of systemic poverty affecting mothers outside the United States. Even if they were able to financially contribute to her well-being and that of her other children, this would not change the system or provide her with more opportunities to earn a living.

Grafting Trees: "We All Coparent One Way or Another"

The story of a grafted family tree provides ways of envisioning kinship that encompass relationships grounded in nature and nurture, while also making power visible. A number of families that used known donors fostered and sustained a broad range of family relationships. As we were interviewing Shelley and Naomi at the gym and outdoor pool that Shelley owns and runs, Naomi pointed across the lawn and said:

> NAOMI: Actually, Ezra's donor's wife and their daughter are here right now.
> SHELLEY: See the blond?
> NAOMI: The blond woman in the dress, and the pink bikini next to her is Ezra's—[pause]
> SHELLEY: Sister.
> NAOMI: That's Ezra's half-sister and we don't have good names for these family members. But we spend a lot of time together.

Naomi hesitates before naming the relationship between Ezra and this child, but Shelley inserts "sister" with ease and comfort. They do not "have good names for these family members" because, as a society, we have few templates for understanding these relationships *as family*. I have similar feelings about my birth parents and their children. We do not have widely available maps or stories to guide us through the complexities of family-making outside the narrowly defined scope of the legitimate heteronormative nuclear family. These families map and name the relations of care connecting children to families, and families to society, in creative ways that speak beyond themselves to family-making practices across a broad range of families.

Queer folks are creating families that do not necessarily look like the nuclear family ideal, yet this is not a new phenomenon. As Queer Latina activist Lisbeth Melendez Rivera describes her family in a 2008 interview with Melanie: "There's three moms. My wife and I are god-mothers to our best friend's child, who lives with us fifty percent of the time. And we are Salvadorian, Puerto Rican, Jewish, and Arab." Her multiracial family of three moms and a kid are what many would call a "chosen" family (Weston 1991). The tensions between this notion of family as chosen and the lack of legal protection speak allegorically to the moment in history that Lisbeth, her partner, and their friend participate in family-making. Their situation highlights gaps between fictions of choice, and the structural context in which actual options are circumscribed by law and thus limited to affective bonds. She continues:

LISBETH: There is *no legal ties* between us and this child. It all exists on the emotional, psychological level. There is *no laws* in Maryland that will allow us to get custody of this child without diminishing the role of the mother, which we are not willing to do. That is not what this arrangement is about. We get scared sometimes that if something happens to his biological mother that we would have a harder time continuing to be a line of support for him, especially since a ruling a few months ago, in June 2008. When the Supreme—the Appeals Court of Maryland ruled that a nonbiological mother had no rights to custody. Especially, since she had been what the court defined as a secondary parent, meaning the mother had gone on to a different relationship. And though the original mother continued to be in the picture, once the bio-mother denied visitation, the non-biological mother *lost all rights*.

Family law and policy not only narrate how families are defined; they also *constitute* and *construct* particular kinds of family units by legislating what families are legitimate social units with full access to the rights, protections, and privileges of citizenship. This family of three mothers is not socially recognized as legitimate, and this erasure is supported by public law.

Yet Lisbeth's performance of family is also a reclaiming of kinship history among families of color. As I have discussed, being denied access to social services, resources, and social institutions, families outside the white middle-class heteronormative ideal have always found creative ways of surviving under circumstances ranging from ambivalence to hostility. Family connections have been used historically as sources of resistance to the lack of family support provided by local, state, or federal laws and policies (Dill 1988). Lisbeth locates herself in a history of family that challenges the ideal:

> LISBETH: What my relationship in my family reminds me of is, you
> know, what my grandmother did with the neighbor's kids when their
> mom was sick. Or what my father did to support his best friend's
> children when he passed away. You know, like it doesn't matter how
> far removed from your biology they are.

Lisbeth's family is, in effect, participating in a Latinx tradition of *compadrazgo*, or "god-parenting," a legacy of Spanish Catholicism in which kinship relations are expanded through symbolic connections between children and adults previously considered "outside" the family (Dill 1994).

Cypress and Kim are raising their daughter Alex in Los Angeles in a multigenerational household that resembles traditional kinship patterns in the Philippines, where Cypress's parents grew up. Cypress explains:

> CYPRESS: We have a really good support network. You know, our family has been just tremendous with their support for us, you know.
> In our house my parents live with us and they are pretty much a
> real godsend helping with Alex. And you know, they just love Kim.
> Ever since—gosh—ever since we were dating they have just been so
> [chuckle] enamored with her. Just think she's so smart and you know,

and she's just you know, really intelligent and sweet and consider-
ate. You know all these qualities they want, especially—well, what
they wanted in a son-in-law and they got in a daughter-in-law. She
completely won them over. Not to mention I have three sisters and
they are so equally fond of Kim, and so we're a very tight family. We
see them all the time. They come over. They live very close to us as
well—geographically they live very close. So we probably see them
every day, if not, you know, over the weekends.

Extended families have been the norm for most of the history of humanity; nuclear families are actually a relatively new phenomenon.[13] In the
United States, families of color have historically been located outside the
social institutions supporting family-making through recognition and
social resources. As Lisbeth explains:

> LISBETH: When we come down to talking about LGBTQ families
> that a lot of the times we forget that as people of color we have been
> *creating families all along that don't fit the norm.* That in order to
> parent, how many of us, when you ask, "Oh, you know, how did you
> grow up?" the answer is, "By my aunt and my grandmother because
> my mom was working and couldn't spend as much time with me."
> Or, you know, my mom, my parents, you know, coparent with my
> neighbors and all four of us—there is four of us kids who spent time
> in one house or the other, depending on whose parents were work-
> ing. You know, we ate at one house or the other. We were just one big
> family. And forty years later *you call them your cousins because you
> don't know anything else.*

The notion of "fictive kin" among people of color intersects with stories
of "chosen families" among queer folks whose families of origin have
rejected them. These two fluid narratives intersect with contemporary
representations of adoption as well.

Lisbeth puts her family in a larger transnational and historical
context:

> LISBETH: There's ways we constantly challenge that notion of normal
> family, which infuriates me when we talk about family because

what they say, the two parents, two-point-five kids, doesn't exist in real life. *We all coparent one way or another.* The concept of it takes a village is not new. And it's—I think that it's being recreated every day in some place in the world. In some place every day we recreate that model. The village may be three of us, but it is what's raising this child.

Parents that participated in this research composed their families through many different means, but, as they did, all of them engaged with templates for legitimate family embedded in social interactions, public media narratives, social institutions, and laws at multiple local, state, national, and international levels. Their stories of family-making challenge genealogical templates for legitimacy and reimagine families and social narratives about them.

Conclusion

These stories of grafted family trees provide a glimpse into the complexities of queer family formation in the contemporary United States, and they function as useful allegories about family-making at the turn of the twenty-first century. These mothers tell stories in which the gaps and erasures necessary to maintain mythologies of white heteronormative families are, nevertheless, made socially visible. These are stories that *out* covert and insidious intersections between white supremacy and its cousin "colorblindness" that work collaboratively with gender and sex to reproduce class inequalities. These mutually reinforcing fictions of family lie at the core of legal definitions of legitimate family and citizenship in the United States, past and present.

These stories point to the importance of exploring the complex ways that reproductive stratification is constructed and maintained in family policy. The mothers we spoke with interacted with social institutions and laws and policies in different ways, depending on their social and geographic locations. I have argued for the importance of exploring same-sex marriage and adoption laws in relation to other laws shaping the lived experience of family. In the next chapter I examine in depth the public policy battles in the 1990s over definitions of legitimate mothers, children, and families. I consider political debates over the passage of the 1996 Defense of Marriage Act alongside policy discussions of welfare reform, immigration reform, and legislation regulating adoption. Exploring the reproductive policy debates of the 1990s in depth lays the groundwork for understanding how the same-sex marriage debate took shape in the twenty-first century.

FAMILY LAW AND POLICY, 1990–2000

May 1993   Hawaii Supreme Court rules on same-sex marriages

October 1994   Multiethnic Placement Act signed into law

March 1995   Utah Governor signs "Defense of Marriage" statute into law

August 1996   Personal Responsibility and Work Opportunity Reconciliation Act (welfare reform) signed into law

August 1996   Interethnic Placement Act enacted as part of the Small Business Job Protection Act

September 1996   The Defense of Marriage Act (DOMA) becomes law

May 1997   Hawaii becomes the first state to offer domestic partnership benefits to same-sex couples

February 1998   Alaska Superior Court rules on same-sex couples' right to marry

November 1998   Hawaii and Alaska voters approve constitutional ban on same-sex marriage

Dec. 20, 1999   Vermont Supreme Court rules in favor of providing same-sex couples' benefits and protections

October 2000   Child Citizenship Act of 2000 signed into law

November 2000–   Nebraska voters approve constitutional ban on same-sex marriage

Adapted from https://gaymarriage.procon.org

4

What about the Children?

Genealogies of Illegitimacy and Reproductive Injustice, 1990–2000

> LISBETH: The first time around I became a parent because we felt that
> we had the time and the energy to help my niece get through high
> school as an African American Latina woman, and assure that she
> would go on to college. It was a great moment for us to be able to pro-
> vide what she needed in terms of structure and stability, as our entire
> family was in transition, and her mother was moving to Atlanta.

Lisbeth and her partner, Gabriella, a Latina couple living in Boston,
became mothers in the early 1990s. Gabriella's sister was a queer Latina
single mother who was having a difficult time financially. The entire
family worried that her adolescent daughter Elena would be "at risk"
socially and academically if she continued to live with her mother. Lisbeth and Gabriella stepped in to make sure their niece was in a stable
environment that would "assure that she would go on to college."

> LISBETH: We ourselves moved to North Carolina to provide a less urban
> environment for her, and then came back to Massachusetts a few years
> later for her to be able to finish high school in the Cambridge, Massa-
> chusetts, system. So, for six years—a little bit over five years—she lived
> with us, and we took care of her needs, and she was the center of our
> world. She—like I said—she's now twenty-seven, twenty-eight—my
> god, I'm old. And she lives and works in Atlanta, Georgia.

Lisbeth and Gabriella were dedicated to providing her with a stable, "less
urban environment" in which she could thrive.

Lisbeth's family-making took place in the 1990s at the height of public policy debates about motherhood and family regarding the Defense
of Marriage Act (1996) and welfare and immigration reform. Conser-

FIGURE 4.1. Lisbeth, Family Pride Week, Provincetown, Massachusetts. Photo credit: Sandra Patton-Imani.

vative politicians defined "family values" through the glorification of heterosexual marriage, hard work, and legal citizenship. This family, by necessity, employed resistant legal and cultural practices in a sociopolitical and historical context in which nonnormative families were cast as deviant and illegitimate. Yet it is also clear that Lisbeth and Gabriella's parenting decisions were informed by mainstream understandings of stability and educational achievement. Lisbeth draws distinctions between an "urban environment" and the "structure and stability" she and her partner provided. Elena's family was "in transition," and her single mother was moving to another state. While their family structure is "resistant" to mainstream definitions of family, they are also enmeshed in the very narratives they work against. Their family-making is a process of cultural navigation and negotiation with competing definitions of parenting and safety in a complex society in which young women of color, in particular, are often vulnerable. Like many parents, Lisbeth draws on sociopolitical allegories about the dangers of urban environments for teens of color to explain the "stability" she and Gabriella provided:

LISBETH: At the time that she was with us I was her legal guardian
mainly because her aunt, which was my partner, had blood ties, and

it was easier to explain than me coming into the schools and making decisions. And so, we had paperwork drawn that said in the absence of her mother I was the person to make decisions. But the reality is that *all of us made decisions as a family.* You know, my niece can say *she was raised by six lesbians.* That was the village at the time. I don't know what it is to parent in a *binary system.*

Elena has six mothers. How are we to understand her family in the sociopolitical context of the United States in the 1990s? How might we read Lisbeth's family story allegorically? We have only the outlines of a child's life in her narrative. I do not know this girl's real name. I call her Elena to provide a link to her story.

The figure of an "at risk" child is at the center of sociopolitical allegories that emerged in news media and policy discussions about families in the 1990s. She is the young teen of color living in poverty that conservatives and liberals alike hold up as a threat to the nation. She is the focus of welfare reform. She is a concern in public policy dialogues focused on immigration. She is at the center of alarm in legislative discussions about DOMA. Some people say she needs to be saved. Others contend that her unwed mother needs to be punished. Politicians warn about the corrupting influence of her lesbian mothers. Some say she is the future to fear. Others know she is the future to ensure.[1]

The focus of sociopolitical debates about "family values" in the 1990s concerned socialization and what politicians called "illegitimacy." Competing visions of the future were embodied in contrasting stories about children in family policy debates in the 1990s. In these narratives, imaginary white middle-class children are envisioned, simultaneously, as those for whom the future must be saved, and those who will do the saving of society. Alternately, this conservative rhetoric about family casts children of color as threats to the social order, deploying images of kids with same-sex parents, children of "welfare mothers," children of undocumented immigrants, children of color in foster care, and transracial adoptees. These representations of children concern illegitimate relationships with the state, and more specifically, their mothers' relationships to family laws regulating access to the benefits and privileges of citizenship.

In the previous chapter I explored stratified reproduction through the lived experiences of families navigating uneven political and legal terrain regulating family-making at the turn of the twenty-first century. In this chapter I deepen my *genealogy of illegitimacy* through a focus on links between law and policy debates and sociopolitical narratives about families who are considered "illegitimate." I trace the lines of argument that facilitated agreement in the 1990s among conservatives, centrists, and liberals that illegitimacy was the fundamental cause of poverty and all of its attendant social problems. These policy dialogues about children present as colorblind, yet the contrasts between narratives about those children who are in need of salvation and those who pose a threat to society betray the racial logic undergirding the US legal system. These contrasts point to the importance of exploring how sociopolitical allegories emphasizing whiteness as salvation and redemption, alongside racialized representations of at-risk children, were crucial to the passage of punitive policies directed at regulating reproduction. Indeed, I argue that sociopolitical allegories about mothers and their children do the ideological work of deploying race in the context of neoliberal denials of the social importance of race and gender in shaping the "family values" political debates of the 1990s.

Race is underexamined in discussions of LGBTQ families, and queerness has been largely ignored in public dialogues about families of color in poverty.[2] Queer mothers of color often fall through the cracks of these analytical categories. When we follow these discussions through the children we see how oppression against some women is enforced by privileging other women. The laws that passed in this era facilitated the transfer of children from women labeled "unfit" to those deemed "fit" to raise the next generation of American citizens. In these policy discussions, race is instrumentalized as an insidious array of forces in the social project of family legitimacy.

I contend that we cannot fully understand the politics of same-sex marriage in the twenty-first century without a critical exploration of the "family values" politics of the 1990s. On a practical policy level, the laws passed in this era overhauled the social welfare system and deepened inequality in ways that public narratives were largely successful at masking. This was a historical moment of *reproductive injustice*: not only was the social safety net for vulnerable families dismantled, but the media and policy discussions about the mothers most deeply affected by these changes denied the existence of inequality and blamed governmental oppression on the women's own bad choices.

On a symbolic level, the social narratives that served to justify these laws further entrenched the heteronormative white nuclear family ideal as the standard by which to judge social inclusion and legitimacy. Focusing solely on DOMA alone, without attending to the race, gender, and class politics of the social welfare and immigration debates, provides a limited understanding of how same-sex marriage came to be a primary focus of political rhetoric. Adoption policies, too, are central to a full accounting of the family politics that characterized the turn of the century, and the ways that these laws continue to function to erase the roles of race, gender, class, and sexuality in the regulation of inequality.

Heather and the Illegits: Socializing Future Citizens

Conservative Christian family activist James Dobson, founder of Focus on the Family, articulates a view of "homosexual[s]" that has been pervasive among conservatives for decades, casting the gay and lesbian "agenda" as literally and figuratively predatory: "The homosexual agenda is a beast. (It) wants our kids. . . . And the only thing standing between them and that agenda are those of us who believe in the Judeo-Christian values of this country" (2006). The "beast" is coming for "our kids." Which children are endangered, and which embody this monstrous threat? At issue are competing assessments of contemporary family politics, visions for the future, and strategies for socializing the next generation of American citizens. The bitter irony in this debate is that this political rhetoric, and the legal inequalities it justifies, pose a more tangible and immediate danger: to the children of same-sex parents.

The queer mothers in this research project cite negative representations of their families as one of the central arenas of struggle in making their families. When Leslea Newman wrote and self-published the children's book *Heather Has Two Mommies* in 1989, she did so to fill a gap in children's literature. She reports her inspiration as the complaint of the lesbian mothers of a toddler that there were no children's books representing two-mom families, and they wanted their daughter to have books that affirmed her family. Children's literature and media are particularly rich sites for exploring what constitutes "appropriate" socialization for children. The public debates about *Heather Has Two Mommies* map out the social investments and stakes in the enculturation and socialization of future citizens.

Queer parents' stake in having LGBTQ-inclusive children's literature concerns their children's safety and self-esteem. Yet they are also invested in educating the current generation, in service of a vision of the future in which all human beings are treated with dignity and respect. Allison, a white lesbian mom, references a media narrative in her discussion of the future:

> ALLISON: It was certainly never a question with us about—that we wouldn't want to have kids 'cause of that reason [oppression]. I always think about—It's super-cheesy, but in *If These Walls Could Talk 2*, that scene where Ellen and Sharon Stone are sitting watching the kids play in the playground.[3] I think it's Sharon Stone says something like, "Well, you know, *what if it doesn't get better?* What if we're raising—bringing a kid into this world . . . ?" And Ellen just looks at her and says, "It always has. *It always has gotten better and. . . .*" *We create this world by all of us having kids*. So, and like I say, as a teacher I have seen so much change in ten years that, you know, I have students—girl students fighting over other girls, and it's, like, cool to be gay in my middle school in some kind of strange way.

This interview with Allison and Lisa took place in 2005 in San Jose, California. The middle school students she refers to were young children in the 1990s, and, in her view, their perspectives on LGBTQ issues reflect a sense of social change toward open-mindedness.

This generation of young adults, often credited with embodying a shift in the acceptance of queer relationships, was born into a United States in which *Heather Has Two Mommies* was the topic of fierce social discussion and political action. The controversy over *Heather Has Two Mommies* focused on the question of the legitimacy of same-sex parents and their families, but it became a larger public issue of what information regarding queer families is appropriate in libraries and school curricula. Earlier in this book I introduced the controversy over *Heather Has Two Mommies* in the context of congressional debates about DOMA to introduce the concept of sociopolitical allegory. I turn now to a consideration of the public debate about family legitimacy, socialization, and citizenship that initially developed in relation to the inclusion of the book in the New York City Public School Curriculum. In 2009, twenty years after its publication, the author commented on its impact: "When I first conceived of the book in 1988, I had no idea that it would be so loved—and so hated. I had no idea it would appear on "most challenged" book lists alongside *Huckleberry Finn* and *The Catcher in the Rye*. I had no idea it would become part of the congressional record and be debated on the Senate floor. I had no idea it would be defecated upon by a library patron in Ohio, stolen by a minister from a library in Texas and the cause of a New York City school superintendent's downfall. Not to mention being parodied on Jon Stewart's *The Daily Show* on a regular basis" (Newman 2009). This public debate was about much more than a children's book. It was a political and cultural battle over visions and strategies for the future of the nation.

In 1992 the New York City Public School District introduced a new "Children of the Rainbow" curriculum, developed by educators to teach "racial harmony" to elementary school students, in response to the 1989 murder of a white teenage boy in the predominantly Black neighborhood of Bensonhurt (Myers, 1992). *Heather Has Two Mommies* and two other children's books about same-sex families were included in an optional reading list for elementary school children focusing on family diversity. The inclusion infuriated a number of parents, school board members, and conservative activists. As the *Washington Post* reported: "Some parents' meetings have ended nearly in fistfights. Last week, (School Superintendent) Fernandez received two threats on his life and had to have security increased. Posters and pamphlets ominously warned about a gay recruitment campaign in the schools—part of what Fernandez calls 'sad' and 'hateful scare tactics.' Conservatives have mailed thousands of letters to parents declaring that the policy would mean first-graders would be shown 'explicitly the homosexual lifestyle, including oral and anal sex'" (Jordan 1992, 1A). These debates, in conjunction with political rhetoric emphasizing family values, put questions regarding queerness and socialization of children at the forefront of political discussion.

Dr. Michael Bauman, Director of Christian Studies at Hillsdale College in Manitou Springs, Colorado, was a vocal critic of feminists and homosexuals. He declared New York City "Sodom on the Hudson" for promoting immorality in public elementary schools.

> Heather doesn't really have two mommies; she's got only one. The other lady is just the woman mommy has sex with. Having sex with mommy doesn't make you a mommy. Otherwise, what would daddy be?
>
> But daddy is the one person missing from this book. And not daddy only. No adult male appears in its pages. Not one adult male is even named. The closest this book gets to identifying any adult male is in passing references like those to Stacy's two daddies. (Yes, two.) Heather, you see, lives in a man-free zone, a gender-cleansed ghetto built and patrolled by feminazis. (Quoted in Beckwith 2008)

This tirade articulates the axis point between conservative critiques of lesbian mothers and of single mothers receiving social welfare support: the absence of a father financially supporting his family and ensuring the socialization of appropriately masculine boys and feminine girls.

The political intersection between welfare reform and same-sex marriage turns on the social, moral, and economic definition of a "legitimate" mother and child through legal attachment to a man. In his testimony in favor of DOMA, Republican Senator Kempthorne of Idaho made clear that *marriage* was the connective tissue between welfare reform and DOMA.

> Mr. President, as part of the welfare reform bill which this Chamber overwhelmingly supported, we stressed the importance of marriage. The first two findings in the bill said, "Marriage is the foundation of a successful society," and "Marriage is an essential institution of a successful society which promotes the interests of children." What we are doing today is saying that we want to protect that institution. We want to maintain marriage as it has existed from the foundation of the United States, and, in fact, as it exists throughout the world today. Establishing a Federal definition of marriage and ensuring that States are not required to accept marriages which violate their public policies are modest, yet very important, parts of that process. (*Congressional Record* September 10, 1996, S10116)

US public discourse in the 1990s divided into two distinct streams of debate about marriage. In one, lesbian mothers are prohibited from marrying because not having a father is not in the best interests of the children. In the other, single mothers are urged to marry as a means of escaping poverty and ensuring their children's proper socialization.

These contradictions are discursively reconciled by a common attitude: that without the presence of a father children cannot be properly socialized into productive citizens.[4] The terms of these two streams of public debate about mothers and marriage have been explicitly linked through the fiercely held belief that this supposed breakdown of the family fails American society through a failure to socialize future citizens.

The public policy debate about same-sex marriage was part of a much larger social discussion in which the cause of contemporary social problems is located in the reproductive and socialization practices of mothers. In his 1995 testimony to the US Senate Finance Committee in favor of the passage of the Personal Responsibility and Work Opportunities Act (more commonly referred to as "welfare reform"), conservative policy advisor Charles Murray articulates what came to be a commonly held understanding of the perceived deficiencies of families without fathers:

> What social workers, pediatricians, and police see today among the children in low income communities is seldom the age-old ravages of simple poverty. Today's children are often going malnourished, malnurtured, neglected, and unsocialized not because their parents have no access to material resources, but because the mother is incompetent and the father is missing altogether. Whether the mother's incompetence derives from youth, drug addiction, low ability, an unjust social system, or defective character makes little difference to the child. Even that the mother loves the child makes little difference if the love is unaccompanied by the steadfastness, maturity, and understanding of a child's needs that transmute love into nurturing. And, finally, the child who grows up without a father, in a neighborhood without fathers, is at risk in ways that even the most loving and competent mother finds it hard to counter. (1995)

In Murray's view, even a mother's love does not overcome the deficiencies brought on by the absence of a father. He proffers an argument that the salvation of "at risk" children from such circumstances is so urgent, both for the children and the nation, that the rights of their mothers must be ignored. He explicitly argues that providing either welfare benefits or jobs—"access to material resources"—would not solve the social problem of illegitimacy.

The promotion of marriage (to men) for single mothers is justified as a means of reducing poverty and improving children's well-being. Historian Gwendolyn Mink discusses the role of marriage in debates over the implementation of welfare reform:

> TANF's (Temporary Assistance for Needy Families) patriarchal solutions to welfare mothers' poverty have enjoyed bipartisan support. Democrats and Republicans did fight over some of the meaner provisions of the 1996 TANF legislation, but both agreed that poor women with children should at least be financially tied to their children's biological fathers or, better yet, be married to them. Endangering poor single women's independent childbearing decisions by condemning their decision to raise children independently, both parties agreed that poverty policy should make father-mother family formation its cardinal principle. (2001, 3)

Single low-income mothers and lesbian mothers are positioned differently in relation to the social promotion of legitimate family through marriage. Yet these are not mutually exclusive categories. The political rhetoric is framed as if all single mothers receiving social welfare benefits are straight, but lesbian mothers of color are vulnerable to the same forces of economic inequality as heterosexual mothers of color, and, likely, more. The category of illegitimacy intersects with these two seemingly distinct groups of mothers in particular ways.

Illegitimate Illegal Invalid: Narratives of Dependent Citizenship

DOMA states, quoting Representative Henry Hyde, the chairman of the Judiciary Committee, that legalizing same-sex marriage "trivializes the legitimate status of marriage and demeans it by putting a stamp of approval . . . on a union that many people . . . think is immoral" (1996, 15). DOMA federally codified the structural status of same-sex couples, and, by extension, children of gays and lesbians, as illegitimate.

In the United States the use of "illegitimacy" to regulate both civil rights and the flow of wealth is deeply gendered and racialized. Legal scholar Zanita E. Fenton explains the relationship between illegitimacy and the presumption of parentage: "Illegitimacy is the offspring of the marital presumption. That is, they are related and generally work together to accomplish the same social purposes. Similar to illegitimacy, the origins of the marital presumption served not only to predetermine intergenerational transfers of wealth, and ensure sexual control over women, but also to continue racial purity through the mythology of White supremacy" (2014, 21). Indeed, the history of the concept of illegitimacy in the United States is structured by patriarchy and deeply entwined with the history of slavery, nativism, and settler colonialism. Illegitimacy functions as what sociologists Michael Omi and Howard Winant refer to as a "racial project" (2014, 125). Thus, the concept can be deployed with subterfuge by the logics of gendered white supremacy; without ever mentioning race, it can be used as a tool of racism.

Yet the consequences of illegitimacy vary profoundly for mothers and children in different social locations. In 1990s family policy debates, mothers were labeled "unfit" for a variety of reasons that converged around "chosen" sexual and economic deviance from the traditional family ideal, and "dependency" on the state rather than on a patriarch. Exploring the ways mothers of different races, sexualities, and classes are located in relation to the state makes evident the largely unacknowledged importance of race to these assessments of the present and prescriptions for the future. Euphemisms like "illegitimate," "dependent," and "illegal" were used to discuss people of color while simultaneously denying the social relevance of race.

The critique of mothers accessing AFDC was bound up in a dystopian view of the future in which public coffers would be drained by children raised to remain dependent on the government, which would supposedly undermine the morals, values, culture, and economy of the United States. This fearful perspective also informed a change in public discussions about immigration. In the 1990s a political shift highlighted undocumented immigrant women giving birth in the United States to children who would be eligible for social welfare, health, disability, and education benefits as a social problem in need of address (Hondagneau-Sotelo 1996; Gutierrez 2009).

Despite the fact that undocumented immigrants were already ineligible for AFDC, a debate ensued over access to welfare for both documented residents and "illegal aliens"—that is, single mothers living in poverty. Representative Elton Gallegly articulated one stream of the argument emphasizing strict regulation of access to a broad range of privileges and benefits of US citizenship: "Further, to reduce the incentives for illegal immigration, I have introduced legislation to prohibit illegal aliens from receiving welfare or other federal benefits, and to deny federal funds to jurisdictions that allow illegals to vote, as has been proposed for the Los Angeles school district. We also must remove the ultimate incentive-guaranteed birthright citizenship for the children of illegal aliens" (*Congressional Record* September 9, 1992, 24291). Latinas and other immigrant mothers are here represented as strategically breaking the law in order to gain citizenship for their children, and, ultimately, access to social welfare services (Hondagneau-Sotelo 1996; Gutierrez 2009; Mayers 2016).

This perspective gained traction with the 1994 passage of California's Proposition 187, a law that sought to deny public education and nonemergency health care to undocumented immigrants. The law was eventually ruled unconstitutional by a federal district court, yet its passage carried profound representational weight in federal policy debates about mothers in relation to a government that deemed them illegal, and thus ineligible for the benefits of citizenship. Let us be clear that their social locations as undocumented immigrants are constructed in relation to laws that restrict and regulate immigrants based on country of origin, wealth, and professional and academic qualifications, in conjunction with the labor needs of the United States.

The structure of this story matches the dependency myths about women receiving welfare: dishonest mothers give birth to children that they use as conduits to government resources. Conservative political commentator Heather Mac Donald extends the discussion of dependency and socialization to include the invalid use of Supplemental Security Disability Income support: "Eulalia Rivera came from Puerto Rico in 1968 and proceeded to raise a welfare dynasty. Her 16 surviving children (the 17th was shot) and their 89 progeny collect $750,000 to $1 million a year in government benefits. Their main form of support, however, is not AFDC, the program for single mothers and children that has been targeted for reform: it is federal disability payments" (1995, 1). Mac Donald's primary complaint is not against people with severe disabilities that prevent them from engaging in productive employment, but it is there that she draws a line. She argues that amendments made to the law in 1984 regarding two primary categories of disability—substance abuse and children's behavioral disabilities—have been defined so broadly as to facilitate unprecedented misuse of the system. She suggests that the function of disability payments has undergone "an unacknowledged shift" in who is served, such that many beneficiaries' "unemployability reflects rampant drug use, a chaotic upbringing, and a lack of education and work ethic rather than any physical impediment" (1995, 1). She not only blames irresponsible adults whose substance abuse renders them unemployable, but also mothers who abuse the system by qualifying their children for governmental support for what she views as bogus behavioral issues that result from bad parenting.

As is clear from the story above, the fears she raises are primarily about rewarding and thus encouraging deviant behavior, and raising children who will in the future be incapable of productive employment. The chief consequence she predicts is a generation of kids socialized into "dependent" adults—the opposite of the productive citizens posited as necessary for a strong national future. Mac Donald's policy prescriptions emphasize the need to redefine disability to only include people whose disabilities are so severe as to prevent them from working and caring for themselves (i.e., invalids). She essentially argues that the majority of recipients of SSDI and SSI are in*valid* in*valids*, and that their "bad choices" should not be rewarded with government support.

"Illegitimate," "illegal," or "invalid" status is tied to an unlawful relationship to the state, and this very failure to achieve economic independence is used as evidence of an inability to appropriately socialize the future citizens of this democracy:

> Although black and Latina women are characterized differently in the family values debate, each group is demonized and their behavior depicted as threatening the basic values of American society. In the case of black, the central threat is single-parent families that produce "illegitimate" children who, according to the conservative and centrist narrative, are likely to become unruly citizens. In the case of Latinas, the threat is

undocumented immigrants who give birth in the United States and create unwanted citizens, who then become a conduit of government resources to a family of "illegal" residents. (Dill, Baca Zinn, and Patton 1998, 20)

Characterizing SSDI and SSI support as an extension of poor mothers' dependency on and abuse of the social welfare system adds disability to the pantheon of shaming practices conservatives employ to represent bad mothers making bad choices as the cause of the most pressing social problems in the United States. Illegitimate and illegal citizenship have historically been coded as *not-white*. Immigrants and people of color are not only cast as illegitimate families, but as signifiers of illegitimate relationships with the state.

It seems clear that "illegals" and "invalids" occupy similar locations to "illegitimates" in the lexicon of US citizenship and belonging. Welfare moms, undocumented immigrants and their "alien children," children receiving disability payments, and innocent orphans in need of salvation emerged in political discussions as characters in sociopolitical allegories about the future of the nation. Each of these populations is used in deployment of the American Dream story to justify the neoliberal economic agenda of privatization. Each character has particular social functions, whether to represent the ills of the contemporary United States, fears for the future, or scenarios of redemption: marriage and adoption.

Sociopolitical allegories about the "bad" socialization practices of lesbians, women receiving welfare, and undocumented immigrant mothers function as a smokescreen for the larger neoliberal economic agenda of the privatization of family care. Fiscal concerns were obvious in welfare reform and immigration legislation. Although less evident in discussions of DOMA, financial concerns still held sway with respect to access to family benefits and services. Conservatives bristled at the prospect of extending the rights and privileges of citizenship to LGBT families. In testimony in favor of DOMA, senator Trent Lott explained the fiscal agenda beneath the moral concerns, explaining that legalizing same-sex marriage would require "redefining eligibility for benefits under those and other programs. Imagine the financial and social consequences of taking such a step" (*Congressional Record* September 10, 1996, 2). In testimony in favor of DOMA, senator Don Nickles of Oklahoma viewed this feared extension of rights to same-sex couples as a challenge to "traditional" definitions of "American identity": "Another reason this bill is needed now concerns Federal benefits. The Federal Government extends benefits, rights, and privileges to persons who are married, and generally it accepts a State's definition of marriage. This bill will help the Federal Government defend the traditional and commonsense definitions of the American people. Otherwise, if Hawaii, or any other State, gives new meaning to the words 'marriage' and 'spouse,' reverberations may be felt throughout the Federal Code" (*Congressional Record* September 10, 1996, 4). The reverberations the senators are worried about are economic. This trajectory of thinking lays bare linkages between the definition and enforcement of traditional marriage and the allocation of citizenship rights, privileges, and family protections. Stories about unmarried mothers being incapable of properly socializing the nation's children drew attention away from neoliberal efforts to privatize care.

I began this chapter with Lisbeth's discussion of becoming one of Elena's six mothers when her birth mother was having difficulties. Was Elena's mother receiving AFDC? Was she on SSDI? Was she an immigrant? Perhaps Elena's mother entered the United States without appropriate documentation and gave birth to her while living here. "At risk" urban youth of color were the subject of great political concern in the 1990s. Politicians and pundits rang alarm bells about the dangers such children and their mothers posed. For conservative policy makers Elena represented a social problem: illegitimate US family and citizenship. Most likely, her mother would have been perceived as a criminal, illegally seeking social benefits through her child, whatever the actual circumstances of their lives might be.

The same dangers Lisbeth and Gabriella worry about, as Elena's mothers, haunt these sociopolitical allegories. Elena is a Black Latina teenage girl in a low-income urban environment. If the conservative anxieties about bad socialization played out, Elena would represent one of the greatest villains imagined: she would have unprotected sex with a "superpredator," "drug dealer," or "gangbanger" that had, like her, been improperly socialized by an unwed mother in a culture of poverty. In this narrative, the cycle of dependency would be reproduced through Elena's pregnancy and subsequent bad mothering.

"Illegitimacy" as Cause of Poverty

While illegitimacy prevailed among politicians and pundits, academics and progressives emphasized poverty as the issue to be addressed, rather than the behavior of individual mothers. Feminists charged that conservatives were scapegoating women of color and ignoring structural inequality. Yet these systemic critiques were largely drowned out by an explanation that was accepted among conservatives, centrists, and liberals: illegitimacy came to be seen as the *cause*, rather than the *consequence* of poverty and the social problems associated with it.[5] There are several versions of the narrative, slightly tinged by different ideologies. Some emphasize immorality while others are more concerned with dependency on the state, but they largely agree that individual deviant behavior must be curbed in order to stem the tide of social chaos.

Heather Mac Donald responded to a *New York Times* op-ed written by Peter Edelman, Georgetown University law professor and former counselor to Health and Human Services secretary Donna Shalala during the Clinton administration.

> To the Editor:
>
> Peter Edelman (Op-Ed, July 8) attacks welfare reform, arguing that "the real issue isn't welfare. It's poverty." In fact, it's neither; the real issue is illegitimacy. The rise in child poverty that Mr. Edelman laments was fueled by the explosion of out-of-wedlock births, particularly among blacks. Children growing up in single-parent households are five times more likely to be poor than children of married parents, and are more likely to fail in school, become delinquent and suffer abuse, regardless of their parents' income, education or race. Do single mothers have a tenuous grip on the job market? Of course. When crisis hits, they have exactly half the resources to fall back on as a married couple. No amount of Government Band-Aids can change this. To end poverty and protect poor children, we should figure out how to revive marriage, not how to resurrect welfare. (July 8, 1999)

Mac Donald draws on an analysis disturbingly common in these dialogues: she confuses correlation for causation. The Personal Responsibility and Work Reconciliation Act ("welfare reform") cited this same litany of social problems in its preamble, declared out-of-wedlock pregnancy the cause of poverty, and enacted policies designed to "combat illegitimacy." This analysis enacts a "culture of poverty" argument, emphasizing individual and cultural behavior as the problem, and marriage and adoption as solutions.[6] In his role as one of two primary Republican advisors on "welfare reform" in the 104th Congress, conservative policy analyst Charles Murray testified to the House Subcommittee on Human Resources: "My proposition is that illegitimacy is the single most important social problem of our time—more important than crime, drugs, poverty, illiteracy, welfare or homelessness because it drives everything else. Doing something about it is not just one more item on the American policy agenda, but should be at the top" (1994). Blaming social problems on the individual behavior of mothers makes a tidy story that contains the cause of poverty at the level of individual choice, morality, and family structure. The villains were clear: lazy, sexually- and gender-deviant mothers, largely of color, milking the system by having babies to profit from it.

This culture-of-poverty argument blames the choices and behavior of poor people for their inability to pull themselves up by their bootstraps: the underside of the American Dream narrative of self-made men succeeding economically through good morals and hard work. The fierce denial of systemic inequality is central to this capitalist ideology. Whether acknowledged or not, race, gender, and sexuality are fundamental to this explanation. There were other voices in the public debate emphasizing discrimination and the need for more jobs and a stronger social safety net. These voices were less audible in the public sphere. Systemic inequality is harder to explain in a soundbite than "bad choices."

Culture-of-poverty explanations are bolstered further by representations of Asian American immigrants as "model minorities," succeeding in America because their "cultural values"—emphasizing family, hard work, and academic achievement—match the demands of capitalist success in the United States (Glenn 1994). Sociologist Lynn H. Fujiwara explains:

Asian immigrants have been precariously situated within a racial discourse that confuses their role and impact. On the one hand, prevailing cultural narratives of the Asian "model minority" have been politically employed to legitimize existing systems and impose "group" or cultural blame on other people of color to justify dismantling federally mandated social programs. At the same time, contrary to popular narratives of "Asian success" is the reality that between 1990 and 1994, poverty among Asian Pacific American families rose from 11.9 in 1990 to 13.5 percent in 1994. (1999, 108)

Deployment of the "model minority" narrative both obscures poverty among Asian Americans and blames African American, Latinx, and Indigenous cultures, families, and individuals for perpetuating poverty through a generational cycle characterized by "bad values" like laziness, irresponsibility, sexual deviance, immorality, and poor work ethic. The key features of this explanation are intractability and generational transmission.

Neoliberal Redemption Through Adoption

These intersecting explanations laid the necessary groundwork for adoption, particularly transracial adoption, to be proffered and largely accepted as solutions to the perceived social problem of illegitimacy.[7] Stories about the necessity of saving children from the horrors of poverty and illegitimacy provided comfortable political fables that allowed for a political agenda that I call *cultural eugenics* to be embraced as salvation for both literal and symbolic children. While the eugenic movement of the nineteenth and twentieth centuries was grounded in biological theories of social inferiority, contemporary versions of such social engineering have expanded to include culture as a nearly intractable feature of racial identity. Indeed, this is central to the culture-of-poverty narrative. In a social and historical moment characterized by understandings of race as cultural rather than biological—the core of the "color-blind" meaning system—the means of generational transmission have expanded from *biology* and *blood* to include *culture* and *choice*.[8]

In this section I critically explore how adoption policies in the 1990s privileged white middle-class people (including lesbians) who wanted to parent. These are also the federal policies that undergird family-making among the mothers we interviewed. I do my best to convey my deep respect for the people who shared their stories with me, while also considering the perilous politics of adoption in the contemporary United States. I want to be very clear that I am not critiquing human beings here, but, rather, the interlocking systems of meaning and power shaping the contours of everyone's family-making practices. One of the pitfalls of writing about adoption—or, I suppose, about all human issues—is that people sometimes interpret critiques of the stratified system as critiques of the people involved in that system. As an adoptee myself, I know how deeply vulnerable both birth and adoptive parents (most often mothers) feel in relation to these issues.

In the 1990s, adoption was promoted as a central policy solution to combat illegitimacy and poverty. Explicitly colorblind adoption and foster care policies were put forward under the banner of the "best interests of children" being saved from incompetent mothers and missing fathers. Adoption became part of the conversation about how to solve the social problem of illegitimacy. As William Bennett testified before Congress: "I believe that making adoption easier is an essential and compassionate part of welfare reform. Adoption is the best alternative we have to protect a child's interest in a postwelfare world. The demand is virtually unlimited (at least for very young children), but current laws make adoption exceedingly difficult. Lifting restrictions on interracial adoption and easing age limitations for adoptive parents will help ensure that large numbers of children will be adopted into good, stable, loving homes" (1996). The sociopolitical narrative that emerged focused in particular on concerns about children of color in a "post-welfare" world. In other words, this seemingly noble policy concern regarded what to do with the children of mothers receiving welfare benefits under AFDC that would no longer be eligible for TANF. Republican Speaker of the House Newt Gingrich infamously proposed that the children of welfare mothers unable to find employment should be removed and placed in orphanages. In the context of such inflammatory rhetoric, making adoption easier seemed like a beneficent effort to save endangered children.

Charles Murray explicates connections between welfare reform, unfit mothers, and adoption: "What about women who can find no support but keep the baby anyway? There are laws already on the books about the right of the state to take a child from a neglectful parent" (1993). Murray argues that the only social policy initiative radical enough to alter the "inevitable" fate of children born into a "culture of poverty" is to remove all restrictions to transracial adoption, and to make all adoptions irrevocable and as easy as possible for two-parent families (Murray 1993; 1994a; Herrnstein and Murray 1994). The story that developed about transracial adoption drew on the discourse of colorblindness to argue that children of color were "languishing" in foster care because "racist" social workers were dedicated to "race-matching" (Patton 2000). It was a deeply appealing narrative. Conservatives also promoted adoption for its government cost-saving measures: "In terms of government budgets, adoption is cheap; the new parents bear all the costs of twenty-four-hour-a-day care for eighteen years or so" (Herrnstein and Murray 1994, 416). Indeed, in many ways, adoption speaks allegorically to the neoliberal political agenda of privatization that characterizes this era of reform.

Legislation removing all barriers to transracial adoption was originally part of welfare reform in the section designed to combat illegitimacy. The Interethnic Placement Act was removed just prior to the last version of the bill and put into the minimum wage bill that was signed the same week. The focus on transracial adoption revealed the primary legislative concern of regulating the reproductive practices of women of color through an agenda of cultural eugenics. The bill sailed through on a wave of feel-good testimony urging colleagues to pass this "happy bill" (*Congressional Record* May 9, 1996, 1). The law empowered prospective adoptive parents to sue adoption agencies for delaying the placement of a child based on race. On the surface the story made perfect sense. The solution was based on the premise that children of color were languishing in foster care because social workers were misguidedly delaying adoption while searching for same-race parents. This premise, however, was flawed, and due to the way the legislation was written it most directly benefitted white middle-class prospective parents. Indeed, as I argue in *BirthMarks*, a more effective approach to concerns with large numbers of children of color in the foster care system would be to consider why so many children in poverty are removed from their mothers in the first place.[9]

The public adoption system has, at least since the 1980s, become primarily responsible for the adoptive placement of children from the foster care system. Healthy infants of any race rarely enter the public adoption system; their adoptions are typically handled through private adoption agencies and lawyers. The children in the public foster care system are there primarily because they have been removed from their parents, many because they are young, poor single mothers of color.[10] Indeed, according to a 1991 US Committee on Ways and Means report, "the majority of children in foster care are from families receiving aid to families with dependent children (AFDC)" (Golden 1997, 2). The policy focus on removing barriers to transracial adoption as a means of combatting illegitimacy makes evident the concern with race and socialization. Adoption, like marriage, is the state sanctioning of relationships that facilitates access to the full rights and protections of citizenship. It establishes an avenue through which children and families receive governmental protections, support, and benefits.

As I have discussed, one of the chief political concerns about children of undocumented immigrants is that they will function as vehicles of government aid and services to their "illegal" families. Senator Chafee introduced an amendment to the PWRA that allowed for "alien children" who did not qualify for AFDC to qualify for foster care and adoption subsidies, effectively laying out a plan facilitating the transfer of these children to foster and adoptive families. In 1997, a year after the passage of the Interethnic Placement Act, which removed "racial barriers" to transracial adoption, the Adoption and Safe Families Act provided tax credits for adoptive parents designed to promote the adoption of children from foster care. The law also shortened the time frame allowed before parental rights can be terminated and created "financial incentives" awarded to states for increasing the number of permanent placements. These policies changed the federal landscape of adoption, effectively making the adoption of children from foster care easier, for those who fit the qualifications. These legislative changes accompanied the end of AFDC as a federal entitlement program, which limited single mothers to a total of five years throughout the course of their lives to Temporary Assistance for Needy Families (TANF). This policy change allowed that children who could not or could no longer qualify for TANF or AFDC could qualify for state support *only* if they were removed from their mothers and placed in foster care or adoptive families. Mayers states it clearly: "Taken together, the elimination of AFDC, the IEPA, and the ASFA support the movement of 'vulnerable' poor children of color into wealthy white families under the aegis of protection from cultural pathology" (2016, 70).

Where did these children go? Reproductive justice scholar Laura Briggs discusses adoption by white queers in the context of neoliberal politics:

> In the 1990s the newly expanded number of children in the child welfare systems in the aftermath of the crack babies "crisis" had begun to take their toll on state budgets. White queers (or those rhetorically imagined as white in policy debate) disproportionately served as the safety valve in this system, unburdening child welfare agencies of their "hard-to-place" children, either as foster parents or as adoptive parents. There was substantial overlap between "hard-to-place" and "kids of color," as even federal law recognized; by the mid-1990s, as we have seen, the federal adoption tax credit allowed those who took in "special needs" children to deduct all the associated costs from their taxes—and children of color were all defined as special needs. (2012, 264–65)

The success of the conservative neoliberal vision was the construction of a system of laws that both facilitated this transfer of children and simultaneously hid the race-gender-poverty politics driving this agenda of cultural eugenics.

Two of the couples we interviewed in Iowa City were foster parents at the time of our interview, and they were friends with each other. Sue, who is a social worker (not in the field of adoption), was clear about the role of queers in the child welfare system.

> SUE: Kim and Mischa—the four of us laugh all the time. If it wasn't for the gay and lesbian community in Iowa City, and throughout the state of Iowa, there would be very few foster families.

Sue and Adrienne, whose twins were toddlers at the time of our interview, regularly cared for children who have been temporarily removed from their parents and have a reunification plan rather than an adoption plan.

> SUE: We currently do not have any foster children; we did until about a month ago—add yet another element to the neighborhood! We just had a sibling set, an eleven-year-old and a six-year-old, girls, African

American, that had been staying with us—oh, I don't know—maybe
the past five or six months.

ADRIENNE: And they have stayed with us before.

SUE: Last spring, for awhile, and then they went back to their mother.

Poverty is the number-one predictor of removal by the child welfare
system of children from their mothers (Roberts 1999). Given the level of
discrimination in education and employment in the United States, it is
not surprising that women of color are disproportionately represented
among mothers experiencing poverty. Though rarely acknowledged in
public dialogues, there are relationships, both literal and representational, between mothers who are unable to raise their children due to
poverty, and white middle-class adoptive mothers whose families have
been constructed through adoption policies promoting the social reproduction of two-parent, middle-class nuclear families. Such relationships
are literally enforced through policies and laws regulating fit versus unfit
parents.[11]

Kelly and Sam, a white middle-class couple that live in San Jose, California, began exploring adoption when they were frustrated at the lack
of results with their fertility treatments. They came upon a Santa Clara
County Child Welfare recruitment booth at San Jose Pride.

KELLY: They have kids that they are pretty sure will be needing adoptive parents, and so you—

SAM: Yeah, yeah. Low risk.

KELLY: If you want eventually to adopt, these are the kids you are
getting—is those kids whose parents look like they're not going to
make it. So, they don't have enough families, so they recruited at the
Pride Festival.

Low risk. This language—adopted from the social workers who ran
the training session Kelly and Sam attended—betrays the neoliberal
consumer logic governing adoption from foster care. Risk assessment
is structured into contemporary adoption practice. Will the child be
released for adoption? What kind of damage has he or she endured? Will
the birth parents let go completely? What about the extended family?
The foster-adopt program is for children removed from birth mothers

whose parental rights are expected to be terminated. What this means in practice is that birth parents (most often single mothers) are given by the courts set periods of time to change whatever behavior prompted the removal of their children. Foster parents hoping to adopt are then in the contradictory position of hoping these children's birth mothers fail in their efforts at getting their lives together. Kelly and Sam were uncomfortable with this and renewed their fertility treatments, which were ultimately successful.

Kim and Mischa, who have four adopted children, were also caring for an infant from the foster care system at the time of our interview in 2007.

> MISCHA: We've been foster parents for some time, and I was a foster parent way back when. And yes, the problem is, is that a lot of the kids in the social system never become available for adoption. They either go back to their own family or they go back to relatives in the family.
>
> KIMBERLY: Before we brought Jonas from Haiti we were trying very hard to adopt from the foster care system. We had, I think, four infants who were placed with us and had to go back to—either to family or to another foster family, being moved to another jurisdiction.

They discussed the difficulty of bonding with children that they hoped to adopt, only to have them removed from their care. They lamented the tensions they experienced between wanting to adopt a child they had cared for and also desiring that the best interests of that child would be served. Tina and Cass, an interracial couple with five children that live in Des Moines, were very clear with the child welfare system. As Tina told us, "We said don't give us a child unless you know for sure. Cause we wouldn't be able to let go."

While conservatives were adamant that the prospect of homosexuals adopting children constituted a terrifying view of the future, LGBTQ activists pushed for the expansion of adoption rights. Many of the changes that occurred in adoption laws were at the city, county, or state levels. A combination of policy changes and practical strategies developed for navigating the uneven legal terrain for same-sex couples at the local and state levels. Some states, like Florida, had laws

on the books banning gays from adoption. Other states and munici-
palities had more ambiguous policies that left openings for queer prospective parents to adopt through a range of legal strategies regularly
shared in queer communities. A few states, like California, had more
flexible laws that were opened up even more by LGBTQ activism and
legal action.

In 2000 the Child Citizenship Act was passed, which provided
that children adopted transnationally who met governmental criteria would automatically become US citizens when they were adopted.
Prior to this, parents had to apply for citizenship status for their
transnationally adopted children in separate legal transactions. In the
context of bitter political debates about immigration that resulted in
restrictive policies for both legal and undocumented immigrants in
the United States, the cultural eugenics agenda seems frighteningly
clear. The only transnational immigrants the United States fully wel-
comes are those adopted by predominantly white middle-class and
wealthy families.

Race functions in deeply covert ways as a signifier of relationships
to the state. Most of the 1990s political discourse avoided explicit references to race, yet reproductive bodies of color were the clear subjects of
political concern. The "colorblind" discourse employed in these policy
debates uses race-neutral language, but illustrates public stories with
unmarried mothers and children of color. Illegitimacy and illegality
functioned as code words that facilitated rhetorical attacks on mothers of color. This strategy of racial evasion depends upon a belief in
the neutrality of government. As critical legal scholar Dorothy Roberts
explains: "More generally, critical thinkers have demonstrated that the
liberal reliance on seemingly neutral principles to judge equality claims
actually legitimates the interests and experiences of white people. The
very language of neutrality used by judges is already weighted in favor
of the status quo. . . . Government neutrality, exemplified by the doctrine of color blindness, conceals the racist origins of social practices
that do not overtly discriminate on the basis of race" (1996, 367). The
ideology of "colorblindness" is structured to obscure systemic power
and deny the importance of race in social organization. When we symbolically remove race as a structural element from this story, we are left
with individual and cultural explanations of bad and good choices.

Conclusion

The family policy overhaul of the 1990s resulted in structural changes in how families are recognized by the state, yet these changes affected families unevenly and inconsistently. Families closest to the patriarchal nuclear family ideal were supported, while those perceived as deviant were penalized. The policies function in relation to each other to both foster and conceal gender, class, and race oppression with the goal of reproducing heteronormative white middle-class families. On one hand, the passage of DOMA limited the family-making strategies of same-sex couples. On the other, same-sex couples with financial and social resources had advantages in adoption policy that came at the expense of the stripping of protections from vulnerable mothers of color. It is important to recognize that these legal changes fundamentally structured what kinds of family-making decisions mothers in different circumstances were able to make. The privileges of some families depend upon the oppression of others, both representationally and literally. Queer of color theorist Roderick Ferguson argues, "As homonormative formations achieve cultural normativity by appealing to liberal capital's regimes of visibility, the immigrant, the poor, and the person of color suffer under the state's apparatuses—apparatuses that render them the cultural antitheses of a stable and healthy social order" (2005, 65). Visibility of white middle-class gay and lesbian couples came at a cost. Policy advances made in opening up adoption to same-sex parents depended upon sociopolitical narratives of poor women of color as a threat to the future of the nation.

Elena and her six queer mothers of color challenge this phenomenon. I have not seen any children's books celebrating characters like pregnant teenagers, drug dealers, and gang members, yet these characters populate the political fictions narrated in the congressional record and news editorials. Political dialogues conjure horror stories of national decline in the figure of a Black Latina teenager in an urban environment. These dystopian scripts are not the only possibilities. I imagine Elena's life as an allegory, too, but one infused with hope. Elena and her six moms envision family in ways that both contest and uphold white patriarchal definitions of legitimacy. Family-making is a process of navigating the push and pull of social expectations and unequal access to opportunities, as well as strategizing about how best to support one's children in a society stratified by race, gender, sexuality, disability, and class. Sometimes that looks like resistance, and at other times like the embrace of mainstream ideals. For Lisbeth and her comothers, raising a child was a communal effort. Her family may seem like a new form of kinship, but communities of people—often women—have raised children together all over the world throughout history. Lisbeth makes clear that these traditions feel familiar to her. These are the familial models she grew up with in Puerto Rico.

Elena's allegory is a coalitional response to the full-blown policy assault on women and children wrought by the family values politics of the 1990s. In the face of attacks on the legitimacy of Elena and her mothers, these queer women of color came together to raise Elena into an adult they could be proud of. My consideration of the intersections of power and social narrative in these bitter political battles suggests possibilities for similar efforts for social and reproductive justice. Divisive narratives of race, gender, sexuality, and class have cleaved tensions and resentments between various contingencies of people seeking rights and protections of citizenship, particularly along lines of race, gender, sexuality, and class.

The political changes I have detailed in this chapter laid the groundwork for the way political battles over same-sex marriage would take shape over the next fifteen years. One of the crucial elements in this formulation was the fetishization of illegitimacy as the cause of poverty and social problems. This agreement among policy-makers justified the dismantling of some families and the reproduction of others, while simultaneously blaming mothers for the poverty and oppression they experience. The sociopolitical narrative that the poor socialization practices of unmarried mothers were a threat to the future of the nation served as the axis point on which much of the same-sex marriage debate would turn. In the next chapter I take up the question of socialization to consider how the mothers we interviewed navigated the pitfalls of swiftly changing and often contradictory laws regulating families outside the heteronormative ideal in the early years of the twenty-first century. Lawsuits in Vermont and Massachusetts legalized same-sex unions at the state level in 2000 and 2003. The legal strategies employed in both cases built on the sociopolitical allegory about illegitimacy to argue for the rights of same-sex couples to marry.

SAME-SEX MARRIAGE, 2000–2003

April 2000   Vermont civil union bill becomes law

November 2000   Nebraska voters approve constitutional ban on same-sex marriage

April 2001   Netherlands becomes world's first country to legalize same-sex marriage

November 2002   Nevada voters approve constitutional ban on same-sex marriage

May 2003   Federal constitutional marriage amendment introduced

June 2003   US Supreme Court strikes down sodomy laws

July 2003   Vatican begins campaign against same-sex marriage

August 2003   Constitutional ban on same-sex unions gathers sponsors

August 2003   Poll shows majority of Americans opposed to same-sex marriage

September 2003   California passes domestic partnership law

October 2003   US President Bush announces he wants marriage reserved for heterosexuals

November 2003   State Supreme Court decision makes Massachusetts first US state to legalize same-sex marriage

Adapted from https://gaymarriage.procon.org

5

Navigating Illegitimacy

Socialization, Race, and Difference, 2000–2003

ADRIENNE: Society is built to support a certain *family structure*, and
that's not the family structure that we have. You know, we're swimming against the tide, and that does make things a little bit interesting. Yeah, you know, people try to be nice, and for the most part,
people are kind, you know, they're not cruel. But you know, at the
same time, they don't understand and they do have preconceived notions about maybe us, our relationship, the nature of our relationship.

Adrienne speaks as an African American lesbian in an interracial relationship with Sue, a white woman. They have biracial twins that were
toddlers at the time of our interview in 2006. Adrienne and Sue also regularly care for children as foster parents for the child welfare system on
an as-needed basis. They live in a predominantly conservative Catholic
neighborhood in Iowa City that has been less than welcoming. Adrienne
and Sue have to regularly negotiate tensions between the purportedly
ideal structure for raising future citizens—white, heterosexually married,
and middle class—and "the family structure that we have": an interracial
unmarried lesbian couple with biracial twins, one of whom has a disability. In family policy debates, "family structure" is shorthand for the
narrative that illegitimacy is the central cause of family breakdown.

Adrienne and Sue's family is legally defined as illegitimate, and the
pervasiveness of this definition is reflected in the social tensions they
experience. At the time of our interview Adrienne and Sue were unable
to marry or have a marriage from any other state recognized as legitimate by the state of Iowa. Sue gave birth to their children, and Adrienne
became their second legal parent through adoption. Their middle-class
status, the cultural capital they bring as a lawyer and a social worker,
and their economic resources provide them with tools and strategies for

navigating social institutions and for obtaining some measure of legal protection for their family.

Legal recognition provides access to social institutions that provide services, benefits, and care. Yet laws and policies alone do not dictate how families are actually treated when they enroll their children in school or seek medical care. As Adrienne says, "[People] don't understand and they do have preconceived notions" about multiracial lesbian-headed families. These "preconceived notions" are informed by political debates and media narratives about what families should look like, what they do look like, and what differences between these two poles may mean. The "tide" Adrienne and Sue are "swimming against" includes tension with neighbors, illegibility in social interactions, political discourse about the evils of queer families, and public laws and policies enforcing definitions of legitimate family and citizenship. The lives of the lesbian mothers and their children that we interviewed were profoundly shaped by the necessity of negotiating both legal limitations on social protections for their families, and public discourse narrating their families as abnormal, wrong, or dangerous to the future of the nation.

The terms of legitimacy are deeply racialized. Whiteness is not only represented in these political dialogues as legitimate, but as a *legitimating force*. Mothers of color are represented as illegitimate and incapable of appropriate socialization. These stories rely on a fictional split between lesbians, who are imagined as white, and women of color, who are represented as straight. This representation rhetorically erases queer people of color and their children. These stories about navigating family life shed light on the complex ways race is used in political discourse to signify deviance while simultaneously maintaining a pretense of equality.

Mothers we interviewed talked about the stark disconnect between sociopolitical discussions about LGBTQ families and their own experiences. They told stories about unpleasant encounters with strangers. They discussed strategies for teaching their children to think critically about social meanings regarding "normal" families and "gay" families. Many of them stressed the importance of educating their children to understand structural inequality and the forms it takes. They told their children about the value of difference from narrow definitions of normal. Mothers did their best to help their children resist and survive in a world that denigrates their families.

In this chapter I enter the historical moment of the first few years of the twenty-first century through a consideration of narrative and representation. If we strip 1990s politics down to the most fundamental sociopolitical allegory of that era, we have a story about the future of the nation as dependent on the socialization practices of US mothers. Competing versions of these stories deployed racialized representations of mothers and children in different kinds of families to support efforts at legal and social change. What were the ramifications of these narratives? How did these political tales shape the lived experiences of families in different locations? In what ways did they influence the ways that lawsuits in favor of same-sex marriage were framed? I further my *genealogy of illegitimacy* by exploring questions of socialization, illegitimacy, and race in two directions: the lived experiences of the families we interviewed, and the political and legal discourse about the legalization of same-sex unions and marriages in the first few years of the millennium. I would like to suggest that examining the ways that representations of mothers and children shape both the lived experience of family-making, as well as the legal strategies employed to argue for same-sex marriage, makes evident how profoundly neoliberal economic and social agendas influenced public dialogues about families of all kinds.

Crossing State Lines: "We're Both His Moms. He's Got Two Moms"

If conservatives thought the 1996 Defense of Marriage Act would preclude the legalization of same-sex marriage, their assumptions were at the very least complicated by the uneven legal developments across the nation. The early years of the twenty-first century were characterized by swift changes and sharp contrasts in laws regulating marriage and adoption in different states. Vermont legalized civil unions in 2000, the same year the state of Nebraska banned same-sex marriage. The Netherlands became the first country to legalize same-sex marriage in 2001. In 2002 Nevada instituted a state-level version of DOMA, prohibiting the performance or recognition of same-sex unions. In September 2003 California established the Domestic Partnership Rights and Responsibilities Act, extending many of the rights of married couples to domestic partners. Belgium, Ontario, and British Columbia legalized same-sex marriage in 2003. On November 18, 2003, Massachusetts became the first state in the United States to allow same-sex couples to legally marry.

Families were strategic in their approach to the contradictory political climate regarding same-sex marriage and adoption. We went to Vermont in 2000 to legalize our relationship, even though our civil union would not be recognized by any other state. Like many of the women we talked with that were married out of state, we had multiple reasons for doing so. For one thing, the timing was right. Vermont legalized civil unions at the moment in our relationship when Melanie and I wanted to confirm our commitment to each other. Yet this was also about subverting sociopolitical narratives denigrating our relationship as illegitimate. In the context of DOMA and all the political fury over the dangers of same-sex marriage, getting "civilly unified" felt, in 2000, like resistance.

While marriage was the primary focus of public news and policy discussions about same-sex parents at the turn of the millenium, this was not the only, or even necessarily the most, important concern of the mothers we interviewed. Marriage was part of a larger landscape of possible legal protections for families. Wedding stories did not necessarily follow mainstream trajectories of love, marriage, and then children; timing was shaped by what legal options were available. Motivation was often more about protecting children than about the state sanctioning their relationships. As Laura Briggs explains, "To a significant extent, the question of gay marriage is centrally about the raising of children, for its supporters among LGBTQ folk, for its Christian Right opponents, and even for the judges writing decisions about it" (2012, 241). The protection and socialization of children that was a fundamental focus of the stories told by parents, activists, and politicians in the family values debates of the 1990s continued into the early 2000s.

Most of the mothers we interviewed were dedicated to legally protecting their families in whatever ways they could. Carol and Cheryl are white middle-class mothers of triplets who live in Boston, Massachusetts. Their babies were born in 2000.

CAROL: We are very fortunate being in Massachusetts.
CHERYL: Even before marriage was legal we were fortunate being in
    Massachusetts.
CAROL: It's a very open state.

CHERYL: We have the youngest triplets ever adopted in Massachusetts. We had all the paperwork done and waiting for the coparent adoption when they were born. We already had our health care proxies in place so that if anything happened to me, there were any complications in delivery, she was recognized as their parent or as their medical-caregiver-proxy right away.

They petitioned the court for what is called "co-parent adoption" in Massachusetts. Their home study was waived based on their demonstration that they had been in a long-term relationship, and that they shared a household and finances. Cheryl submitted an affidavit stating that she was the children's biological mother and she wanted Carol to be their legal second parent. In many states this is called "stepparent adoption." The benefit of co- and step- over second-parent adoptions is that there is no home study required.

Laws regulating second-parent adoptions varied dramatically between states and within states. In some jurisdictions, like Florida, all adoptions by gays and lesbians were outlawed. In other states there were no laws prohibiting second-parent adoptions, so some couples worked with lawyers to find the right judges—those who had previously approved of guardianship rulings and second-parent adoptions. Once legal precedents were set, changes in adoption laws happened gradually and unevenly. Yet even in states with LGBTQ-friendly laws, finances determined which families could afford to exercise the available options. Carol and Cheryl felt fortunate to live in Massachusetts, where coparent adoption was allowed, but also that they had the resources to be able to take advantage of this option.

Like many of the mothers we interviewed, Cheryl and Carol made every effort to protect their family. They took a deep breath after the adoptions were final, assuming that their relationships were legal and, thus, would not be challenged.

CHERYL: 'Cause then we just relaxed. We didn't have to worry about anything anymore. That was it. [Pause] Until we went to Florida.

When their children were just over one year old they painfully discovered the limitations of legal protection, and the dangers of crossing state lines.

CHERYL: We spent six weeks or eight weeks living in Florida for Carol's work. At the time I wasn't back [to work] full time yet.

CAROL: So we were in Tampa.

CHERYL: We were in Tampa, and Florida is not known to be necessarily the friendliest place for our families. But we had all the birth certificates and adoption certificates and everything all lined up. Carol had all of our insurance at that time. She was providing the insurance through her job. Jake, well—they all got RSV on the plane ride there. They were only fifteen months. They were over a year but because they were over a year they couldn't have the shots anymore.[1] And Jake developed a pneumonia complication. So we're away as it was. My sister was visiting us, but it was scary. We were away from home. I took him to the emergency room. And in the emergency room I provided the health insurance card. And as you're registering, "Well, what's your relationship?"

I said, "I'm his mother."

They said, "Okay."

And then when I handed them the insurance card they said, "Well, then, who's this?"

I said, "Well, that's his other mother."

"Well, do you have a birth certificate? *How*? What do you *mean*?"

"We're both his moms. He's got two moms."

"Oh. [Pause] Can I see your driver's license?"

I said, "Would you like to see the C-section scar as well?" I was so floored. And here I was scared as it was. He wasn't doing well. And they were gonna start to question whether we were both his parents.

This kind of policing of family could happen in almost any state, whatever the laws. Yet the fact that they were in Florida was significant; the social and political context differed dramatically from Massachusetts. Adoption by gays and lesbians was banned in Florida by a 1977 law ushered in by the antigay "Save Our Children" campaign headed by Anita Bryant. This law remained in place until 2010. The most relevant document in Cheryl's transaction was the medical insurance card, yet it was not enough to guarantee adequate medical care unless backed up by an array of legal certifications proving the legitimacy of mother and child.

CHERYL: And so here we were thinking we were safe. We were this
family. We were adopted. We were accepted. We had next to no issues here. We go to Florida for six weeks, he needs medical care, and
someone's gonna start questioning us. And that night I turned to
Carol and I said, "I don't care how much they offer you. I don't care
how great a job it might be. We can't live here. This isn't a place that
feels safe for our family." So we came back to Massachusetts, even before marriage. And said we're just gonna be *here*. And we, you know,
we came from here anyway. So it's not like it was a big transition. But
it was important for us to have that safety and that feeling for our
family. So we might *visit* Disneyworld every now and then but we
won't think about living elsewhere.

Their stories demonstrate the complicated relationships between laws,
their application, and public responses to them. Even with a handful of
legal documents verifying their family's legal status, Cheryl and Carol's
legitimacy as mothers can be challenged on a regular basis. Their experiences reminded them of the tenuousness of family protections for
nonheterosexual parents and their children, even for white and middle-
class folks with the socioeconomic resources to purchase every available
protection. Even with these protections, Cheryl and Carol did not feel
safe crossing state lines. In 2000 families that were struggling financially
had lost access to a social safety net through welfare reform. Lack of
legal recognition often led to hostility in settings like hospitals during
a family's most vulnerable moments. As Laura Briggs explains, "Family
was the only obvious means for queer folks to care for dependents, and
it needed to be a 'legal' family" (2017, 175). Mothers without legal and
social recognition were in need of it.

Tensions between state and federal laws produced a morass of inconsistencies and restrictions. Yet these complications also created openings
for LGBT families with the financial means and geographic privilege to
attain some measure of protections for their family relationships. Unless
one lived in Vermont or Massachusetts, options for recognition of same-
sex relationships were minimal. In fact, until the state changed the law
in 2008, marriage in Massachusetts was only available to state residents.
Traveling to another state or country to get married means having the
finances to do so. For most of the mothers we interviewed, the availability

of civil unions in Vermont or marriages in Massachusetts meant little or nothing in a practical sense. Even those of us who took advantage of these opportunities gained no rights from them unless we lived in that state. Yet legal protection was not our only motivation. These opportunities to legalize our unions and protect our families changed the lived experience of legitimacy for families headed by same-sex couples whether we exercised these options or not. The range of relationships considered legitimate slowly expanded, and this shaped the ways families lived their lives.

At the level of family-making and legitimacy, adoption was often considered more important for family protection than marriage. Cheryl and Carol knew that crossing state lines could be dangerous, so they traveled with documents declaring their legitimacy as a family. Adoptions and marriages were often represented by the mothers we interviewed against the grain of media narratives celebrating romantic love. Instead, they were often seen as markers of legitimacy and social belonging for their families.

> CHERYL: So July 31st, which we then made our wedding anniversary. 'Cause we've always called it *family day*. So that was the—
> CAROL: So that was the day I coparent adopted and then four years later was when marriage was legalized in Massachusetts, in May. And we talked about we wanted to get married but we didn't want to just pick a random date that didn't mean anything. So, we kind of tossed around what would it be so we decided that since July 31st was already family day that's what we should do. And so that's what we did. That's what we did. And July 31st truly became family day for us.

While Carol and Cheryl did take advantage of legal marriage in Massachusetts, their reasons for doing it were about both family protection and celebration. The stories they crafted about it were part of a *family story* that is resistant to how they are represented in political discussions and treated in some social interactions.

> CHERYL: They (the kids) talk about it as *our* marriage—as the five of us. "Remember the day we got married?" is what they talk about. "Do you remember our wedding?" And "I did this at our wedding," and so they think of it—again it's family day. It's all part of our family story. I think that's what we've done is *we've tried to write a family story*.

FIGURE 5.1. Carol, Cheryl, and the triplets, Family Pride Week, Provincetown, Massachusetts. Photo credit: Sandra Patton-Imani.

"Family day," for them, marks two performances of legitimate kinship— adoption day and marriage day. This was both about family protection and about celebrating their family in the context of a society that labels them illegitimate. Their "family story" reclaims their sense of legitimacy in the face of discriminatory laws and attitudes.

Being Schooled: "There Are Too Many Moms!"

When children begin school they encounter kids and adults with a broad range of belief systems about homosexuality and what counts as a "normal" family. Parents frequently wonder if other children will tease their kids for having two moms. They worry that teachers will treat them differently. Kimberly and Mischa discuss what is a common issue for them:

KIMBERLY: One ongoing thing that I found frustrating there was, they knew who the moms were, and they knew the kids had names for the moms. You know, I'm Myo, she's Mimi. And in general, they called any of us Mom. But whenever the kids would write out things—like Sophie would write out "Myo did so and so," her teacher would cross out Myo and write Kim instead. And I talked to the teacher about it repeatedly and she said, "Well, the other kids won't know what she's talking about. And they won't understand if she just says Mom, they won't know which mom she means. It's really better for her to just use first names."

MISCHA: Well, this has been an issue everywhere. I mean, we had this with the public school with my oldest also. Where the teachers, the aids, any of them will refer to the parents by their first names to the child. You know—

KIMBERLY: For us, but not for other—

MISCHA: You know, "Tell Mischa about what you did today." Not "Tell Mom." Or you know—and it's happened at the daycare too with one of the workers, and I don't know what that is, why people feel they can't refer to you as—it's as if they don't know what the kids call you and mom isn't good enough—because there are too many of them. *There are too many moms!* [Chuckle] When the kids would be just fine. They would know who they were talking about in a second.

Even when Kimberly and Mischa discussed the issue with teachers the behavior did not change. This educator marked these mothers as different—not blatantly, but perhaps that is the point. While this teacher did not explicitly object to the presence of lesbian moms, she found ways of making clear to everyone that she did not see them as "real" moms.

The gayby boom increased the number of children with same-sex parents attending school in the United States, and uneven legislative changes in same-sex marriage and adoption laws raised the visibility of these families. How such differences are addressed (or not) is shaped by the attitudes of individual teachers and administrators, education policies, and curriculum needs, among other factors. Education scholar Rita M. Kissen explains:

These children bring a new identity to the diversity equation. Their presence challenges teachers and administrators to rethink traditional assumptions about family and community, to examine their commitment to honor the safety and integrity of all students, and, at the deepest level, to confront their own homophobia. But the heterosexist assumptions implicit in most early childhood teacher education programs, and in society at large, leave most teachers ill equipped to meet this challenge, and even the best intentioned may feel uneasy about having a child with two moms or two dads in the classroom. (1999, 165–66)

This polite homophobia pairs effortlessly with polite racism and sexism to police family legitimacy in social interactions. This exchange carries more weight than comments made in grocery stores or stares from people in church. The teacher is an official representative of the education system; thus, she signals to this family that they do not fully belong there. She reminds them that their family relationships are not recognized as legal. Indeed, she acts as if she is doing them a favor by tolerating them at all. Perhaps even more important is the fact that this woman is teaching all the young children in her class that two-mom families are not legitimate. Educator and activist James T. Sears argues for a critical queer approach to the way diversity is taught in elementary school classrooms: "Queer elementary classrooms are those where parents and educators care enough about their children to trust the human capacity for understanding, and their educative abilities to foster insight into the human condition. Those who teach queerly refuse to participate in the great sexual sorting machine called schooling wherein diminutive GI Joes and Barbies become star quarterbacks and prom queens, while the Linuses and Tinky Winkys become wallflowers or human doormats" (1999, 5). Sears's vision of an inclusive classroom challenges the compulsory heterosexuality of standard education and curriculum practices that only represent heteronormative families as acceptable.

In the face of isolation and indifference in the education system, the parents we interviewed searched for queer-friendly spaces. They were deeply invested in revising the political narratives about their families. As Sears writes, "Teaching queerly demands we explore taken-for-granted assumptions about diversity, identities, childhood, and prejudice" (1999, 5). But the experiences of the mothers we talked with rarely lived up to his expectations. As Mischa and Kimberly made clear, sometimes they had to *school* the teachers about inclusiveness.

A larger symbolic pastiche punctuates the passage of time in families, in societies, in movements for social change: lullabies, bedtime stories, and counting songs are part of the soundtrack of making family in society. As children learn their ABCs and 123s, they also learn what makes a family. They internalize what counts as normal and natural and what kinds of people are valued. What was it in *Heather Has Two Mommies* that convinced conservatives it would endanger the innocence of schoolchildren? How did this children's book narrate LGBT families?

The plot revolves around Heather's first day at preschool, and her discovery that not all families look like her two-mommy family. The teacher reads "a story about a little boy whose father is a veterinarian" (Newman 1989, 12). Several children talk about what their daddies do. "'I don't have a daddy,' Heather says. She'd never thought about it before. Did everyone except Heather have a daddy? Heather's forehead crinkles up, and she begins to cry." The teacher resolves the tensions by having all the children draw pictures of their families, which include a broad range of family forms: "Molly hangs up all the pictures and everyone looks at them. 'It doesn't matter how many mommies or how many daddies your family has,' Molly says to the children. 'It doesn't matter if your family has sisters or brothers or cousins or grandmothers or grandfathers or uncles or aunts. Each family is special. The most important thing about a family is that all the people in it love each other'" (22). The book taught children that family "difference" didn't matter. What matters is *love*.

Queer writer Dervla Shannahan's analysis of *Heather Has Two Mommies* and other children's books written about gay and lesbian families emphasizes the recuperative neoliberal narrative at the heart of these stories: "A very definitive version of the queer family emerges; it is coupled, monied, depoliticised, middle-class, identified through consumption capabilities and above all, is represented as overwhelmingly white. Furthermore this ideal/ized version of family is firmly located within dominant terrains of contemporary queer culture; it engages in middle-class leisure and lifestyle pursuits, glosses over multiple lines of difference and abounds with heteronormative trappings whilst furthering an explicit form of homonormativity" (2010, 8). While considered radical by conservatives for including attention to gays in children's books, these stories also might be read from the left as an assimilationist manual for passing as closely to the white middle-class family ideal as possible.

This imaginary community of homonormative families is in good company. In the sixteen children's books about LGBTQ families that Shannahan explored in depth, 89 percent of the adults represented were white (2010, 6). Queer activist and researcher Jazmine Lester found, in her study of sixty-eight books with "queer characters" written for children that "representation of queer identities in children's literature upholds more than challenges heteronormativity" (2014, 245). She characterizes the "non-threatening queers" in children's books as "people who conform to expected gender roles, who have a vested interest in parenting, and who are White and upper middle class." Where are the people of color in this array of queer families? This erasure of lesbians of color mirrors the absence of attention to queer moms of color in mainstream discourse. What about the children whose families are not represented in books and songs? How does this shape their senses of themselves in the world? Raising children happens in contexts of social interaction and cultural meaning, of songs and stories and pictures, of words about identity, family, nation, and belonging. Mothers talked about the necessity of exposing their children to a broad range of people, families, and places. Family-making is about *meaning-making* in particular social, cultural, and legal contexts.

When our kids were toddlers and we were about to move into a new neighborhood, I shared with a friend of mine that the political signs on the lawns seemed to indicate "liberal tolerance." She asked me if that was what we wanted. I said, "No. We really want leftist and embracing. But we'll settle for liberal and tolerant." This characterizes the experiences of most of the families we talked with about interacting with the education system. We did not hear any dramatic horror stories about children's experiences in school. There were no public protests about the dangers of exposing children to books like *Heather Has Two Mommies*. Few of them talked about their children being bullied for having two moms. No one was run out of town. Yet they did not share stories of inclusiveness either. Very few of the mothers reported having other families headed by LGBTQ parents attending their children's schools. For the most part, mothers reported experiencing "tolerance."

While tolerance may not be what parents are searching for, it is what we often have to settle for. Denise and Rachel are a white lesbian couple with three young children. Each of them gave birth to one of their two oldest children, using the same sperm donor, and they adopted their daughter from Guatemala. Here they discuss their reasons for attending Family Week in Saugatuck, Michigan, in 2004:

> DENISE: We live in a little tiny town in northern Illinois, and there are no other gay families in town. And we wanted our kids to see other two-mommy and two-daddy families, 'cause they *never* see that in their neighborhood. Where we live is all relatively afflu-ent, white—no, that's not true. There's two biracial families in our neighborhood, but they're all mommy-and-daddy families where the mommies stay home and the daddies go off to work. And, you know, we're not like that. She's a social worker and I work in publishing so neither of us make any money. And, you know, we wanted them to see that there's other families that are like ours in the world, and that they're not the only ones.

Their reasons for attending Family Week were similar to those of most of the parents we talked with there: they feel isolated where they live and they want their children to know that they belong somewhere, "that they're not the only ones." Many of the workshops held at the Family Week events we attended as part of this research project focused on socialization. Parents would sit in small groups discussing their experiences and fears, sharing their strategies, and carving out a sense of belonging with other same-sex parents. Socialization and survival strategies for coping with discrimination and oppression both subtle and overt were fundamental concerns of the parents in these groups. These concerns were also articulated by most of the mothers we interviewed.

Denae was nine years old when we interviewed her Latina mothers, DeAnn and Bekka, over dinner at their house in Albuquerque. While we talked with her moms, she played with our kids and her little sister, all three years old at the time. A vivacious and happy kid, she was eager to talk on camera about her experiences.

SANDI: Has anybody ever teased you about having two moms?

DENAE: No. It's just nobody at my Catholic school is really open to it. They never, like, seen anybody with that. So, I was kind of like different.

SANDI: How did that feel?

DENAE: I don't know. Weird. I wanted to be like a normal family. But I think it's good to be kinda different.

She primarily lives with her two moms and her little sister, and she spends every other weekend with her dad and her brother. Denae's father is the ex-husband of her mother DeAnn. They split when Denae was very young, and Bekka has been her mom since she was a toddler. Though DeAnn and Bekka no longer attend a Catholic church, Denae's dad participated in the decision to keep her in parochial school. While Latinx tradition and religion may have been part of the decision, Albuquerque's poorly rated public school system was a significant factor as well.

Denae is trying to figure out where she and her family belong in the landscape of "normal." She has internalized social understandings of normal and different. She knows what feeling "kinda like different" is supposed to mean.

SANDI: What does that mean to have a normal family?

DENAE: To have a mom and a dad in the same house. And to have them supporting at all your stuff. And I think I like having two moms at events and at school stuff.

SANDI: Does your dad go to stuff?

DENAE: Yeah.

SANDI: So you end up having three parents there?

DENAE: Yeah. [Big smile and giggles]

SANDI: That could be a bonus!

DEANN: Exactly. Three parents, a sister, a cousin, an aunt, and usually three sets of grandmas and grandpas, right?

DENAE: And a brother.

DEANN: And a brother. She has an entourage, usually.

She glows as her mom talks about her "entourage," for Denae is active in a dance team and *loves* the attention and support from her extended family at her performances and school events. Denae can easily recite her understanding of a "normal" family, and this is clearly shaped by her experience in Catholic school as the only student with two moms. Yet she redefines what that means for her: "I think I like having two moms at events and at school stuff." It seems clear that having an "entourage" of family feels even better to Denae than having a "normal" family.

This negotiation of meaning characterizes the experiences of the families we interviewed. All of them were positioned as different in relation to mainstream views of families, and all of the mothers we interviewed were concerned about how that would affect their children's senses of self. Whatever the specifics of their interactions with the education system, the common factor was the need to be vigilant about what their children were learning and how it might affect them. Mothers taught their children critical thinking skills and resistant understandings of "difference" and "diversity." Gender and sexuality studies scholar Maria Pallotta-Chiarolli characterizes such socialization practices as *queer*: "To be 'queerly raised' is to be in motion. Not only and not necessarily geographical motion, but shifting and sliding, negotiating and maneuvering, between and within 'lifeworlds.' . . . These sociocultural constructs and sites are based on categories such as gender, ethnicity, and sexuality. To be 'queerly raised' is to interrogate the taken-for-grantedness of such fixed categories and the way society divides people into 'normal' and 'abnormal,' 'natural' and 'unnatural,' according to their locations within those categories" (1999, 71). "Insider-outsider identity" is the term I use to discuss such "shifting and sliding, negotiating and maneuvering" between varying "lifeworlds." While Pallotta-Chiarolli emphasizes raising her daughter "queerly," this strategy is not exclusive to families headed by LGBTQ parents.

By this definition, I was "queerly raised," though that is not how my parents would describe it. Because our family was shaped so profoundly by adoption and disability, we developed survival strategies for redefining "natural" family relationships and "normal" people. My parents were not educated people, but their life experiences taught them that these words needed to be redefined in social interactions on a regular basis. Parents outside social definitions of normal have always found ways of instilling in their children survival skills for navigating illegibility, illegitimacy, and inequality. W. E. B. Du Bois coined the term "double consciousness" to characterize the insider-outsider identity Black folks have historically developed to navigate the "sense of always looking at one's self through the eyes of others, of measuring one's soul by the tape of a world that looks on in amused contempt and pity" (1903, 2). As Bonnie Thornton Dill's work demonstrates, mothers of color have had to teach their children both how to survive oppression by strategically conforming to white folks' views of them, *and* how to preserve their senses of self through everyday acts of negotiation and resistance. What that process looks like is shaped by the specificities of family lives. The question of how to instill in children "survival skills" for coping with racism and oppression is particularly important for transracially adoptive parents.[2]

Race, Socialization, and the Privatization of Care

> KIMBERLY: We do as much as we can to celebrate the kids' back-
> grounds. And you know, it was very important to me to travel to
> Cambodia, to travel to Haiti. I know some people will have kids
> escorted back. And it's very important to me that I got to travel there.
> We would love to get the kids back to Cambodia when they're about
> eleven and twelve, and do some travel there. Let them get a feel for
> it. So that's important to us. There's only so much you can give. You
> know, you've taken them out of their birth cultures. You can't give that
> back to them. But you can certainly try to give them the curiosity and
> love for what they did leave behind. And that's important to us.

Questions of socialization and race have been central in policy discussions about domestic and transnational transracial adoption since awareness of these issues was first raised by social workers of color in the 1970s (Patton 2000). As the oldest generation of transracial adoptees has grown up, they have spoken out about the need for social workers to provide training for white couples adopting children of color, emphasizing the importance of exposing adoptees to their racial-ethnic histories and cultures of origin.[3] Awareness of this need has become standard in social work discourse, which was reflected in the stories we heard. Kimberly and Mischa paid close attention to the ways that race impacted their children's lives. They discuss the differences in how their children are seen and treated:

KIMBERLY: Having Asian kids versus having an African American child, it's a different experience as a parent. And it'll certainly be a challenge to, you know, raise a young Black man, and be able to give him all that he needs to grow up as a strong Black man. And, you know, I hope we can do that.

How parents understand race and inequality profoundly influences their ideas about what a "strong Black man" is and how to raise one. These concerns shaped the ways that many transracially adoptive parents raised their children.

Family Week workshops often include sessions on racial identity socialization in transracial adoption and multiracial families. Parents regularly referred to their families as "rainbow families," emphasizing both queerness and racial harmony, a language fostered by the organizers of these events. Mothers of all races were concerned with how their children would be treated, yet they articulated a range of understandings about how race shaped their children's lives. Parents of color often discussed these issues in terms of structural racism, while white parents of kids of color more often invoked "ignorant people" that "didn't understand" their families.[4]

There were times when we listened to parents talk about race in problematic ways, and we did our best to speak from our own positions as Black and white mothers with biracial children. Sometimes I also had to, as Melanie puts it, use my "professor voice," particularly in workshop settings. I had to stop being the mom and be the expert on transracial adoption. I felt a responsibility to draw on my research with adult transracial adoptees to explore what the parents' words and actions might feel like from their kids' perspectives. My views were usually welcomed. But there were other, more uncomfortable situations, too. One white adoptive mother explained at length why we could not film her African American daughter. We agreed immediately, without question. Yet she felt the need to tell us her story about the "dangers" of her daughter being photographed. The threat of a Black man—her birth father—absconding with their daughter was the centerpiece of her disaster scenario. She had clearly internalized sociopolitical narratives about dangerous Black men as superpredators. How might such stories inform this child's sense of self as she grows up? Representations of men of color as criminals and women of color as bad mothers living in poverty set up the framework for a story about children of color as "vulnerable" that must be rescued. These views cannot help but shape children's understandings of themselves and their places in the world.

As I have discussed, sociopolitical allegories also have profound effects in the realm of politics and law. My analysis of the political debates about family policy in the 1990s and early 2000s emphasizes the ways that both sides of these debates have utilized narratives about children to justify their political agendas. Conservatives tell stories casting illegitimate parents as dangerous to innocent children and the future of the nation. LGBTQ parents argue that discriminatory laws and the sociopolitical narratives deployed to support them endanger their children. If Black children are figured as illegitimate, and white children are represented as innocence itself, mixed-race children and transracial adoptees come to signify a future of racial inclusion and equality, representing the mediating force between these divergent visions. Adoption across racial boundaries is a story both conservatives and liberals can get behind. Transracial adoptions symbolize racial harmony being achieved while also shifting financial support of children from the child welfare system to families invested in raising productive citizens.[5]

Throughout this book I discuss ways that representations of children have functioned to disguise the politics of race and reproduction. The transformation of imaginary children of color threatening society into productive future citizens relies on representations of white motherhood as a civilizing force. Transracial adoptees are often framed by allegories of assimilation into the national family through entrance into the world of middle-class whiteness. As historian Robin Bernstein writes: "Childhood innocence provides a perfect alibi: not only the ability to remember while appearing to forget, but even more powerfully, the production of racial memory through the performance of forgetting. What childhood innocence helped Americans to assert by forgetting, to think about by performing obliviousness, was not only whiteness but also racial difference constructed against whiteness" (2011, 8). Transracial adoptees embody this "alibi." They represent "biological" Blackness at the same time that they signify "cultural" whiteness. They speak to "the performance of forgetting"—racial oppression, economic inequality, reproductive control—embedded in adoption stories. Images of brown children raised by white parents obscure the market relations at the heart of the social practice of adoption and deny the realities of violent global economic inequality. They embody innocence through the erasure of racial-ethnic memory as all evidence of illegitimacy is buried in sealed adoption records. The absence of origin stories leave gaps to be filled by sociopolitical narratives about illegitimate mothers of color unable to care for their children. Children of color are often represented as magical signifiers of colorblind innocence. Bernstein's cogent research demonstrates that representations of childhood "figured pivotally in a set of large-scale US racial projects" in the nineteenth and twentieth centuries, including the civil rights movement. Illegitimacy is at the center of these redemption tales, which became central in lawsuits aimed at legalizing same-sex marriage in the early years of the twenty-first century.

Illegitimacy as Injury: *"You Know What Happens with Kids Who Don't Have Fathers"*

Heather and Sara, who are both white, discuss their frustrating interaction with the child welfare system in Las Cruces, New Mexico. Sara gave birth to their son, and Heather was required to adopt him as his second parent in order to gain parental rights. This was not an easy process.

> HEATHER: Yeah, we had to go through two social workers. And even though we got asked questions about—oh for god's sake. You know, like the whole—It made me kinda laugh when you [Melanie] said, "I'm from a two-female household, my mother and my grandmother." Because one of the questions in the adoption was—she said it in this way, which really pissed me off. She said, "Well, you work out there at the jail so you know what happens with kids who don't have fathers." And she said, "So who will be the *male role models in his life*?" And I was like, I want this adoption so let me bite my tongue really hard.

The social worker conveys a pervasive story about the dangers of raising a child without a father ("Well, you work out there at the jail so you know what happens with kids who don't have fathers"). Even though their second-parent adoption was approved, the messages Heather and

Sara received reinforced the idea that their family and their citizenship were not valued without legal attachment to a man.

In this cautionary tale, the social worker deploys the conservative sociopolitical narrative that was used to justify the punitive family laws enacted in the 1990s, connecting the socialization of their future child with the threat of social chaos. Her narrative suggests that not having the proper male role models for their son will divert him from becoming a productive citizen toward the path of crime and imprisonment. The moral of the story is that good mothers marry fathers. These tales were told in primarily race-neutral language, but they were animated in racialized hues. As legal scholar Zanita Fenton astutely argues, contemporary discussions of illegitimacy function as a "form of racial classification and a vestige of slavery" (2014, 12).

This social worker assumes a shared racial narrative with Heather and Sara because all three of them are white, and because Heather "work(s) out there at the jail." She misreads Heather's understanding of race, incarceration, and the dangers of fatherless families. In fact, Heather is a professor who does feminist research on race, gender, and poverty. Rather than embrace the social worker's narrative, she is critical of it, and of the ways it is used to justify inequality and blame poor mothers for systemic social issues.

Instead, Heather aligns her family experiences with Melanie's story of being raised by her African American mother and grandmother. She reframes the social worker's racial narrative, emphasizing the legitimacy of families headed by women. In contrast to the stock sociopolitical narrative, Melanie's mother was married to her father and lived with him for several months. She was pregnant when he hit her. She packed her bags and boarded the Greyhound bus in Chicago to return to her mother in St. Paul. Melanie was raised by two mothers, just as her own mother had been. Her mothers were not illegitimate. They were not unfit. They both worked. Indeed, Melanie's grandmother was among the first classes of African Americans to be admitted to and graduate from Macalester College in St. Paul in the 1930s. She became one of the first Black librarians in the city. She completed her master's degree in library science at the University of Minnesota while she was in her fifties, and she became the first African American head librarian in St. Paul in the 1960s. Melanie grew up with one of her mothers going to work *in a suit as the boss.*

Stories like this are obscured by sociopolitical narratives about the dangers of illegitimate mothers and their children. In connecting her own two-mom family with Melanie's African American female-headed two-parent family of origin, Heather asserts a story about strength and resistance among women in the face of racism, sexism, and economic inequality. The social worker's narrative does the work of racializing deviance without ever needing to mention race. Even as individual mothers like Heather and Sara reject them, these stories are reproduced by social institutions, lawsuits, family policies, news media, and political dialogues.

Lawsuits seeking to overturn bans on same-sex marriage, for instance, did not challenge these stories. Rather, they *relied* on them. Critical legal scholar Melissa Murray highlights an argument that emerged in same-sex marriage lawsuits at the turn of the century that she calls "illegitimacy as injury": "The marriage equality campaign's use of illegitimacy as injury challenges same-sex couples' exclusion from marriage by contrasting their conformity with marriage's norms of respectability and discipline with the deviance of those who could marry and do not" (2014b, 423). This is evidenced in the Vermont and Massachusetts same-sex marriage cases. "Family values" politics had successfully positioned the concept of "illegitimacy" at the center of social debates about family. These were the terms of engagement following the policy overhaul of the 1990s; therefore, same-sex marriage lawsuits employed these narratives. The case made in these lawsuits was to make this ideal family structure inclusive of same-sex parents by legalizing same-sex marriage.

The fight for legitimate family status by (predominantly white) gay and lesbian couples with the economic means to hire lawyers and sue the state further entrenched templates for legitimate family and citizenship at the turn of the twenty-first century by deploying illegitimacy as a racialized trope. The Massachusetts lawsuit states: "Individuals who have the choice to marry each other and nevertheless choose not to may properly be denied the legal benefits of marriage. But that same logic cannot hold for a qualified individual who would marry if she or he only could" (*Goodridge v. Department of Health* 2003, 328).[6] This notion of equality turns on "choice." Within this logic, the harms of illegitimacy affecting straight people who could get married but do not are considered the result of their own bad choices. Gay and lesbian parents that want to marry are positioned as innocent victims of an unjust system.

Discrimination is defined in this context as not having the choice to marry and thereby access rights and benefits. The Vermont lawsuit that created civil unions frames the desires of same-sex couples in the language of national belonging and inclusion: "The essential aspect of their claim is simply and fundamentally for inclusion in the family of state-sanctioned human relations" (*Baker v. Vermont* 1999). *Baker v. Vermont* was filed against the state by three white middle-class same-sex couples living in different cities. Two of the couples were raising children together. Each couple had attempted to obtain a marriage license and was denied. The 1999 Vermont Supreme Court decision stated clearly that a central purpose of marriage was legitimating children. The Court stated: "If anything, the exclusion of same-sex couples from the legal protections incident to marriage exposes their children to the precise risks that the State argues the marriage laws are designed to secure against. In short, the marital exclusion treats persons who are similarly situated for purposes of the law, differently" (*Baker v. Vermont* 1999).

The argument for inclusion is based on sameness. If same-sex couples are "no different from opposite-sex couples," then, under the legal framework of equal protection, they deserve access to the safeguard of marriage (*Baker v. Vermont* 1999). The sameness emphasized with straight married couples was dependent on constructions of difference from mothers of color living in poverty. Both the Vermont and Massachusetts decisions reaffirm one of the central purposes of marriage as the legitimation and protection of children, and they take this recognition a step further by arguing that disallowing same-sex marriage harms both same-sex couples and their children. The Massachusetts Supreme Court made clear that "it is not permitted, to penalize children by depriving them of State benefits because the State disapproves of their parents' sexual orientation" (*Goodridge v. Department of Health* 2003, 337). This argument represents children of same-sex couples as innocent victims of discriminatory laws.

These arguments rely on polarized representations of good middle-class mothers fighting for their children's rights versus imaginary mothers living in poverty causing their own misfortune and endangering their children through bad choices. This ideological tale ignores the structural inequality and discrimination that limits the range of options available to people of varying socioeconomic status in different social and geographic locations. As Murray further explains:

> The notion of illegitimacy as an injury associated with racial minorities who can get married but do not, further marginalizes racial minorities within the LGBT rights movement. It disassociates the LGBT rights movement from those most closely associated with illegitimacy—African Americans. In so doing, the illegitimacy as injury argument helps construct a portrait of gay life in which those who are both sexual minorities and racial minorities are rendered liminal, while highlighting the distinction between respectable gay couples and those who willfully live and raise children outside of marriage. (2012b, 427)

Emphasizing bad or deviant reproductive decisions deflects attention from the social circumstances that prevent women excluded by definitions of legitimacy from being able to access options that are technically available, but financially inaccessible. This is not only true for queers of color, but for all families outside the heterosexual patriarchal nuclear family norm.

This legal strategy positions LGBTQ parents (imagined as white) against unwed mothers experiencing poverty (imagined as straight and of color). In order to argue for equality in access to legal marriage, the lawsuits deployed a sameness argument that paved over gayness by emphasizing commonalities between white middle-class same-sex couples and the traditional American family. The terms of the narrative make no room for people that challenge representations of LGBTQ folks as white.

E/racializing "Marriage Equality"

The Vermont court argues that marriage is a "vital personal right" that fundamentally shapes the lived experience of citizenship (*Baker v. Vermont* 1999). *Goodrich v. Department of Public Health* (2003) built on this view of marriage as a right by linking the decision legalizing same-sex marriage to court decisions overturning bans on interracial marriage. In the interracial marriage cases, they explain, people were prohibited from marrying "because of a single trait: skin color," and in this case that trait is "sexual orientation" (*Goodridge v. Department of Health* 2003, 328–29). The Massachusetts Supreme Court emphasizes parallels between discrimination based on race and on sexual orientation and rules that, like interracial couples, same-sex couples must be allowed to marry each other.

Prior to *Goodridge v. Department of Public Health*, the legal arguments in same-sex marriage cases had focused on the right to privacy as the basis for legal marriage.[7] *Goodrich*, in contrast, emphasized the right to equal protection guaranteed under the Fourteenth Amendment. This shift contributes to the use of analogies with the civil rights movement as precedent and supports a narrative of colorblind and gender-neutral progress toward equality for all. A new emphasis on "marriage equality" emerged as part of this narrative. Communications studies scholar Michelle Kelsey Kearl explains: "The Supreme Court's comparison of gay marriage to miscegenation in the *Goodridge* decision, however, spurred a shift in rhetoric from privacy to a more fully developed civil rights argument. The discourse moves from the 'freedom to marry' to 'marriage equality'" (2015, 66). This comparison between the civil rights movement and the movement for legalizing same-sex marriage emerges as a simple and convenient story in that it relies on a conceptual split between African Americans and LGBTQ folks. In other words, this analogy only fully makes sense if all Blacks are straight and all gays and lesbians are white.

On the face of it, "marriage equality" as a political strategy seems to make sense. Yet, as I have demonstrated, this view is dependent on racialized narratives about illegitimate mothers and their children and the deviance of "choosing" not to marry when one is legally able to do so. The gradual development of this line of argument served to further entrench middle-class white nuclear family ideals into laws legalizing same-sex marriage and to further marginalize the most vulnerable families in the United States. These families were largely ignored in public discussions of same-sex marriage, and this absence was crucial to the argument that same-sex marriage would provide equality for gays and lesbians. Race was simultaneously deployed and denied in public dialogues about same-sex marriage laws. If political strategies for supporting LGBT couples were grounded in the lived experience of the majority of queer parents, the policy solutions would likely include attention to poverty, employment discrimination, housing discrimination, racism, sexism, and basic human rights. Briggs makes clear that "the politics of raising children in same-sex relationships" signals not only a shift in what has traditionally been considered "gay politics," but also a change in the population of LGBTQ folks who were concerned and engaged (2017, 175). Class, race, and gender distinguished this constituency from previous LGBT rights movements: "By the 2000 census, it was clear that the urban white queer folks in New York and San Francisco who had long been the center of LGBT political movements were not also the center of the gayby boom. Gay parents were disproportionately likely to be Southern, rural, and people of color. The census found 2 million children being raised by two same-sex parents. Their families were disproportionately poor, about twice as likely to live in poverty as the children of married, heterosexual couples" (2017, 175). These were not the parents filing lawsuits based on the harms of illegitimacy, nor would they necessarily benefit from these lawsuits. The legal changes in Vermont and Massachusetts were practically significant for only a small percentage of LGBTQ parents in the United States. The steps taken through state legitimation of same-sex civil unions and marriage were largely symbolic.

Conclusion

Legitimacy is not only enforced by laws, but imposed on families as they live their lives. Daily experiences like picking children up from school or reading a bedtime story involve political battles over legitimacy and belonging. Interactions in the education system contribute to the social policing of inclusion and difference. Changing public understanding of the ways that inequalities in law and policy threaten mothers and children is, I believe, crucial to shifting from a model focused on deviance from natural, normal, and legitimate families to one that emphasizes that all families are constructed through laws and policies, in profoundly different ways.

Legal changes in Vermont and Massachusetts not only expanded the representational legitimacy of same-sex couples; these laws were also significant in what became the political shift toward the federal legalization of same-sex marriage. What are the ramifications of the illegitimacy as injury argument? If we take this narrative to its logical conclusion, we see justification for the neoliberal economic agenda of privatization of care. Arguments for the legalization of same-sex marriage drew on and reproduced sociopolitical narratives stigmatizing children born out of wedlock as the central cause of social chaos. Racialized narratives of illegitimate mothers once again served as a foil for arguments reinscribing white middle-class privilege.

In the next chapter I deepen my analysis of the ways that queer mothers living in different areas of the country navigate the lived experience of citizenship in a context of shifting laws. I explore stratification in access to social rights and resources in narratives of the mothers we interviewed living in California, New Mexico, and Iowa in the early years of the twenty-first century. I consider inequalities experienced by mothers living in different states, but I also explore stratification among mothers of different racial-ethnic identities, tribal affiliations, and economic circumstances in one region.

SAME-SEX MARRIAGE, 2004–2007

February 2004   City of San Francisco begins marrying same-sex couples

February 2004   The New Mexico County of Sandoval Begins Issuing Marriage Licenses to Same-Sex Couples

February 2004   President Bush Announces Support for Constitutional Amendment Banning Same-Sex Marriage

February 2004   New York Town of New Paltz Begins Marrying Same-Sex Couples

February 2004   Activists in Iowa City, Iowa Attempt to Marry

March 2004   Gays Wed in Portland, Oregon

August 2004   California Supreme Court voids same-sex marriages

April 2005   Connecticut Approves Same-Sex Civil Unions

April 2005   Navajo Nation Bans Same-Sex Marriage

July 2005   Canada Legalizes Same-Sex Marriage

September 2005   California legislature first in the United States to approve same-sex marriage legalization

August 2005   California Supreme Court establishes coparenting rights for same-sex couples

November 2005   Texas Voters Approve Constitutional Amendment Banning Same-Sex Marriage

June 2006   Alabama Voters Approve Constitutional Amendment Banning Gay Marriage

July 2006   US House Rejects Constitutional Amendment to Ban Gay Marriage

October 2006   New Jersey Supreme Court Orders Legislature to Recognize Same-Sex Unions

November 2006   Voters in Seven States Approve Constitutional Ban on Same-Sex Marriage

November 2006   South Africa Legalizes Same-Sex Marriage

Adapted from https://gaymarriage.procon.org

6

Making Family Legal

Border Crossings and Other Perils, 2004–2007

> RONNIE: We're with the Navajo Nation. They banned gay marriages as soon as Bush kind of banned gay marriages all over. So, the Navajo Nation kind of took that route. Before, it was never banned. So now that it's banned, it's kind of hard for us.

Ronnie is referring to President George W. Bush's 2004 push for a constitutional amendment banning same-sex marriage in the United States. She cites this unsuccessful federal amendment as influential in the 2005 Diné Marriage Act, which banned recognition of same-sex marriage and adoption in the Navajo Nation. Prior to its passage, cohabitating same-sex couples were recognized as married by the Navajo Nation under tribal common law, the same as heterosexual unmarried couples. Ronnie, Yvonne, and their son Arnold live on the reservation in Tsaile, Arizona. Their sense of belonging there has been challenged as the national same-sex marriage debate has shaped the Navajo Nation's laws regulating same-sex marriage and adoption. Ronnie concisely details the political process among Diné lawmakers:

> RONNIE: But as far as Navajo Nation there's a group called the Navajo Council Nation Delegates. They're against gay marriages, actually—I guess homosexuality in general. But the president of the Navajo Nation, his personal opinion was that you're yourself, and who you are is who you are. But then they kind of overridden him and banned gay marriages anyway.

The Diné Marriage Act and the Federal Marriage Amendment were part of a series of legal and policy proposals to regulate marriage and family at local, state, federal, and international levels in the early twenty-first century.

Ronnie and Yvonne were making a family in a political moment characterized by stark regulatory differences based on where they live, intersected with gender, sexuality, class, race, and tribal identity. Border crossings, and the perils they engender for vulnerable citizens, are central to this story. The rights and protections available to families headed by gays and lesbians depended most fundamentally, in this era, on geographic location. Yet Ronnie and Yvonne had to navigate more than legal inconsistencies across borders. Even within one location there were multiple, and often conflicting, arenas of jurisdiction. Legal demarcations followed national borders and state lines as well as tribal nation boundaries and county jurisdictions. Socioeconomic limitations continue to deepen stratification of access to legal protections for mothers who are not middle class or wealthy. Like all of the mothers we interviewed, Ronnie and Yvonne's available options for protecting their family relationships in the early years of the twenty-first century were limited. In this chapter I deepen and extend my analysis of stratified reproduction among queer mothers through an exploration of family-making in three different US regions.

In the first few months of 2004 same-sex marriage events in five cities—three of which were among my research sites—garnered significant media attention: San Francisco, California; Sandoval County, New Mexico; New Paltz, New York; Iowa City, Iowa; and Multnomah County, Oregon. It was an exciting moment of possibility for LGBTQ couples and families. Melanie and I, like queer couples all over the United States, watched news coverage of weddings on the steps of San Francisco City Hall with rapt attention. I use these events as lenses through which to explore inequalities between families living in different states, under varying social, economic, and political circumstances, in this historical moment. For mothers residing in different states, there were clear differences in the lived experience of citizenship, but there were also significant differences between mothers of different racial-ethnic identities and socioeconomic circumstances within each state.

Exploring microlevel politics through the stories of mothers in different locations demonstrates three particular points. The first point is that marriage is just one part of the story, and, as I have argued, must be considered in relation to other laws shaping the lived experience of family. Second-parent adoption, health insurance, domestic partner benefits, wills, and powers of attorney are the more practical concerns of the parents we interviewed. Each state regulates access to each of these family protections differently. The second point is that these legal discrepancies reveal the ways these laws deepen inequality. This stratification of access to reproductive and family supports is rooted in historical inequities that have privileged white families while disadvantaging families of color in the name of strengthening the future of the nation. Living at the intersections of multiple jurisdictions both amplifies oppression and makes border crossings dangerous.

My third point is that these mothers' narratives challenge standard constructions of assimilation and resistance and therefore reshape the contours of the public debate in the early years of the twenty-first century. This snapshot moment of family politics was largely narrated through tensions between conservatives and liberals in the ways I have discussed in previous chapters: as diagnoses of the state of the nation as either progressing or declining. Yet the public debate became more complex at the turn of the century. Leftist and queer critiques of same-sex marriage as an assimilationist project increased as more opportunities for legalizing same-sex unions became available. Sociologists Mary Bernstein and Mary C. Burke make clear that queer leftist critiques of marriage in the media increased in frequency and gained a new level of credibility following the Vermont Supreme Court decision that led to the creation of civil unions in 2000.[1] Liberals discussed same-sex marriage as the path to equality; conservatives saw it as deviance; leftist queers called it assimilation. The lived experience of negotiating power inequalities is more complex than how these issues are represented in public discussion.

San Francisco, California: "You Have to Be Able to Adopt"

On February 12, 2004, the City of San Francisco, under the direction of mayor Gavin Newsom, began issuing marriage licenses to same-sex couples. Newsom justified his actions on the basis of equal protection under the California State Constitution, arguing that the denial of marriage to gay men and lesbians "is wrong and inconsistent with the values this country holds dear."[2] While Newsom was instrumental in this brief legalization of same-sex marriage in San Francisco, a history of activism shaped the performances as well. As sociologists Verta Taylor, Katrina Kimport, Nella Van Dyke, and Ellen Ann Anderson explain:

In San Francisco, the tactic of same-sex couples showing up at City Hall to demand marriage licenses originated on February 12, 1998, when the Lambda Legal Defense and Education Fund, a national organization of the lesbian and gay rights movement, sponsored "Freedom to Marry Day." Gay rights groups held small actions in more than forty cities that year. In San Francisco, Molly McKay and her partner Davina Kotulski went to the marriage counter at City Hall to request a marriage license. When they were denied, they decided to make it an annual protest. (2013, 239)

Between 1998 and 2003 activists showed up at San Francisco City Hall every year on February 12 requesting marriage licenses. In 2004 Newsom's actions changed the outcome of this tradition. Over three thousand same-sex couples were issued marriage licenses by San Francisco in the first week they became available, including a number of high-profile celebrities who flew in for weddings and photo opportunities on the steps of city hall. The city resorted to making appointments for same-sex couples seeking marriage licenses in order to accommodate the steady demand. Indeed, giddy people from all over the country flooded San Francisco City Hall seeking state sanction of their unions.

I draw here on the voices of mothers we interviewed in the San Francisco Bay Area in 2005. All of these families were middle-class parents of toddlers. I draw on the family-making stories of Angela and Michelle, an interracial (Chicana and white) couple who lived in the East Bay. The other mothers we interviewed at this time in the Bay Area were members of an internet listserv in San Jose called Lavender Moms. All of the parents from this group that agreed to be interviewed are white, middle-class parents of toddlers that lived in Silicon Valley. Each of these families had the economic and cultural resources to undergo fertility treatments and to secure legal recognition of their family relationships through adoption.

We interviewed Vickie and Pam—white, upper-middle-class lesbian parents of toddler twins—at their home in San Jose, California. We sat in their backyard, enjoying the sunny day, as our toddler twins ran around with theirs. They did not participate in the San Francisco weddings, primarily because they heard that these marriages would interfere with their legal status as domestic partners under the 2003 California Domestic Partnership Rights and Responsibilities Act. This was a crucial consideration, as the family's medical coverage (for Pam and their children) was secured through Vickie's employer on the basis of this law, and their daughter has health issues and disabilities that require ongoing medical care. This was not a risk they felt they could take for what might turn out to be a purely symbolic act, if the marriages were not recognized by the State of California.

Vickie had undergone in vitro fertility treatments and had several ova harvested and implanted in Pam. While Vickie is the genetic mother of their twins, because Pam gave birth to them, Vickie was required to adopt her own children to become their legal parent. Had she not done this she would have been considered an "egg donor" with no legal recognition of her relationship with her children.

> PAM: Obviously, we'd like to see some laws enacted so that she didn't have to adopt her own children and we could both be on the birth certificate. I mean, in reality we are both their moms. She is genetically their mom, and I was their birth mother. So, yeah, I would like to see some legislation take place to help families out in that way, obviously.
>
> VICKIE: That's pretty much it. I think it would just be easier all around if they would just accept gay marriage, and then they wouldn't have to worry about the fact that—whose kids they were. They were born within the marriage, so guess what? They are both of ours.

The connection between marriage and the presumption of parentage encapsulates the logic undergirding the argument that same-sex marriage is the key to equality. If legal marriage were available to all couples, regardless of gender or sexuality, second-parent adoption would be unnecessary (at least when children are born after the couple is married).

Jamie and Lorie viewed adoption as a burdensome requirement necessary to protect their entire family:

> JAMIE: That's why I said you have to be able to adopt. It's like you have no power if you can't. You're totally helpless. You can't do anything with your children if you can't adopt.

When we interviewed them at their home in San Jose in 2005, their oldest child was five years old and their twins were a year and a half. The interview was punctuated by requests for snacks, outbursts of crying, and the blur of motion caused by a five-year-old trying to corral two sets of toddler twins. The four moms in the room eagerly talked about family-making and took turns dispensing snacks and managing crises. Jamie and Lorie had completed second-parent adoptions for all three of their children, in order to ensure that Jamie was a legal decision-maker in contexts like public schools and doctor's offices. Despite this legal protection, they encountered problems. They shared a story about when their oldest child was a toddler and had to be rushed to the emergency room for a serious head injury:

> JAMIE: So they ran a CAT scan on him. We were there a good couple of hours. So the doctor comes in and he goes, "Well, who's the parent?"
>
> LORIE: "Who's the *mother*?'
>
> JAMIE: "Who's the mother?" I said, "We are." And he goes, "No, who's the real mother?" And I said. "*We* are." He said, "Who gave birth to him?" Oh, that ticked me off. I was set off in a big-time way. I said, "Does it make any difference? We're both legally his guardians." You know. So he goes, "Who's the birth mother?" And Lorie goes, "I am." And he says, "Will you come with me?" And he takes her down the hall to look at the CAT scan, you know. So she went to go look at it and came back and he goes, "Now you can come look at it if you want." You know? I was—ooooh. If it hadn't have been the situation it was in I'd a-been all over that.
>
> LORIE: Usually that's when it happens, too. It's hardly ever happened, but it generally happens when you're really powerless because you want your child to be like safe and cared for and taken care of. And that's when it's pulled. Normally, you would not stand for it, [but] you allow it a little more. Because I'll be like, "Babe, let's just, let's just let them say whatever so we can find out what's going on with our kids." You know, we're a little bit more willing to not make a big fuss out of it.

As Lorie said, interrogations about your legitimacy as a mother are "the last thing you want when your kid is sick." Melanie shared with them a story about a narrow-minded nurse's response to our family when our children were in the neonatal intensive care unit after they were born nine weeks prematurely. We talked about the difficulties of navigating power inequalities when your children are vulnerable, and about how resistance to oppression has to be finessed strategically. Lorie and Jamie emphasized the need to choose their battles carefully.

For Lorie and Jamie, and families like theirs that had already completed or were in the process of completing second- or stepparent adoptions, the possibility of getting married in San Francisco—about an hour's drive from San Jose—was exciting, but ultimately would have been more symbolic than practical. When the City of San Francisco began issuing marriage licenses to same-sex parties, each of the couples we interviewed considered the prospect, yet none of them actually did it. They all wanted familial rights, but none of them were confident that the San Francisco weddings would achieve that. Many of them feared that these licenses would not be legally recognized or might even be annulled (which, in fact, they eventually were). The other primary consideration was the worry that a San Francisco marriage would nullify their domestic partner status under the Domestic Partnership Rights and Responsibilities Act (2003). Not only was health insurance at stake; the new law provided that couples that had been registered as domestic partners for one year were eligible for stepparent adoption, a legal process much less expensive and invasive than second-parent adoption.

Sam and Kelly were in the final stages of Sam's stepparent adoption of their son Jackson when we interviewed them in their home in San Jose in 2005. As we watched our toddlers play together, they explained to us that after they had been registered with the State of California as domestic partners for one year they became eligible for a stepparent adoption as opposed to a second-parent adoption. Stepparent adoption has historically been used by heterosexual married couples to legalize the relationship between a child and a stepparent that has assumed a primary parental role. In the past this was only possible when the birth parent of the same gender relinquished parental rights; the US adoption system has historically been regulated through gender, meaning that a child may only legally have one mother and one father. Second-parent adoption reaches beyond this gender polarity in allowing children to have two mothers or two fathers. The most significant difference from second-parent adoption is that no home study is required. All the women we interviewed described the home study as highly intrusive. At the time of this interview in 2005, stepparent adoption for gay and lesbian parents was still extremely rare.

SAM: I found it interesting that Kelly needed to be fingerprinted, in the process. And Kelly has always brought up a good point about some of the things we had to go through to become legal parents of what is by all rights our child. Is you know, she could have gone into a club and had a one-night stand, and it would have been no problem, with, you know, that person's rights. So you know, it's funny that—

KELLY: Well, it's sort of like, I chose Sam just like anybody chooses their partner and that should be good enough. I think that should be good enough because he's my child. Biologically, he's my child so it should be good enough that I say she's the parent I want for my child. I definitely put a lot more thought into it than some people that get pregnant.

Choice is the theoretical grounding upon which Kelly constructs her argument for equality under the law. As a California resident legitimized by the Domestic Partnership Registry, she does have the option to designate Sam as Jackson's second parent; that is in fact, what their stepparent adoption in California has allowed them to do. They downloaded a form from the state's website, filled it out, got fingerprinted, and sent in the materials with a twenty-five-dollar filing fee. The upcoming court date for finalizing the adoption was circled in red on their refrigerator calendar, alongside family photos and magnetic alphabet letters. We shared with them the costs of second-parent adoptions (which also require home studies conducted by social workers) in Iowa and other states (three to six thousand dollars were the amounts we heard most commonly). They were shocked by this, and grateful for the liberal California laws; they would not have been able to afford a second-parent adoption if that were the cost. Sam is a full-time student and does in-home day care to contribute to the family income. Though Kelly works full-time, they can really only afford to live in their modest San Jose home with help from her parents. These laws are accessible only by those with both the geographical proximity and the financial resources. California was, in these early years of the new millennium, one of the few states in the United States where second- and stepparent adoptions were this available. Yet the laws were confusing, contradictory, and shifting quickly. The second-parent adoptions of the other families we interviewed in the Bay Area all required home studies, lawyers, and large sums of money.

Angela, who is Chicana, and her partner, Michelle, who is white, live in the San Francisco East Bay area. They found the second-parent adoption process for their twins frustrating. It cost them between three and four thousand dollars for a lawyer and for the social worker's home study. The social worker wanted to charge them double, yet the report was exactly the same, the only difference being the children's names. They bargained her down a bit, but it was still very expensive.

> MICHELLE: I think from the onset it just felt a little ridiculous that we have to spend all this money and time for something that you know, should just be . . .
> ANGELA: Should just *be*.
> MICHELLE: Yeah, should just *be*. And of course, now kids born in the state of California you can get 'em on the birth certificate without this process, but they're still recommending the process.

The Bay Area is a very expensive place to live, and most of the families we talked with struggled financially in their early years of family-making. Some had family members helping them. Others detailed their cost-cutting measures, like buying toys at garage sales and shopping at stores with twin discounts. Some worked multiple jobs. Having children is expensive enough, and even in California the added costs of legally protecting family relationships that are not already recognized by the courts are burdensome. In addition to adoption, families paid lawyers for name changes (so the entire family would have the same last name), preparation of wills, powers of attorney, and guardianship assignations.

According to a study released by the Williams Institute in 2009, lesbian couples are more likely to be poor than heterosexual couples. The study, which draws on 2000 census data on LGB couples, also demonstrates that children of gays and lesbians are twice as likely to live in poverty as those in families with heterosexual married parents. It states, "The social and policy context of LGB life provides many reasons to think that LGB people are at least as likely—and perhaps more likely—to experience poverty as are heterosexual people: vulnerability to employment discrimination, lack of access to marriage, higher rates of being uninsured, less family support, or family conflict over coming out" (Williams Institute 2009). Legal marriage would not resolve these inequalities, yet it remained at the center of political discussions of LGBTQ rights discourse during this era.

The steps of San Francisco City Hall were a stage to a morality play at every level of discourse. This performance of citizenship garnered attention from protesters as well as marrying couples from across the country. The *Washington Post* reported:

> About 15 protesters from Christian conservative groups in Louisiana, Pennsylvania and Wisconsin came to City Hall with placards calling homosexuality a sin and urging gay people to repent. They were confronted by counterprotesters who carried signs such as "straight guys in favor of free choice" and who offered coffee and doughnuts to waiting couples, reporters and police.
>
> At one point, the anti-gay-marriage protesters blocked the door to the clerk's office that issues marriage licenses, kneeling down and singing prayers. The protesters were drowned out by waiting couples, who began belting out "The Star-Spangled Banner" as sheriff's deputies escorted the protesters from the building. (Nieves 2004, AO1)

This clash of beliefs is deeply enmeshed in neoliberal language of American democracy and freedom. Indeed, even the "straight guys" in support of same-sex marriage celebrate and defend it in the language of neoliberal choice. These protests were formalized in a series of lawsuits, rulings, and appeals. The legal volleys ended in August 2004 when the California Supreme Court voided all same-sex marriages performed in San Francisco. The symbolic significance of these marriages indeed ended up being greater than their legal value.

Conservatives were joined in their opposition to same-sex marriage by some unexpected allies. From the other end of the political spectrum emerged a fierce critique of same-sex marriage as a strategy for achieving equality for gays and lesbians. Academics, feminists, queers, and leftists have been critical of efforts to legalize same-sex marriage because it reinforces inequality for low-income people, has historically functioned as a regulatory gatekeeper of citizenship against people of color, and fosters assimilation to a white, heteronormative, middle-class family ideal.[3] In 2004 blogger Matilda (Matt) Bernstein Sycamore wrote:

The violence of assimilation lies in the ways the borders are policed. For decades, there has been a tension within queer politics and cultures, between assimilationists and liberationists, conservatives and radicals. Never before, however, has the assimilationist/conservative side held such a stranglehold over popular representations of what it means to be queer. Gay marriage proponents are anxious to discard generations of queer efforts to create new ways of loving, lusting for, and caring for one another, in favor of a 1950s model of white-picket-fence, "we're-just-like-you" normalcy.

Sycamore argues supporters of same-sex marriage have been co-opted by conservative definitions of traditional family—a narrative that became more prevalent in the early 2000s.

While marriage was front and center in news and social media, the stories of the mothers we interviewed undermine the notion that their desire for marriage is simply a performance of normative family. Indeed, their perspectives on same-sex marriage were more complex than what is generally represented in news coverage and policy debates. Underlying this discourse is a more intricate discussion of adoption as a strategy for legalizing family relationships.

New Mexico and the Navajo Nation: "This Act Is against Tradition"

Meanwhile, in Bernalillo, N.M., a rural town just north of Albuquerque, dozens of gay couples flocked to the Sandoval County Clerk's office after the clerk announced she would grant marriage licenses to same-sex couples. Clerk Victoria Dunlap, a Republican, said she decided to grant the licenses after the county attorney determined that New Mexico law is unclear on the issue. County Attorney David Mathews said state law defines marriage as a contract between parties but does not mention gender. (Nieves 2004, AO1)

Sixty-four same-sex couples were married on February 20, 2004 before the New Mexico State Attorney General stopped the granting of marriage licenses. The marriage event was initiated by a request by a same-sex couple for a marriage license earlier that week to the Sandoval County Clerk's office. Upon analysis of the New Mexico marriage statute the county clerk and county attorney determined that, in fact, the only place the gender of prospective spouses was specified was on the marriage license application form. The county clerk proceeded to grant marriage licenses for several hours before the attorney general required them to cease.

In the summer of 2007 we interviewed twenty-six lesbian mothers living in Albuquerque, Taos, Santa Fe, and Las Cruces, New Mexico, and Tsaile, Arizona.[4] Ten of the mothers were white, eight were Latina, four were African American, and four were Indigenous. These families had vastly different experiences of family-making that are linked to long histories of oppression against families of color in the Southwest.

Sonia and Renee, a white, middle-class couple with two kids who live in Sandoval County, were among the same-sex couples that raced to the courthouse during the brief window the day the weddings took place.

> SONIA: I woke up one morning and they said, "News flash! There's a place in New Mexico where gays and lesbians can get legally married." I heard it from the bathroom—we have a TV in the bedroom. I'm like, "Turn that up!" It was right in Sandoval County at our courthouse in our county in Bernalillo, New Mexico.

Sonia is an educator and administrator at a prominent private day school for grades six through twelve in Albuquerque (approximately a thirty-minute drive south of Bernalillo), where she has a number of lesbian coworkers.

> SONIA: My friend Janet, who's the scheduler—she's a couple offices down from me over there—said, "I think we better hustle. There's a rumor going around that the state attorney general is gonna shut this down as soon as possible."

Several of them left that day to get married.

> SONIA: And so I left work and met Renee at the courthouse, and we did the application. And there was a minister down there from umm, I can't remember—one of the gay churches in town, I think it was the Metropolitan Community Church. And we went downstairs and our friends Janet and Dawn were our witnesses. And we got legally married. We got all our paperwork filed in time, and about twenty minutes after

our paperwork had been filed the attorney general's letter came to the
courthouse saying that she was shutting down all the ceremonies, that it
violated New Mexico law, in her legal opinion. So, then they quit doing it.

The legal status of these marriages, like those performed in San
Francisco, was uncertain. Yet Sonia and Renee were more concerned
with getting married as an act of civil disobedience than with the rights
they might acquire or with the social approval or inclusion that might
accompany legal marriage. They had never had a commitment ceremony, "because it felt false to us":

> SONIA: You know, we considered ourselves married in the sense of we
> have a home together that we own jointly. We have children together
> that share our names. We're a family, and it didn't matter what people
> thought, so. But [big smile] we did run and get the marriage license.

Her comments articulate the ambivalence many of the mothers we
interviewed felt about getting married. Legal marriage simultaneously
did not matter *and* was profoundly significant. A traditional marriage
ceremony was not important to Sonia and Renee, nor were they confident that their marriage would actually provide any family protections.
Yet the opportunity to participate in a political performance of marriage
that might contribute to larger legal changes was appealing.

While queer critics of same-sex marriage viewed this rush to the altar as
assimilation to a heteronormative family model, Sonia and Renee viewed
their nuptials as resistance to discriminatory laws. Their sense that the
media coverage they received might contribute to a larger movement for
social change was shared by many of the mothers we interviewed. This is
consistent with research conducted with same-sex couples following their
marriages in San Francisco. According to one study, "For most partici-
pants, the weddings were not meant to embrace the institution of marriage as traditionally defined"; rather, weddings were public performances
designed to "gain visibility for their relationships, stake a claim to civil
rights, contest discriminatory marriage laws, and challenge the institu-
tionalization of heterosexuality" (Taylor, Kimport, Van Dyke, and Anderson 2013, 239). Feminist scholar Shannon Weber argues that the activism
of the marriage equality groups in California with whom she conducted

research "revise queer theoretical arguments about marriage equality activism as by definition assimilationist, homonormative, and single-issue" (2015, 1147). Her research found a heterogeneous, coalition-based network of organizations focused on social justice that engaged in creative modes of political protest. Discrete categorizations of assimilation versus resistance in political commentary do not adequately account for the multiple political strategies employed by individuals or organizations working for social justice for queer folks. Taylor and Bernstein are clear that "the current debate among LGBT activists over whether marriage is assimilationist or transformative is far too simplistic" (2013, 3).

At the time of our interview in 2007, Sonia and Renee were still unsure about the legality of their marriage or whether they had actually gained any rights through it. The federal government's denial of recognition, however, was unequivocal, and the gap in protection made the inequity starkly clear. Sonia and Renee participated in this performance of marriage because they could; geographically, they were in the right place at the right time. Sonia has a law degree and works as an administrator in a private school, so taking time off from her job to get married on the spur of the moment was not an issue, as it likely was for many working-class people. Renee was able to meet her there that day because she works on their ranch and determines her own working hours. Sonia describes Renee as a "ranch woman" that "has really taken to the New Mexico lifestyle." Their participation spoke to their social location: they are by no means wealthy, yet their race and middle-class privilege clearly facilitated their access to legal marriage at that time. It is important to remember that these privileges have been secured and maintained for Anglo ranchers through the history of settler colonialism that made these lands available to whites by violently removing Indigenous peoples from their homelands. Whether white folks are aware of it or not, these histories shape contemporary power relations in complex ways that obscure attention to systemic inequality.[5]

The Perils of Border Crossings

The legal discrepancies and contradictions within New Mexico, between New Mexico and other states, and between state and federal governments fomented a lively set of issues, which played out differently in varying social locations. The *Washington Post* reported that "the same-sex couples married last week in Sandoval County, N.M., cannot cross into any bordering state and be recognized as wed" (Von Drehle 2004, A08). Lack of recognition across state lines was a fundamental issue for same-sex parents in this political moment; many mothers worried about travel. As Jamie and Lorie's story in the last section reminds us, it is typically in moments of vulnerability that parental legitimacy is questioned. Caution is advised in unfamiliar territory.

Border crossings have particular salience for Yvonne and Ronnie. Navajo Nation lands cross the corners of three states: New Mexico, Arizona, and a small area of Utah. Even if Ronnie and Yvonne had decided to travel the almost four-hour drive from the reservation in Tsaile, Arizona, to the courthouse in Bernalillo, New Mexico, the marriage would not have been recognized by Arizona state law. Contradictorily, in 2004 the Navajo Nation recognized cohabiting couples—whether heterosexual or same-sex—as married. It was the passage of the Diné Marriage Act in 2005, less than a year after the Bernalillo weddings, that denied tribal recognition of same-sex marriages, whether common-law or legal in another state.

These lands are divided by colonial histories etched into the demarcations of states, territories, and nations. The Diné Marriage Act is consistent with the federal Defense of Marriage Act and the ban on same-sex marriage passed in Arizona in 1996. Utah, which includes a tiny portion of Navajo lands, banned same-sex marriage through a series of laws passed in 1977, 1996, and 2004. In contrast, New Mexico, the third state the Navajo Nation overlaps, has never legally restricted marriage to heterosexual couples. Borders overlap with histories of belonging and dispossession, layered by contradictory jurisdictions and boundaries of citizenship.

A week or so after the weddings, the *Farmington Daily Times* published a letter to the editor declaring a moral war over same-sex marriage. Farmington, New Mexico, is approximately a two-and-a-half-hour drive west of Bernalillo, just outside the borders of the Navajo Nation. In her letter, Cecelia Tsosie writes: "Marriage is more sacred than those trees, those mountains, those animals, those ceremonies in the churches and outside the churches, and those religious things. God's word is sacred ground; we are ignoring his word and his warnings about homosexuality" (2004, 4A). This narrative is familiar, but Tsosie's Navajo identity puts this tale celebrating (heterosexual) marriage as sacred into a particular context. Tsosie continues: "Homosexual marriages are running rampant across America. Very soon San Juan County and the Navajo Nation will be issuing licenses. In time homosexuality will reveal those who practice it in secret. Homosexuality is a gender confusion. Confusion does not come from God, but from Satan himself." Tsotsie's worries about the legalization of same-sex marriage align explicitly with mainstream Christian views of deviance from traditional gender identities as a danger to family and nation. This perspective on homosexuality embraces Christian colonial patriarchal definitions of family, gender, and sexuality over Diné cosmology. As feminist Navajo scholar Jennifer Denetdale argues, "Tradition becomes a tool that Navajo men and women use to legitimate claims about appropriate gender roles" (2006, 17).

The Diné Marriage Act proposal was introduced in January 2005. Ryan Hall of the *Farmington Daily Times* reported: "The purpose of the act, according to the legislation, was to promote strong families and to preserve and strengthen family values" (Hall 2005, A1). The *Navajo Times* reported on the introduction of the legislation and community response to it: "Orlanda Smith-Hodge (Cornfields/Greasewood Springs/Klagetoh/Wide Ruins) also spoke in support of the legislation. 'Many tell us our teachings come from our home,' she said. 'Our elders have taught us much and unfortunately it appears that we are leaving our traditional values. Mr. Anderson is moving in the spirit of preserving cultural teachings. We must create policy so that when we are challenged, we can have a policy to stand by. Many of our children are not learning our ways. We should teach from this legislation'" (2005, 3A). On both sides of the political debate the focus was on preserving Diné traditions. What constituted "tradition," however, was the subject of dispute. Supporters of the Diné Marriage Act defined it through Christian patriarchal meaning systems grounded in settler colonialism. Those against the legislation emphasized a precolonial definition that embraced ancient matrilineal kinship organization, women as leaders in the tribe, fluid understandings of gender and sexuality as articulated through the embrace of Nadleehi tribal members, and a disregard for legal marriage.

Queer Diné activist Sherrick Roanhorse argued that "this act is against tradition, our own culture and our way of life" (Hall 2004, 1A). As Ryan Hall reported in the *Farmington Daily Times*, "Roanhorse also said to set guidelines for marriage is to define a tradition that is not Navajo in origin, thereby taking another step towards assimilation by white society, as opposed to the sovereignty the Navajo Council is supposed to represent" (2004, 1A). Assimilation and resistance are woven through this discourse in what might seem like opposing ways. From the perspective of the law's supporters, homosexuality is assimilation to white ways and a betrayal of Diné tradition; those against the law define the emphasis on Christian patriarchal marriage as the larger assimilationist project affecting Native traditions. The article continues: "'(The act) is taking away from the whole concept of self determination. It is saying we will embrace the western concept of marriage,' Roanhorse said. He noted that marriage did not even exist in Navajo culture until it was introduced by the Anglo Christians" (2004, 1A). This articulation of Navajo tradition and culture clashes with the version of history Ms. Tsosie and other supporters of the act engage. The Christianized, family-values side ultimately held sway.

The passage of the Diné Marriage Act on April 22, 2005, articulated and enacted a regulatory system for family legitimacy that obscured attention to power inequality through the assertion of celebrations of traditional family and culture. Denetdale explains: "While the law claims to draw upon tradition, it actually serves to affirm Western gender ideals and American values as normative for Navajos. The conflation of Navajo traditional values with mainstream American values gives credence to the multicultural narrative that America has created about itself and renders invisible the links between the past and the present, wherein Native people still live with the consequences of dispossession and disenfranchisement" (2008, 289). "Tradition" is a contested category in this social narrative about "American values," and this version of it renders Indigenous histories invisible. This very old story speaks to a history of material and cultural domination that has characterized white settler colonialism. Much of that regulatory practice has focused on reproduction and family.[6]

This law is not just symbolic for Ronnie, Yvonne, and their son. Family legitimacy is regulated through this law that bans same-sex marriage and adoption. Yvonne works at Diné College, the Navajo two-year college in Tsaile, Arizona. She would be eligible to live in traditional "Hogan-style" campus housing with her family if she were legally married. The Diné Marriage Act prohibits them from marrying each other, so their family is not allowed in campus housing. The law also limits the right to adopt children to husbands and wives, unmarried and divorced persons at least twenty-one years old, and "in the case of a child whose parents are not married, the child's unmarried father" (Title 9 Navajo Nation Code, Domestic Relations).

This law would not necessarily ban queers from adopting as single people. The law's implementation would likely be dependent—as many family law decisions are—on the beliefs and practices of the social workers and judges involved. The delineation of eligibility for adoption under the Diné Marriage Act does, however, preclude same-sex partners from legally adopting the biological or adopted children of their partners. This intersection of laws prohibiting same-sex marriage and adoption leaves Yvonne, Ronnie, and their son legally vulnerable.

Borders are not just lines on a map or signs we pass while speeding along the interstate. Geographic demarcations mark deep and complex histories of dispossession and oppression, just as laws act as boundaries of community and national belonging. The Diné Marriage Act tells a story about what kinds of families *belong* in the Navajo Nation and defends who gets included through its definition of "traditional." The DMA enacts a colonial definition of traditional marriage and family through Christianity, heterosexuality, and marriage, effectively erasing the history of Navajo matrilineal kinship, Nadleehi tribal members, and Diné pre-Christian cosmology.

The reclaiming of Nadleehi history is important to Ronnie and Yvonne, and to other queer Indigenous people, because it locates them in a gender-queer, matrilineal, extended-family tradition in Navajo history. This history challenges contemporary conservative views of the patriarchal, nuclear, heterosexual family as natural, traditional, and unchanging over time. It is an origin narrative that includes them in their own community, culture, and history. Denetdale explains: "Contemporary gay and lesbian Navajos regard the creation stories as proof that Navajos recognized more than two genders and that third, and possibly fourth, genders were accepted and celebrated. They have embraced the *nadleehi* as evidence of acceptance in Navajo society and as a model for their own lives" (2008, 294). This political debate about same-sex marriage within the Navajo Nation articulates ongoing debates over meanings of family, tradition, colonial power, assimilation, and resistance. Ronnie and Yvonne's embrace of Nadleehi and matrilineal history resists assimilationist projects focused on family and the transmission of cultural identity. Their resistance aligns with leftist critiques of same-sex marriage as assimilation, but their particular social and geographic location problematizes simple polarities. While they are resistant in claiming the legitimacy of Nadleehi history over the colonial version of a patriarchal, Christianized family narrative, at the same time they say life has been more difficult for them since the passage of the *Diné Marriage Act.* They wish they could be legally married, and that Ronnie could be the legal parent of their son. They do not like feeling like outsiders in their own tribe. Their desire for social and legal recognition of their family, and their anger over the lack of it, is both resistant *and* assimilative, emphasizing the inadequacy of the false dichotomy for understanding the lived experience of family-making and belonging.

Contradictory laws and tribal conflict over definitions of tradition put Ronnie and Yvonne in an insider-outsider position as citizens and family; they are not fully at home anywhere. Ronnie is neither Yvonne's legal spouse, nor her son's legal parent. In the event of a medical emergency for either of them, Ronnie would face the possibility of being kept out of the hospital room, refused health information by the doctor, and denied the ability to make medical decisions for her family. If Yvonne were for any reason unable to care for their son, the likelihood is high that he would be removed from Ronnie by child welfare authorities. There is a long history of children being removed from lesbian mothers, whether by child welfare or through custody battles with fathers. There is also a disturbing history of children being removed from Native mothers.[7] These laws function as borders of family, tradition, and belonging, and as barriers to inclusion, rights, and resources.

Inconsistent marriage and adoption laws characterize this historical moment, but Ronnie and Yvonne's family-making takes place in a social location in which contradictory laws are not necessarily new. Inadequate and uneven legislation regulating families across racial-ethnic identities and geographic locations are not unique to queerness, but, in fact, characteristic of US legal jurisdiction. The rule of law applies to various populations in different places in remarkably inconsistent ways. Indigenous studies scholar Alyosha Goldstein makes clear: "The United States encompasses a historically variable and uneven constellation of state and local governments, indigenous nations, unincorporated territories, free associated commonwealths, protectorates, federally administered public lands, military bases, export processing zones, *colonias,* and anomalies such as the District of Columbia that do not comprehensively delineate an inside and outside of the nation-state" (2014, 1). Laws and policies regulating family relationships have always varied by region. Focusing here on society's most vulnerable families provides a view of history and society that reveals how consistently inequality is obscured. Oppression has always been here for some groups.

In the United States, family and marriage law have historically functioned as a means of regulating access to the full range of citizenship rights. As sociologist Bonnie Thornton Dill's work demonstrates, race and ethnicity have been central factors shaping the legal recognition of families and the social resources accorded them. Well before intersectionality became a popular framework for feminists, Dill's historical research on African American, Chinese American, Mexican American, and white families insisted on the importance of exploring the ways that structural issues of race and economy intersect with gender to reproduce inequality. In her groundbreaking work "Our Mothers' Grief: Racial-Ethnic Women and the Maintenance of Family," Dill explains: "From the founding of the United States, and throughout its history, race has been a fundamental criterion determining the kind of work people do, the wages they receive, and the kind of legal, economic, political, and social support provided for their families. Women of color have faced limited economic resources, inferior living conditions, alien cultures and languages, and overt hostility in their struggle to create a 'place' for families of color in the United States" (1988, 166). Dill's comparative historical analysis highlights how white patriarchal nuclear-family ideology was used as a measuring stick against which all families were judged, while only white middle-class and wealthy women were provided access to the cultural and economic resources necessary to embody constructions of ideal mothers devoted to raising the next generation of United States citizens.

Stratified Reproduction and the Child Welfare System

The mothers we talked with in the Southwest navigated family-making in a landscape of legal, cultural, and representational stratification grounded in histories of racial-ethnic conflict and colonization. The cultural regulation of boundaries and borders of national identity have historically involved assimilation projects targeting family and reproduction; mothers of color in the United States have had a particularly brutal relationship with the child welfare system. As historians David Wallace Adams and Crista Deluzio describe: "For Mexicans, as well as Indians, the promise of genuine citizenship was anchored to their acceptance of their colonizers' prevailing gender, racial, and moral codes, including dominant modes of family life. If the institution of the family was an essential source of moral character, the child's first window on home life and social living as well as the wellspring of identity, then surely, it was reasoned, society was justified in efforts to improve the Mexican family's suitability in the American fold" (2012, 6). The reproductive capacity of women of color has been consistently narrated as the root of social problems and targeted for regulation. Historian Meg Devlin O'Sullivan explains that for Native American women resistance and activism took the form of fighting to keep and raise their children:

> The legacies of settler colonialism—including the boarding school system, coerced sterilizations, and child removals—rendered the right to bear and raise children as not a limiting framework but a desired expression of personal autonomy and tribal sovereignty. Thus, within larger more familiar portrayals, there existed a very different struggle for rights and justice particularly around mothering. For many indigenous women, political action regarding children was not about campaigns for subsidized day cares or cultural arguments about gender, work, and parenting. Child welfare was a literal fight to keep Native children in their homes and in their nations. (2016, 20)

The history of Indigenous women under settler colonialism in North America is a history of fighting for the right to mother and raise children in which the child welfare system has figured prominently. Latinas, too, have been targeted by social welfare practices and laws aimed at policing rigid definitions of legitimate mothering.[8]

Family has always been a site of political contention, and this plays out in the narratives of the mothers we interviewed. I turn now to the family-making stories of Betty and Edna, a working-class Hispanic couple living in Albuquerque, New Mexico.[9] At the time of our interview in 2007, their daughter was grown and out of the house, and their son Andrew was a young teenager.

Their family origin story is punctuated by interactions with the child welfare system, lawyers, and the capitalist marketplace. They became parents when Betty's niece asked her to adopt the baby she was about to give birth to.

> BETTY: My niece was pregnant with her first, and she was gonna you
> know, give me the baby. And then she met this guy and then they
> changed their minds. And then she became pregnant again, and asked
> me if I wanted to adopt the baby. Um, and I told her no because, I
> said, "You're not gonna break my heart again." And so she decided
> that no, that she just did not want—her and the guy had already
> broken up—and she just did not want this baby, you know. And I told
> her, "No, I don't want it." [Big smile] And that was my Jamie.
> EDNA: You got that wrong. She's *my* Jamie. [Both laugh]

Betty and Edna were interested in adopting this child, but wary of their niece's reckless behavior. They began exploring options. The first lawyer they consulted, whom they were told was an expert in adoptions in Albuquerque, would have charged them five thousand dollars. This was unaffordable on their salaries as a truck driver and janitor. They eventually found a lawyer willing to complete the adoption at a cost they could afford. They went through the home-study process, signed the papers, and paid the fees. Betty became their daughter Jamie's sole legal parent.

Several years after their daughter was born, Betty and Edna received a phone call informing them that Betty's niece had given birth again.

> EDNA: So we went down to the hospital to see him, and it was too late.
> He had already been placed in a foster home. So it just happened
> that—we started talking to everyone, you know, and trying to you
> know, to find where he was and all. When we—when finally they let
> us see him he was already almost two and a half months old, by the
> time we got to see him.

They had been on vacation when the baby was born, and by the time they arrived at the hospital he had already been removed from his birth mother and placed in foster care.

FIGURE 6.1. Edna and Betty, Albuquerque, New Mexico. Photo credit: Melanie Patton-Imani.

BETTY: Well, at the very beginning I talked to the welfare worker and I told them that I wanted to know where he was at. And they told me he was at a foster home. And I said, "Well, I want him." And they kept arguing with me that he was in a foster home. And I says "Now I know damn well if I go to a judge, the judge is going to give him to family before he gives him to foster care." And so I fought with them for two months, and then finally . . .

This struggle suggests, at the very least, reluctance on the part of the social worker to place this infant with Betty. It is impossible to untangle race, class, gender, and sexuality as forces shaping this interaction, but it is likely that some combination of these factors shaped the social worker's reluctance to even let them see the infant. He had been placed with a two-parent heterosexual white middle-class married couple. Betty and Edna have no way of knowing whether or not the foster parents hoped to adopt him or not. This is certainly a possible reason the social worker was resistant to Betty's petitions for custody.

Her adoptions of both children were processed through the child welfare system as single-mother adoptions. Though Jamie and Andrew have only one legal mother, there are three mothers in this family story. Jamie and Andrew do not have a relationship with their birth mother, though they have met her at a few family functions. She is their biological mother whose parental rights have been severed—once through relinquishment, and once through removal by the child welfare system at birth. Betty is both their legal and relational mother. Edna is not recognized as a mother by the state, yet she clearly has a deeply loving relationship with her two children. She has participated in their care and financial support all of their lives. She was omitted from the family in the adoption home-studies and represented as an "auntie" in the schools their children attended.

This is, in part, a story of regulatory relationships between state definitions of "fit" parenthood and these three mothers, codified by money, class, and patriarchy. Both financial and legal constrictions kept Edna from being able to legalize her connection to their children. Second-parent adoption was not explicitly prohibited in New Mexico in the 1980s; however, access to it was largely dependent on judicial discretion, and it was not a common practice. The most significant barrier for Betty and Edna was financial. These economic issues were shared by many of the families we interviewed.

Questions of assimilation, belonging, and normative family structures wind their way through all of these discussions. Betty locates herself not only through geography, but through race and connection to her family tree. Boundaries are enforced within families as well as among them.

> BETTY: I'm a native New Mexican. I was born and raised here in Albuquerque. I'm what in New Mexico they call a "coyote," which is a half-breed. I'm half Spanish, half white. But I lean more to the Hispanic because they're the ones that have always loved me whole-heartedly, you know, no questions asked. You know, I am [pause] from my *mother* [with emphasis]. The Okie side of my family, they didn't want to have anything to do with us because we were half-breeds and we were Catholic, at the time.

These stories reflect layers of history and power. As she says, "I am [pause] from my *mother*," Betty actively embraces her mother's "Spanish" family tree, as the "Okie" (white) branch rejected her on racial, ethnic, and religious grounds. However, her embrace of her mother's language is not free from traces of colonial power. Betty, like many New Mexico residents, regularly uses "Spanish" as the term to describe people whose family histories are grounded in Mexico; language supersedes geographic boundaries. Colonization effectively wrote this narrative of kinship rejecting "half-breeds" to enforce boundaries of nation and citizenship.

Betty and Edna became mothers through familial caretaking that was legally codified through Betty's single-parent adoption. Their experiences are vastly different from those of Ronnie and Yvonne, or of Sonia and Renee. Betty and Edna had the same second-parent adoption laws available to them as Sonia and Renee, but were not able to afford second-parent adoptions. Ronnie and Yvonne, living on the reservation, did not have the option of legalizing Ronnie's relationship with their son. These differences are rooted in long histories of stratification between white middle-class mothers, Indigenous mothers, and mothers of Mexican origin in the Southwest. These historical tensions and inequalities focusing on family are reproduced in the different family-making experiences among white, Latina, and Indigenous lesbians.

Iowa City, Iowa: "There's a Thousand and One Benefits"

Kimberly and Mischa were married in Toronto, Canada, but at the time of our interview in 2007 their marriage was not legally recognized by the state of Iowa or by the US government. For them and many others, family protection was not acquired through marriage. They did their best to legitimize their relationships through adoption and other legal means, but these strategies fell far short of what they considered adequate protection. Mischa and Kimberly adopted their youngest child, Jonas, from Haiti in 2004 (prior to the adoption scandals that emerged after the 2010 earthquake), but because of laws against same-sex couples adopting together, he had to be adopted by Kimberly as a single mother. At the time of this interview they had not yet been able to afford a second-parent adoption, so Mischa has no legal relationship with Jonas. She also has no legal relationship with Sophie and Theo, the two children Kimberly legally adopted with her first partner, because in the state of Iowa children cannot legally have more than two parents.[10] In spite of this, it is through Mischa's employer, Linn County, that Sophie and her siblings receive health insurance. Mischa explains the contradiction in county and federal tax law: "The county recognizes our domestic partnership, but I have to pay taxes on all that medical because they are not—they are not—acknowledged as family members, really. They are just—the city acknowledged them, acknowledges my domestic partner and her children, essentially. But I have to pay tax on all that medical and other families don't." At that time, the benefits Mischa received for her family at the county level were taxed as income at the federal level, unlike that of straight couples. Mischa explains, "I travel a lot for work and I worry about if anything ever happens to me." Queer parents are cautioned by legal experts, LGBTQ organizations, and other queer parents that they should carry all their legal documents— adoption decrees, guardianship papers, marriage licenses, civil union documentation, domestic partner registrations, power-of-attorney papers, and even wills—with them when they cross state lines. That certain citizens must carry identification papers to travel safely within their own country signifies their lack of full citizenship rights.

The couples we spoke with, in Iowa and across the country, that wanted to get married to demonstrate their commitment to family and friends or to have a religious ceremony commemorating their relationships, had already done that. Some had nonlegal commitment ceremonies; others, like Mischa and Kimberly, were legally married in other states or countries, without legal recognition in their home state or nation. Their ceremonies were symbolically important for their sense of social recognition, but many of them also articulated the importance of recognition by the state in which they live:

> SUSAN: We have friends that have gone to Canada. We have friends that have gone to Massachusetts. And they ask us what—We actually went on vacation to Massachusetts last June, and people were like, "Oh, are you gonna get married?" And we were like, "Nope. We're gonna wait 'til it's legal right where we live." If we move to Massachusetts then we'll get married, obviously, but 'til Iowa has it we're not gonna bother doing it. Because we've heard it's hard to get recognized even if your state does it. So we'll just bide our time.

Susan and Dana, a white lesbian couple with two children, had a nonreligious commitment ceremony several years prior to our interview and were registered as domestic partners in Johnson County, Iowa. We interviewed them in their home in Iowa City in March 2007, two years prior to legalization of same-sex marriage in Iowa.

SUSAN: I think we are just gonna to have to take care of things through lawyers. I mean, you have to get all those documents and make sure you have them when you travel.

Susan has been active in political organizing in Iowa City, so she extended her activism to include marriage equality. Dana explains why legal marriage matters practically for their family:

DANA: I would like for it to be legal. I mean I understand not everybody wants to have like a church wedding. But to have a union of some sort recognized by the state, by the country, would be nice. As well as all the legal benefits that go along with it, you know, power of attorney, just being a given that I am her spouse and that if something happens I could make decisions at a hospital. Um, there's however many—[she looks at Susan]
SUSAN: There's a thousand and one benefits at the federal level. It's the general accounting office, the GAO, counted them up, and that is how many benefits you just get the minute you are married as a couple at the federal level.

Susan explains that she learned about the rights, privileges, and benefits of citizenship that are regulated through federal marriage law through her involvement in the 2004 attempt by "thirty or forty" lesbian and gay couples in Iowa City to obtain marriage licenses (prior to marriage legalization in 2009). They were at a baby shower talking about same-sex marriage:

SUSAN: New Paltz was doing it, San Francisco was doing it. And I was just like, why doesn't Johnson—why don't we just do it here? I thought we had to go to city hall. *Why don't we go to city hall?!*

Susan's idea sparked excitement, and her friend Janel organized the event for the next week. They spread the word for LGBTQ couples to request marriage licenses at the county recorder's office.

SUSAN: We were shooting for five couples, you know tops, and it ended up being you know, thirty or forty.

Kim Painter, the Johnson County recorder, was an out lesbian herself, and she made no secret of her support for same-sex marriage. As each same-sex couple requested a license, she dutifully read the text of the law restricting marriage to opposite-sex couples: "Due to the Iowa code of the state of Iowa, marriage is only allowed between a man and a woman, and I am not allowed to issue you a license" (Witosky and Hansen 2015, 57). No one was married that day. The cover of the *Iowa City Press Citizen* on February 28, 2004, featured the faces of Dawn and Jen BarbouRoske, a white lesbian couple, who later became plaintiffs in *Varnum v. Brien*, the lawsuit that legalized same-sex marriage in Iowa.

The rest of 2004 would see more ups and downs in state and federal legislation, including the passage of bans on same-sex marriage in thirteen more states, the failure of the Federal Marriage Amendment, and the refusal of the US Supreme Court to hear arguments challenging the legalization of same-sex marriage in Massachusetts.

Conclusion

While marriage was front and center in public discourse, the stories of the mothers we interviewed challenge the standard arguments about same-sex couples' desire for marriage, framed variously as the key to full equality for gays and lesbians, the work of the devil and the end of civilization, and as assimilation to heterosexual "normalcy" contributing to the demise of queer culture. None of these perspectives adequately represents the family-making stories of the mothers we spoke with. Yet each of these views has profoundly shaped their family lives.

Political scientist Paisley Currah suggests that queer academic critiques of homonormativity reify the power of the state through an overemphasis on "activities regulated by the federal government (commerce, war, immigration, national security, etc.) and national discourses of American identity (marriage and family)" (2012, 5). Currah's argument suggests that even those to the left of these partisan lines have placed too much emphasis on a macroview of law and politics: "Fetishizing a generalized idea of the state—the conceptual state—obscures what is actually happening in the local, micro, particular sites where public authority is being exercised" (2012, 6). Clearly "the state" is not one thing; fighting it would be easier if that were so. Its tendrils are far-reaching, and mothers in different social and geographic locations negotiate the law in many different ways.

These family-making stories deepen and advance my analysis of stratified reproduction based on intersections of geography, race, ethnicity, tribal status, socioeconomics, gender, and sexuality. Differences in laws in California, New Mexico, and Iowa clearly demonstrate the ways that geography fundamentally shaped access to family rights and protections in the early years of the twenty-first century. These contrasts are not difficult to see, although stratification among mothers of different racial-ethnic identities and socioeconomic status is often more difficult to identify. Deep racial and colonial histories in the Southwest, in particular, fundamentally shape access to social resources and family protections. While the mothering practices of white women have been celebrated as foundational to the nation, the family-making practices of women of color have been under constant regulation, as is evident in the family-making narratives of Indigenous, Latina, and white queer mothers I interviewed. This critical intersectional analysis demonstrates the importance of exploring the multiple axes of power shaping the lives of individual women and their families. At the same time, it makes evident the relationships between inequality and privilege, between queer mothers of different racial-ethnic groups and economic circumstances, that are deeply rooted in settler colonialism, patriarchy, and capitalism. All of these families were shaped by the fact that they were headed by two women, but how that queer gendered identity is experienced differs across geographic, racial-ethnic, and economic borders.

In the next chapter I consider the 2008 presidential election outcome as an allegory about the politics of family. I focus in particular on the politics surrounding the passage of Proposition 8, a ballot measure in California that declared same-sex marriage unlawful, nullifying the California Supreme Court ruling, just six months earlier, that ruled same-sex marriage legal.

SAME-SEX MARRIAGE, CALIFORNIA, 2004–2010

February 2004   City of San Francisco begins marrying same-sex couples

March 2004   California Supreme Court orders halt to San Francisco same-sex weddings

August 2004   California Supreme Court voids same-sex marriages

March 2005   Judge rules California same-sex marriage ban is unconstitutional

September 2005   California legislature first in the United States to approve same-sex marriage legalization

August 2005   California Supreme Court establishes coparenting rights for same-sex couples

September 2005   California legislature first in United States to approve same-sex marriage legalization

September 2005   California governor Arnold Schwarzenegger vetoes bill to legalize same-sex marriage

May 2008   California Supreme Court overturns ban on same-sex marriage

November 2008   California voters approve a constitutional ban on same-sex marriage

August 2010   US District Judge rules California Proposition 8 unconstitutional

Adapted from https://gaymarriage.procon.org

7

Irreconciliable Differences

Socialization, Religion, and Race, 2008

> KIM: I did work on the "No on 8" campaign. I did the phone bank
> a couple of times. And I was outside the polling center, like, a few
> blocks away. And, you know, verbally abused by a few people in the
> neighborhood.
> CYPRESS: [Chuckles] Especially when Alex and I came to visit her one
> night because it was really cold. And we came to visit.

November 6, 2008, was a particularly chilly night in California. Kim
and Cypress are an Asian American couple that live in the Los Angeles
area with their five-year-old daughter Alex and with Cypress's parents.
The 2008 California ballot initiative Kim worked against was officially
titled "Proposition 8—Eliminates Rights of Same-Sex Couples to Marry."
It was designed in response to the California Supreme Court ruling in
May of that year overturning the state ban on same-sex marriage passed
in 2000. Kim and Cypress, like thousands of other same-sex couples
in California, had been married following the 2008 ruling, and they
were deeply committed to safeguarding the rights they had gained. If
Proposition 8 were to pass, the legitimacy of their marriage would be
threatened. Kim continues her story about election night 2008:

> KIM: So we had the signs, and . . . I was trained in how to do the polling
> thing. And [you] walk in and introduce yourself and explain what
> you're going to be doing. And you want to confirm the distance from
> the polling place so that we are in complete compliance with the
> law. . . . I mean, I got a couple looks. . . . "You shouldn't be here" was
> mostly what we got.
> CYPRESS: And "I'll pray for you." She was like, "I'll pray for you. I'll
> pray for your daughter."

KIM: The one woman flipped her lid . . . like stormed in, "You shouldn't be here. I'm gonna have them move you. You need to leave right now. You're disgusting." And then she walked into the polling place, got the guy to come out. And he said, "No," like, "Yes, I know them. They came in. They have a legal right to be here. They are within the distance. They are in compliance." And she goes, "Well, that's just not right." And then she goes, "I'm gonna go make a sign and come back." And she did.

This performance of citizenship and belonging was shaped by the deep investments different voters had in this ballot measure. Kim's efforts were aimed at fighting what she viewed as an oppressive attempt to renege on rights that had already been granted by the state. This woman did not just disagree with the stance Kim was advocating; she did not see Kim as a fellow citizen exercising her right to free speech. She said, "You're disgusting," and tried to have Kim removed from outside the voting center. When that failed, she made her own sign and began advocating for the passage of the restrictive measure.

Proposition 8 quite likely did not directly affect this woman's life, yet her behavior suggests she believed otherwise. Her emphasis on praying for their daughter makes her stakes in this debate clear. The campaign for passage of Proposition 8 was almost exclusively funded by conservative religious organizations that argued same-sex marriage was a danger to children, family, and the future of the nation. Religion and queerness were prominent themes in this political battle. Race and gender were also profoundly important, yet articulated in more covert ways. This experience can be read as an allegory for the irreconcilable differences that characterized the campaign rhetoric that saturated media in the months prior to the election.

Kim and Cypress's family-making narratives are bound up in the social, political, and legal terrain regulating same-sex marriage and adoption in California and the United States in the early twenty-first century. They, like mothers we interviewed all over the country, have had to navigate legitimacy as a family in a political and legal context in which neoliberal policy agendas intersect with conservative Christian representations of "traditional" families to justify laws and policies designed to restrict access to social rights and resources. At the same time, they have had to construct and maintain a sense of belonging as a family in the larger LGBTQ community in which whiteness is reproduced as the norm, and queers of color seem not to exist representationally.

Kim and Cypress are socially located in complex ways in relation to the No and Yes on Prop 8 arguments. They clearly side against the restrictive measure, yet their relationship to the rhetoric of the No on Prop 8 campaign is more complex than unproblematic acceptance. Kim volunteered for the campaign in order to do as much as she could to protect the legitimation their family had been granted through legal marriage, but her and Cypress's stance as a queer family of color is also shaped by the whiteness of the mainstream LGBTQ population, and the ways that race is deployed on both sides of the debate. I argue that the emphasis on family, socialization, and children in the political debate about Proposition 8 facilitates the deployment of racialized and gendered narratives of blame. While denying the social and political salience of race and gender for queer families of color, these sociopolitical narratives profoundly shape their lives on multiple levels. Navigating family-making can be challenging in predominantly white settings, even when the group is LGBTQ. Mothers of color often discussed feeling like outsiders at Family Week or Pride events. Their lives were also affected in material ways by the laws and policies put into place that legally define family legitimacy through patriarchal white supremacy.

I draw primarily on interviews with mothers of color living in California and several other states. I focus on the politics surrounding the proposition to ban same-sex marriage after it had already been legal in the state for several months. This chapter is not only about California, however, but about the politics of marriage and family more broadly in 2008. Proposition 8 threatened a rollback of marriage rights that had already been legally granted by the California State Supreme Court. This was state politics, but it was also national news. California is often regarded as a bellwether state, given its large and diverse population, and this battle was closely watched as a portent of how the rest of the country might vote on same-sex marriage.

I draw on these narratives, along with news reports and letters to the editor concerning Proposition 8 to explore the irreconcilable differences over social meanings of same-sex marriage, parenting, and race. I approach the arguments raised in the 2008 California Proposition 8 campaign as a lens through which to consider the competing sociopolitical narratives that characterized the volatile politics of family in the United States. Proponents of Proposition 8 argue that same-sex marriage is a danger to children and traditional families and thus constitutes a threat to the future of the nation; opponents of the proposition deployed rhetoric of equality through language largely borrowed from the civil rights movement. This familiar narrative of progress posits marriage equality as the fulfillment of the promise of US citizenship.

Though each movement framed their campaign distinctly, both focused on what the legalization of same-sex marriage might mean for the nation's future. Each invoked a narrative about the meaning of "America" as justification. Both the No and the Yes sides of the debate emphasized the importance of rights: while conservatives framed the issue as a denial of religious rights, liberals insisted that same-sex marriage would grant gays and lesbians the rights necessary for full equality as citizens. In letters to the editor in newspapers throughout the state, both conservatives and liberals routinely cited the Declaration of Independence, the Constitution, and the Bill of Rights in their arguments for and against same-sex marriage.

Queer families have to maneuver their way through these competing stories about rights, which is made more difficult by the obfuscation and erasure of race and gender on both sides of the political debate. In this chapter I narrate the political battle over the passage of Proposition 8 to explore the conflicting and complementary meanings of race, gender, religion, and queerness in the United States at the turn of the twenty-first century, as well as the ways that mothers in different social locations navigate the lived experience of citizenship as a negotiation of belonging.

Shifting Marriage Laws in California: Reading Allegorically

The first decade of the twenty-first century was characterized by dramatic shifts in California state law regulating same-sex marriage. The legal changes in California were more frequent and uneven than any other US state. Between 2000 and 2013 same-sex marriage in California

was alternately outlawed, performed legally, forbidden and delegiti-
mized, legalized, banned, and finally legitimated by the US Supreme
Court.[1] While important in California, this was also the subject of a
national discussion that both shaped and was shaped by larger tensions
over meanings of US citizenship.

Kim and Cypress, like approximately eighteen thousand other same-
sex couples, were legally married between June and November 2008,
when same-sex marriages were lawfully performed in California. The
California Supreme Court ruled that same-sex marriages could begin at
5:01 p.m. on June 16, 2008, and couples all over the state began a steady
parade toward churches and courthouses. Kim and Cypress also sprang
into action the day the ban was lifted.

> KIM: I called all around in LA County and the courthouses were
> booked solid. But we're up in the San Fernando Valley, so I thought
> why don't we just drive up to Ventura County? And we drove up
> there and there was no wait at all, no line. We just walked right in.
> CYPRESS: It was pretty cool. We grabbed our—my two sisters as our
> witnesses, and Alex came with us. And so we got married with her
> there. It probably took less than an hour. [Laughter] We're fortunate.

Stories like theirs about dropping everything and rushing to a courthouse to get married were common for gays and lesbians in this era.
Stacey and Jess, a white couple living in Massachusetts, told us an almost
identical story about the day marriage was legalized in their state in
2003. Stacey called Jess at work and told her to get ready to jump in the
car so they could go get married. The way Stacey told the story conjured
a vision of her speeding to Jess's place of work, screeching to a stop just
long enough for Jess to get into the car, and tearing off to the courthouse
to have their relationship sanctioned by the state. Same-sex marriage
laws and court decisions were so tenuous that couples often rightfully
feared they would be challenged or revoked. Opportunity prevailed over
long-term wedding planning.

Like many of the women we interviewed, Cypress and Kim had a
commitment ceremony earlier in their relationship, prior to having children. As Kim said, "We had the ceremony. We got the house. We had
the kid." They viewed a legal marriage as something separate from their

commitment to each other. Like most of the mothers we talked with, having children was the primary factor in deciding to become legally married.

> CYPRESS: [Nodding] Yeah, I think that commitment ceremony we had was pretty much—
> KIM: That took enough energy and money as it was. We didn't want to do it again.
> KIM: Well, we had a daughter, so it was more important for legal reasons that we be legally married. [Pause] In case anything would happen to one of us. When she was born though—
> CYPRESS: They'd just passed that legislation.
> KIM: Yeah, they did put Cypress on the birth certificate as parent. We had to strike through, like, "father."

The California Domestic Partnership Registry (2005) made step- and second-parent adoption unnecessary for Cypress. Because the law passed right before Alex was born, Cypress was listed as her parent on her birth certificate. Even so, they felt an imperative to marry when it became legal in order to protect the three of them, particularly Alex.

The May 2008 court ruling making same-sex marriage legal and available throughout the state was not the final word; conservative forces were poised for battle. The *San Francisco Chronicle* reported that "conservative religious groups have submitted more than 1.1 million signatures on petitions for an initiative that would enshrine the ban on same-sex marriage as a state constitutional amendment" (Egelko 2008). The possibility of the proposition being passed fostered a sense of urgency among LGBTQ couples. In a letter to the *Chico Enterprise-Record* on October 13, 2008, James Wilkerson expresses anxiety over the initiative: "If Proposition 8 passes, all of those marriages, which are now legal, will be in legal limbo as the courts try to determine what to do." The vitriolic debate took shape in local, state, and national news from June to November 2008.

Activists in favor of and against Proposition 8 were fiercely opposed, yet, for all their differences, the claims made by each side were grounded in a common emphasis on rights—often characterized as "life, liberty, and the pursuit of happiness"—and what it means to be an "American

FIGURE 7.1. Kim, Alex, and Cypress, Los Angeles, California. Photo credit: Sandra Patton-Imani.

citizen." Both sides deployed race-evasive, gender-neutral language to argue for laws grounded in race, gender, and class politics. The No on 8 campaign, specifically, narrated the battle over same-sex marriage as key to the promise of "American equality."

Yes on California Proposition 8: "No One Has Two Mommies"

Arguments in favor of Proposition 8 (against same-sex marriage) that focused on children and socialization proved to be persuasive as the campaign progressed. Conservative political arguments were framed through the right to religious freedom and the right to raise their children as parents see fit. Families headed by same-sex couples were cast as the villains in this morality tale. Queers were blamed for threatening the rights of Christian heterosexuals and for poisoning the minds of innocent children. In a letter to the editor published in the *Contra Costa Times* in the weeks prior to the election, Karen Reyna of Brentwood articulates her opposition: "If Prop. 8 is defeated, you will have no right to protect your children in the public classroom from the teaching that homosexuality is normal and acceptable" (October 18, 2008). This side of the debate focused on protecting children, echoing the rhetoric the 1990s in discourse about DOMA. According to the *San Jose Mercury News*, "The race began to tighten when the Yes on 8 campaign began running ads that suggested that churches could lose their tax-exempt status if clergy refused to do gay weddings and that second-graders would be taught about gay marriage" (Swift, November 8, 2008). The conservative articulation of rights in relation to the politics of family was a slightly new twist on the families-are-endangered storyline that was so dominant in the "family values" discussions in the 1990s.

Betty and Edna, a Latina couple in Albuquerque, were raising young children in the 1990s (Jamie was born in 1986 and Andrew in 1992). When we interviewed them in 2007, Andrew was a teenager, and the family was still bombarded with political rhetoric damning families headed by same-sex parents. Betty and Edna felt they had no choice but to find ways of affirming their family in a political context that cast queer parents and children as illegitimate. They used humor and critical thinking as strategies for navigating the land mines of public media, including challenging social definitions of "normal" and *questioning everything*.

EDNA: Jamie, one time she said, um, that someone had asked her, you know, "What is it like being raised by two women?" And she's like, "Well, what's it's like being raised by a mom and dad?!" You know, she says, "*It's normal to me.* It's my life."

This redefinition of "normal" was precisely what conservatives feared. Betty continues:

BETTY: And years ago, you know, people used to say that *lesbians* used to have children because they were recruiting. And as you see [gesturing toward a photo on the mantle], we recruited our daughter to be straight [laughter all around].

Such accusations of recruitment were popular scare tactics in 1990s family values rhetoric. This theme was vigorously renewed in news media discussions about Proposition 8.

The most frequently broadcast ad of the campaign focused on the dangers to children of teaching acceptance of homosexuality in public schools. It was produced by iprotectmarriage.com, an organization formed to support the passage of Proposition 8.[2] The commercial focuses on an elementary-school-aged girl of indeterminate racial-ethnic identity. She could be read as Latina, Indigenous, or as mixed white and Asian American; some people would also likely read her as white. The girl runs into a kitchen and says, "Mom, guess what I learned in school today!" Her mom, standing at the kitchen counter sorting mail, looks up and says casually, "What, sweetie?" The girl excitedly hands her mother a colorful children's picture book with the title *King and King* and says, "I learned how a prince married a prince, and I can marry a princess!"

The camera pulls back to a god's-eye view of the mother and child from above, as Richard Peterson, professor at Pepperdine University School of Law, is superimposed over the left third of the screen. He says, "Think it can't happen? It's already happened! When Massachusetts legalized gay marriage, schools began teaching second graders that boys can marry boys. The courts ruled that parents had no right to object." Graphics read "NO LEGAL RIGHT TO OBJECT," over a shot of a judge's gavel and a file folder labeled "*Parker v. Hurley* 514 F.3d 87" (1st Cir. 2008). The scene cuts to a shot of the cover of a copy of the California Education Code. A disembodied hand opens the book and points to a highlighted section. A woman says, in voice-over, "Under California law public schools instruct children about marriage." Graphics read "S51933, 7 Instruction and materials shall teach respect for marriage . . ." The woman's voice continues, "Teaching children about gay marriage will happen here unless we pass Proposition 8. Yes on 8."

For conservatives, this ad represents a dystopian future in which homosexuality is normal and acceptable—so normal it is taught in elementary schools. The tone of the ad suggests that the only appropriate response to this threat to the future is horror and outrage. Critics of this perspective pointed out that acceptance of same-sex marriage was already being taught in California, and that the passage of Proposition 8 would not influence the curricula. *Parker v. Hurley* (2008), the lawsuit referenced in the ad, was filed by two sets of white middle-class same-sex parents in Lexington, Massachusetts, after same-sex marriage was legalized there in 2003. The parents objected, on religious grounds, to three children's books about same-sex families being included in their children's elementary school curriculum. A Massachusetts federal appeals court ruled in favor of the school district, making clear that the religious objections of parents cannot control public school curriculum. *King and King* (2000), the children's book used in the Yes on 8 advertisement, was one of the texts the parents objected to.

According to the language of the lawsuit, the two sets of parents involved "assert that the defendants' conduct violates their rights under the United States Constitution to raise their children and to the free exercise of their religion."[3] On January 31, 2008, the US Court of Appeals for the First Circuit ruled that "public schools are entitled to teach anything that is reasonably related to the goals of preparing students to become engaged and productive citizens in our democracy. Diversity is a hallmark of our nation" (Supreme Court of the State of Massachusetts 2008). This ruling contradicts conservative arguments that a traditional family structure is necessary for socializing the next generation of US citizens. The court's decision aligns with liberal arguments that children in US schools need to learn about "diversity" in order to be prepared for the future, yet there is more going on here than first appears. The decision links education about a diverse range of people and families to socialization of "productive citizens." As I have discussed, the use of this term deploys a narrative about single mothers of color as inadequate socializing forces for the next generation. This court's argument in favor of diversity is supported by a sociopolitical story grounded in the covert denigration of unmarried mothers of color living in poverty.

This legal challenge to parental authority was a central point of contention in Proposition 8 debates. The message rang true for conservative voters, and it became a prominent theme in letters to the editor in newspapers all over the state. *Molly's Family* (2004) was one of the children's books cited in *Parker v. Hurley* (2008), and the plot is quite similar to the story in *Heather Has Two Mommies* (1989). Each is set in a classroom of young children and focuses on the legitimacy of a family with two moms through a story about a child's drawing of her family. One notable difference between the Heather's and Molly's stories is that the challenge Molly faces to the legitimacy of her family is much more explicit than that experienced by Heather. When Molly is done drawing a picture of her family, several boys in the class begin questioning her about who the adults in the picture are.

> Tommy looked at Molly's paper. "That's not a family," he said.
> "It is so!" said Molly. "It's my family."
> "Where's your daddy?" asked Tommy.
> "I don't have a daddy" said Molly. "I have Mommy and Mama Lou and Sam [their dog]."
> 'You can't have a mommy and a mama, can she Stephen?'
> Stephen shook his head. "I don't think so," he said. "But you don't have to have a daddy. I don't have a daddy."
> He showed Molly his picture. "This is our classroom. And this is my mommy and my sister Jackie."
> "See," said Tommy, "Stephen's only got one mommy. That's all you can have."
> "It is not!" said Molly.
> Tommy laughed. "Molly says she has a mommy and a mama," he told everyone. "There's no such thing."
> "I have a mommy and a daddy and a grandma and two brothers," said Tanya.
> "I just have a daddy," said Adam. "Daddy and me."
> "And I have a daddy and a mommy," Tommy said. "No one has two mommies."
> Molly tried hard not to cry. (Garden 2004)

These children call her out on the legitimacy of her family. She becomes the "no one" that has two mommies, the illegitimate child. Indeed, in English common law, on which the US system is based, illegitimate children were labeled *filius nullius*—child of no one.[4] Not having a father was legally equated with being the *child of no one*; mothers were symbolically erased. It is significant that two boys lead the charge of family illegitimacy in this story. The absence of a patriarch is incomprehensible to Tommy, the spokesman for traditional families: "There's no such thing." Molly is told her family is not real.

The tension in *Molly's Family*, like that in *Heather Has Two Mommies* and many other children's books published during this era, is resolved with a lesson about accepting all kinds of families. The message is that two-mommy families are just like any other kind of family. This emphasis on sameness is consistent with the colorblind, neoliberal framing of race in this era; difference is repackaged as sameness to resolve tensions between divergent definitions of family legitimacy.

The classroom interaction in *Molly's Family* raises a key issue for families headed by same-sex parents—questions about legitimacy are often framed through the notion of *realness*. As Angela and Michelle discuss:

ANGELA: Or they'll say, "Who's the *real* mom?"
MICHELLE: Yeah, we get that of course. Who's the real mom?

This question suggests that strangers recognize the existence of families with two moms. Yet people often still cling to models of family legitimacy that distinguish between which mom counts as real. Families formed through adoption also have to deal with questions like these in everyday social interactions. When people asked about the "real" or "natural" mothers of the children she had adopted, my mother used to say, "Who am I, the *unnatural mother*?" As I have discussed, same-sex families are not unique in having two moms or two dads. As an adoptee and as a parent, I have been navigating versions of these social interactions throughout my life. Like many of the mothers we interviewed, Angela and Michelle received questions about who counts as a legitimate mother on a regular basis.

On a breezy summer afternoon, they walked with their twins to a local park in their East San Francisco Bay area neighborhood, likely not thinking about how their family was being seen. As the parents of active toddler-twins, they were probably focused on making sure the kids had enough exercise to settle in for their afternoon nap.

ANGELA: *Who's the real mom?* We were at a playground, actually, and
     some kid's like, "Who's the real mom?" And I'm like, "We both are
     the real mom." And he was like. "Oh." But I think he was a little con-
     fused. You know, you have those rewind moments, when I wish you
     could rewind and say, "You know, you might have a mom and a dad,
     and they have too, they have a mama and a mom."
MICHELLE: Yeah, we haven't hung out much with older kids and we're
     just kinda getting used to how to deal with that.

The questions children ask often highlight discrepancies between the social narratives they have learned and the social interaction they are currently trying to understand. The boy at the playground had internalized social definitions of family that included only one "real" mother. Like most children living in the contemporary United States, he has probably been exposed to kids with more than one mom before; he himself may even have a mom and a stepmom. He may have read some books about families with two moms.

That he asks which is the "real mom" suggests he is trying to reconcile two conflicting sets of meanings about family. One set emphasizes sameness, with narratives like the ones in the children's books: families come in lots of different forms, but they are all united by love. This narrative gestures toward "diversity" but makes clear that what really matters is what all families share. Social narratives about biology, genetics, and illegitimacy qualify stories celebrating diversity and difference with delineations of who counts as real. In other words, this child recognizes the fact that there are two moms, but seems to assume that traditional understandings of motherhood preclude the complete and unqualified acceptance of both of them on equal terms. The way such questions function linguistically and socially—regardless of intent—is to reinforce the presumption that children can only have one real mother. "Real" is defined in public narratives through both heteronormative templates of legal and social legitimacy, as well as biological assumptions about family, inheritance, and sameness. This microlevel interaction about the legitimacy of queer families speaks allegorically to the stakes in the political debate about socializing children and the future of the nation.

Many of the families we talked with emphasized how coming out shifted profoundly for them when they had children. Michelle explains:

MICHELLE: But we're very used to the grocery store coming out, and having to explain the fact that. . . .
ANGELA: That took some getting used to—outing yourself every time you're introducing your family—
MICHELLE: Constantly, not even introducing your family, just buying bread—
ANGELA: —diaper cream or something.

MICHELLE: Everyone's in your business. "Oh, twins? Oh, who's the mom?"

ANGELA: We both are. "Oh, yeah, how did that work?"

They both shake their heads and Angela lifts her hands up like 'Oh well.'

MICHELLE: Or, like, "Do twins run in the family?" and the whole loaded sort of question about fertility, and you just wanna say yes.

ANGELA: They do now! [Gesturing toward the toddlers running across the room]

The way this plays out in social interactions is often shaped in particular ways by race. Angela, who is Chicana, describes common social interactions in which she is read through hackneyed racialized narratives:

ANGELA: We went to the farmer's market and this woman said, "Can you weigh this for me?" *To me.* And I, I . . . For a second I thought she was just trying to be nice. I didn't get it. And then I did, and I got really mad. And I was like, "You know, I don't work here." And she went, "Oh," and she was somewhat embarrassed.

This woman assumes that Angela works at the produce stand where she is shopping because she is Mexican American. In this example Angela is illegible behind this woman's deployment of images of women of Mexican origin as agricultural workers. In other situations, her identity *as a mother* is not legible. She and Michelle chose a Mexican American sperm donor so the kids would look like both of them. Their twins, however, inherited Michelle's blonde hair and fair skin and are often perceived as white. Angela continues her discussion of race and legibility:

ANGELA: You know, it's just things like that. And then being with, especially my son. I was somewhere with him, and I was holding him. . . . And just how people look at him and then look at me and then look at him, trying to figure out if am I the n[anny]—I think there's questions when I'm walking with my kids whether I'm their mom.

These experiences rang true for us, as well as for other interracial couples we interviewed. Contemporary ideas about family have been expanded to include multiple forms, yet exchanges like these demonstrate how deeply entrenched social beliefs about legitimate families continue to be reproduced in everyday social interactions.

Liberal Deployment of Race: "Truly Pro-American"

The No on 8 campaign deployed an argument that legalizing same-sex marriage would represent the achievement of the "American Dream" of equality for all people. In a letter to the editor published in the *San Jose Mercury News*, David J. Patterson of Mill Valley writes: "I AM voting no on Prop. 8 because I believe in equality for all Californians. Californians can be proud of our state's leadership to legalize interracial marriage, 19 years before Loving v. Virginia, with the California Supreme Court's 1948 holding in Perez v. Sharp" (2008). Those against Proposition 8 grounded their arguments in analogies with the civil rights movement. In a letter to the editor in the *Chico Enterprise-Record*, Jim Radke of Chico explicitly makes the connection: "Proposition 8 supporters say the 'rule of the people' was overruled by the California Supreme Court when they legalized gay marriage. If popular opinion dictated constitutional rights and equality then we would still have 'whites only' drinking fountains, interracial marriage would be unlawful, Rosa Parks would have died at the back of the bus and women would not be casting a vote to elect a president. If Proposition 8 were about denying Hispanics or African-Americans or women a civil right, people would be up in arms" (November 1, 2008). Radke argued that voting no on Proposition 8 would preserve "the freedom we know as America." As he articulates, the rallying cry of "marriage equality" is grounded in sociopolitical allegories about what it means to be "truly pro-American." The logic of this widely embraced analogy is sameness: discrimination, it asserts, is discrimination, whether based on race, gender, or sexuality. In practice, articulations of this analogy often ignore queers of color, avoid systemic analyses of racial inequality, and reaffirm representations of gays and lesbians as white and middle-class.[5]

The No on Prop 8 movement's framing of the legalization of same-sex marriage as the fulfillment of the promise of US equality depended on the ideology of colorblindness to deploy covert narratives that relied on racial meanings. At the same time, this ideology denied the existence of racial discrimination. Voters of color were identified early on in the campaign as a possible problem for the No on 8 campaign. Strategists feared that a large percentage of people of color would turn out to vote for Barack Obama as president, who would also vote yes on Proposition 8. Tony Castro of Ontario, California, reported in the *Inland Valley Daily Bulletin*: "Call it an election year twist of fate: Even as Barack Obama's historic candidacy is expected to draw a record number of Latinos and blacks to the polls, those same voters could help pass the statewide measures that oppose gay marriage" (October 30, 2008). In fact, the Yes on Prop 8 campaign attempted to build on this by aligning themselves with predominantly Black and Latinx churches. As *New York Times* reporter Jesse McKinley writes: "The Obama/Proposition 8 situation appeals to those opposed to same-sex marriage, who are banking on a high turnout by blacks and conservative Latinos. 'There's no question African-American and Latino voters are among our strongest supporters,' said Frank Schubert, the co-campaign manager for Yes on 8, the leading group behind the measure. 'And to the extent that they are motivated to get to the polls, whether by this issue or by Barack Obama, it helps us'" (September 21, 2008). The No on 8 campaign also sought to build alliances with communities of color, but critics noted that these efforts were not extensive.

In a commercial that first aired on October 30, 2008, African American and presumably heterosexual actor Samuel L. Jackson's voice lends authority to the analogy. He narrates a succession of black-and-white images of Japanese Americans in internment camps; newspaper clippings about housing discrimination against Armenian Americans; and Mildred and Richard Loving, the plaintiffs in *Loving v. Virginia*: "It wasn't that long ago that discrimination was legal in California. Japanese Americans were confined in internment camps. Armenians couldn't buy a house in the central valley. Latinos and African Americans were told who they could and could not marry. It was a sorry time in our history. Today the sponsors of Proposition 8 want to eliminate fundamental rights. We have an obligation to pass along to our children a more tolerant, more decent society. Vote no on Prop 8. It's unfair and it's wrong."[6]

The push for equality is not only about equal treatment for same-sex couples; defeating Proposition 8 is posited as necessary "to pass along to our children a more tolerant, more decent society." As Jackson's voice moves us beyond that "sorry time in our history," to the threat Proposition 8 represents to "fundamental rights," we see contemporary images of same-sex parents with their children. *All of them are white*. As communications scholar Michelle Kelsey Kearl astutely notes, "This logic underscores a view of racism as only or primarily historical, and places white families as the rightful inheritors of the benefits of the CRM" (2015, 70). By framing the movement for legalizing same-sex marriage as the natural evolution of "American equality" from the civil rights movement, a narrative emerges that constructs people of color and queer folks as separate categories. Queerness is defined as white, and racism is framed as a social problem that was solved by the movement. Sociologist Jane Ward explains: "By comparing gay rights with the civil rights movement and appealing to white politicians by demonstrating that 'we are just like you,' LGBT movement leaders have indirectly constructed people of color and lesbians and gay men as mutually exclusive groups. Such strategies have built upon an imaginary 'shared whiteness' to appeal for equal rights, helping to reinforce the enduring notion that being queer is 'a white thing'" (2008a, 33). The terms of the narrative make no room for people that challenge representations of LGBTQ folks as white.

Mothers of color we interviewed in multiple locations articulated their struggle in finding a sense of belonging in predominantly white LGBTQ settings. Like many of the white mothers we interviewed, women of color talked about attending LGBTQ events in order to foster a similar sense of belonging with other families headed by same-sex parents. This was not always a comfortable process. In the summer of 2008 we attended Family Week in Provincetown, Massachusetts, where we conducted participant-observation and interviews. The political turmoil of the debate over Proposition 8 in California dominated discussions among families there in both structured and casual settings. The Family Equality Council organized workshops for attendees, as well as events for kids, parents, and families. I participated in a roundtable discussion focused on raising children in the context of political narratives demonizing queer families. Lisbeth was the director of the Rainbow Families Initiative, a new project of the Family Equality Council designed to increase participation of families of color in the organization. She introduced the project and talked about her queer multiracial family. I told our story about the YMCA. Corinne, a queer mom of South Asian descent, talked about socializing children in a homophobic environment, as the daughter of a clergyman. After the roundtable, attendees were asked to join smaller discussion groups.

In one group, mothers of color discussed feeling like outsiders among the predominantly white attendees. Sharon, who is African American, asked another Black queer mother:

SHARON: [We know] how it feels to be a family of color at Family Week, and its so predominantly white and . . . I mean, do you feel like you're finding a space?

REGINA: All the time.

SHARON: Yeah?

REGINA: Last year was our first time here. And we walked around, and I was kidding, and I started calling us the anomaly. I said, "We are the anomaly." It's just sort of a—as long as you're comfortable in your own skin, you know, you can go with the flow. But you know, we said, as we keep coming and we keep bringing our son, and I said, in that particular space we're just going to be who we are, you know. And people do take a double-take, you notice, just walking down the street.

SHARON: Okay, 'cause we're traveling with our dear white friends and, you know, their white baby. And they are feeling such amazing acceptance. And it's so interesting to us to feel kinda like, whoa, we're a little resistant, a little . . .

REGINA: Well, we look at people's hesitation to come over to us, but . . .

This question sparked a lively discussion among the predominantly Black women in this breakout group. All of them emphasized the stressors of participating in a week-long series of events that purported to be for all LGBTQ families, but felt very white-centric. The Family Equality Council was aware that their organization was predominantly white, and they were making efforts to address race. Melanie and I were asked to be on the advisory board of their Rainbow Families Project. These tensions were not isolated to the political debates in California; they were part of national issues that were articulated through the Proposition 8 debate.

The emphasis on sameness in the civil rights language in the No on 8 campaign essentially precludes attention to a queer politics of color. The logic of sameness in this analogy suggests that all inequality is identical and thus collapses significant differences between African American movements for civil rights and gay and lesbian activism. Kearl's important intersectional analysis argues that this "reductive understanding of race perpetuates the racism it strives to historicize" (2015, 78). Framing racism as an issue of the past denies the continued effects of systemic racism that shape the daily lives of people of color. Emphasizing sameness obscures attention to the ways that queer families of color continue to be vulnerable to structural racism and inequality. Together, these ideas converge into a framework that ignores the ways that gender, sexuality, class location, and disability shape the lived experience of citizenship for people of color. Focusing on the civil rights movement also reinforces a narrative of race that frames tensions through a polarized construction of whites versus African Americans, ignoring Latinx, Native Americans, and Asian Americans. The logic of the neoliberal agenda depends upon the demarcation between race, gender, and sexuality.

Race-Gender Blaming

I began this chapter with Kim's election night story about the Yes on 8 voter that objected to her presence outside the polling center. When the disgruntled woman returned with her hastily made sign opposing same-sex marriage, Kim called Cypress, who was at home with Alex just a few blocks away.

> KIM: I said [with a mischievous smile], "Come on over. I'd like to see you right now. Bring Alex."

Kim had a sparkle in her eyes as she told this story. She had every intention of disrupting this woman's conservative perspectives with a resistant performance of family. Kim knows she and her family challenge mainstream views of "gay families." Even in their current circle of friends in

214 IRRECONCILIABLE DIFFERENCES

the Los Angeles area, they are the only queer Asian American mothers. They have lesbian and gay friends that are also parents, but none of them are Asian American. They have queer Asian Pacific Islander friends, but none of them are parents. To what extent did race shape this exchange between Kim and the white Yes on 8 voter? Her clash with this woman was not only about a difference of beliefs; Kim wanted to challenge this woman's perceptions.

> CYPRESS: And it was funny because she [the Yes on 8 activist] approached me—
> KIM: As they were walking toward me she was, like, trying to get to people before we would say, "Oh, vote no on 8." And she was talking to Cypress, like, "Vote yes on 8." And Cypress was like, "What?!" And then I walked by—
> CYPRESS: And then Kim introduced me!
> KIM: I'm like, "This is my wife. This is my daughter." And [she said], like, "I'll pray for her."

As she approached voters walking into the polls in this middle-class, racially mixed neighborhood, this woman likely assumed that Cypress was a heterosexual mother with her child. When Kim introduced Cypress and Alex as her wife and daughter the woman was shocked. Their family quite likely violated her expectations about same-sex couples, and race as well. Additionally, the woman's declaration that she would pray for their daughter makes clear her investment in sociopolitical narratives about the dangers to children posed by gays and lesbians. In this context, Kim, Cypress, and Alex performed their family as legitimate and deserving of the right to legal protections of marriage.

That night, November 4, 2008, was indeed momentous. The country elected Barack Obama, its first African American president. Liberals celebrated the victory as a milestone for racial progress in the United States. Yet, for the LGBTQ population, there was also reason for deep disappointment. Despite the efforts of Kim and other activists, Proposition 8 did pass, reinstating the statewide ban on same-sex marriage first instituted in 2000. Legislation restricting the rights of gays and lesbians to marry was passed in Arizona and Florida, and a ban on unmarried people adopting children was passed in Arkansas.

African American—and, to a lesser extent, Latinx—voters were initially blamed for the success of Proposition 8. On the morning following the election, Dan Savage, a white, gay, Seattle-based writer and activist for the legalization of same-sex marriage, set an inflammatory tone for the post-election night discussion: "African American voters in California voted overwhelmingly for Prop 8, writing anti-gay discrimination into California's constitution and banning same-sex marriage in that state. *Seventy percent* of African American voters *approved Prop 8*, according to exit polls, compared to 53% of Latino voters, 49% of white voters, 49% of Asian voters [emphasis original]" (2008). Savage's excoriation of the Black community as homophobic was based on what was later revealed to be faulty analysis of data gathered by the National Election Poll. But the damage was done. This early interpretation set the tone for a problematic discussion that blamed people of color for the passage of Proposition 8. Savage continues: "I'm not sure what to do with this. I'm thrilled that we've just elected our first African-American president. I wept last night. I wept reading the papers this morning. But I can't help but feeling hurt that the love and support aren't mutual."

Savage's logic here is grounded in the civil rights movement analogy that dominated the No on 8 campaign. He displays his liberal credentials with a story about weeping over the election of the first African American President; in the postracial narrative evoked here, Savage understands the election of Barack Obama as evidence that racism is a thing of the past. He is "hurt," however, that African Americans did not share "love and support" for gays and lesbians by defeating Proposition 8. Within the logic of the analogy, white LGBTQ folk imagine that the invocation of equality and rights for all would ally the No on 8 campaign with communities of color. "I do know this, though," Savage says. "I'm done pretending that the handful of racist gay white men out there—and they're out there, and I think they're **scum**—are a bigger problem for African Americans, gay and straight, than the huge numbers of homophobic African Americans are for gay Americans, whatever their color" (2008).[7] Savage's language focuses on men; he contrasts "the handful of racist gay white men" with "the huge numbers of homophobic African Americans." In so doing, he makes lesbians of all races invisible. Liberal reliance on civil rights analogies laid the groundwork for the blaming of Black and Latinx communities for the passage of Proposition 8 and for the virtual erasure of women of color. This belief only works when paired with the myth that racial inequality was eradicated by the movement, and when African American straight men are unproblematically represented as symbols of American freedom and equality.

Blaming people of color for the passage of Proposition 8 served to deflect attention from two other more significant factors shaping the outcome: religion and parenthood. Once polling data was examined in more depth, researchers found that, in fact, religion was the most salient feature of Yes on Prop 8 voters. The National Gay and Lesbian Task Force Policy Institute, with funding from the Evelyn and Walter Hass Jr. Fund in San Francisco, commissioned a study of the voting patterns that led to passage of Proposition 8. The study's authors, political scientists Patrick Egan and Kenneth Sherrill, make clear that the narrative blaming African American and Latinx voters was inaccurate and misleading. They explain: "Controlling for frequency of religious attendance helps explain why African Americans supported Proposition 8 at higher levels than the population as a whole. Among Californians who attend worship at least weekly, support for Proposition 8 was nearly uniform across all racial and ethnic groups. Among those who attend worship less than weekly, majorities of every racial and ethnic group voted 'no' on Proposition 8. The differences that remain among groups are not statistically significant at the 95% level of confidence" (2009, 11). The initial story that African Americans were the reason Proposition 8 passed was incorrect and inflammatory. It echoed a convenient narrative of racialized blame that paralleled culture-of-poverty explanations, explaining poverty through the individual behavior of unmarried mothers of color. The intersection of religion and race made evident that the decisive factors in the Black vote in favor of Proposition 8 were Christian beliefs that homosexuality is sinful and wrong.

Parenthood was another significant factor in the election outcome. The narrative that same-sex marriage presents a threat to the socialization of children into productive citizens was apparently successful. The *Los Angeles Times* suggested that a significant shift in voting patterns at the end of the campaign was explained by the success of this story: "The numbers are staggering. In the last six weeks, when both sides saturated the airwaves with television ads, more than 687,000 voters changed their minds and decided to oppose same-sex marriage. More than 500,000 of those, the data suggest, were parents with children under 18 living at home. Because the proposition passed by 600,000 votes, this shift alone more than handed victory to proponents" (Fleischer 2010). The shift in votes, it turns out, was greatest among parents with children under eighteen years of age living at home, many of whom were likely white Democrats. These two factors in the election outcome—religion and parenthood—suggest that the conservative narrative linking same-sex marriage with a threat to children was effective at swaying a range of voters. Indeed, both liberal and conservative perspectives laid the narrative groundwork supporting the absence of attention to queer mothers of color in public debates. This erasure facilitated that gap being filled with sociopolitical allegories blaming the deviant reproductive practices of unmarried women for social problems resulting from systemic inequality.

Blaming the Black and Latinx communities for the passage of Proposition 8 allies effortlessly with sociopolitical allegories that blame unmarried women of color for the social problems associated with poverty and urban blight. While conservative narratives construct "illegitimate" mothers as sinful, deviant, and not "real," liberals focus on "equality" and "diversity." Yet, as I have discussed, the liberal narrative about equality also functions as a means of excluding queer mothers of color through the denial of differences. Gender, race, and reproduction are key to understanding how each side's exclusion of queer moms of color functions as an opening for sociopolitical narratives about social problems being caused by irresponsible parenting by women of color. These narratives for and against same-sex marriage converge to justify and support the neoliberal economic agenda of privatization of care. This racial bait-and-switch was accomplished by the deployment of narratives about children and family legitimacy as stand-ins for social concerns about race. The emphasis on children and family facilitates a policy discussion focused largely on race, gender, and class without ever stating that explicitly.

Funding sources for the campaign testify to the national stakes in this state ballot measure. Geographer Michael Shin explains that 30 percent of the unprecedented $83 million raised by the Yes and No on Prop 8 campaigns came from out-of-state donors. There were patterns in the distribution of donations: Utah was the source of a large percentage of the funds donated to help the proposition pass, while the northeast was the source of most out-of-state donations against the state constitutional amendment. While a few large donations to the No on Prop 8 campaign came from outside of California, the majority of funding in favor of the issue came from out of state: "Of the top 30 contributors opposed to Proposition 8, these (the Human Rights Campaign and two out-of-state businessmen) were the only three out-of-state donors. Of the top 30 contributors in support of Proposition 8, more than one-third were from out-of-state. Furthermore, the top three donors to the 'Yes on 8' committee originated from outside of California" (Shin 2009, 6). Geography was not the only salient factor. 40 percent of donations—within and outside California—in favor of Proposition 8 came from members of the Mormon Church. As Shin points out, most voters do not seek out financial disclosure information; therefore, much of this information remained hidden until after the election. The importance of the outcome of Proposition 8 for people and organizations outside of California is evident in the funding sources for this political campaign. The funding patterns lend credence to a view of this political battle as a sociopolitical allegory about the future of the nation, while these state politics speak to larger national issues emphasizing tensions between religion, sexuality, race, gender, and class.

Conclusion

The public erasure of lesbians of color in debates about the passage of Proposition 8 maintains the illusion that legal marriage for same-sex couples provides access to full equality as citizens. What is the social function of narratives ignoring queer moms of color? This erasure bolsters the sociopolitical narrative that the civil rights movement eliminated racial inequality in the United States, supporting the ongoing national narrative of progress. I read this political moment as a set of allegories about social tensions over liberal narratives about race and equality versus conservative Christian stories about deviant sexuality and family legitimacy. Each of these narratives both depends on and reproduces the illusion of governmental neutrality through denials of race and gender inequalities. Putting the family-making narratives of queer mothers at the center of this racial project fundamentally challenges American myths about governmental neutrality and equality for all. This political moment speaks to social tensions over meanings of race, gender, and equality, the power of conservative Christian interpretations of family and legitimacy, and visions for the future of the nation.

In the next chapter, I further my analysis of local politics through a focus on Iowa. I narrate the 2009 legalization of same-sex marriage in Iowa, drawing in particular on the voices of queer mothers of color to consider the state legalization of same-sex marriage from an insider-outsider perspective.

SAME-SEX MARRIAGE, IOWA, 2005–2009

December 2005   Lambda Legal files *Varnum v. Brien*

August 2007   Iowa District Court rules in favor of same-sex marriage; a stay is issued immediately, halting marriages

December 2008   Iowa Supreme Court hears oral arguments in *Varnum v. Brien*

April 2009   Iowa Supreme Court overturns ban on same-sex marriage

April 2009   Vermont legislature legalizes same-sex marriage

June 2009   New Hampshire legalizes same-sex marriages

November 2009   Maine voters repeal state's law allowing same-sex marriage

Adapted from https://gaymarriage.procon.org

8

Queer in the "Heartland"

Allegories of Family, Race, and Equality, 2009

At the public celebration rally in downtown Des Moines the night the Iowa Supreme Court ruling that legalized same-sex marriage was announced, one of the speakers, Nancy, a white lesbian mom, told the story of a conversation she'd overheard that morning while walking in the downtown skyway system. Nancy and her partner were active members of the LGBT community and had completed the first second-parent adoption in Iowa, many years before.

> NANCY: After our wonderful decision this morning, of course, I had to go to work. But I got on the skywalk behind this—of course on cloud nine. I got behind this woman who was talking to her friend and she said—[clears throat and looks down at notes]. She remarked to her friend, she says, "Now our sons will come home and say, 'Billy has two moms or two dads.' And what am I going to say?" And you know what I realized? That even though it was a wonderful morning this was just the beginning. We have a lot of educating to do that we—[pause] that we aren't, you know, terrible people. That we're just like anybody else.

In Nancy's anecdote, the overheard mother worries about the implications of the same-sex marriage ruling for her children. How will she answer their questions about homosexuality? What effect will this new recognition of the legitimacy of LGBTQ couples have on the way she raises them? Nancy's last line is striking and, perhaps, somewhat unexpected. She echoes the mainstream logic governing "difference"—first, that it is "terrible," and second, that the resolution to the social tension it creates is to emphasize sameness.

Each of the parents in this story was profoundly shaped by political rhetoric citing homosexuality as a threat to children's moral development, but in distinct ways. The mother overheard in the skyway articulates fears echoing conservative rhetoric regarding the dangers of homosexuality corrupting innocent children. Public recognition of families with two moms and two dads is a challenge to parents who have never acknowledged to their children the existence of LGBTQ people ("And what am I going to say?"). In the version of the world one can imagine she conveys to her child, queer folks are illegitimate and thus not socially legible. In all likelihood, by 2009, even in Iowa, her children were already going to school with mythical "Billy." Her real objection is likely the social and political legitimation of what conservatives often call the gay "lifestyle": prior to the legalization of same-sex marriage, parents could easily cordon LGBTQ folks off as deviant and not worthy of comment, but the new law would, in some senses, force them to socially recognize the legitimacy of families headed by same-sex parents.

Nancy knows which "terrible people" are seen as a social threat, and she draws upon widely available liberal narratives about difference to counter this belief ("We're just like anybody else"). "Anybody" doesn't really mean *anybody*, or *any body*. It means, primarily, straight white middle-class mothers. Nancy is white, too. She is middle-class. She is a productive citizen on her way to work. She is a mother of two sons that she, too, would like to protect from negative influences. "(W)e're just like anybody else" is, in fact, the foundation of the argument in favor of legalizing same-sex marriage.

In this chapter I explore the ways sociopolitical narratives of sameness have paired with calls for marriage equality. This emphasis on sameness depends upon a denial of the social salience of race, gender, and class. These stories, paired with narratives about innocent white mothers and vulnerable children, facilitate the symbolic redemption (i.e., inclusion) of white queer moms in the sociopolitical allegory of the national family. Transracial adoption was both practically and symbolically important in these public discussions. I argue that the story of same-sex marriage legalization in Iowa can be usefully read as an allegory of how sociopolitical narratives about white motherhood figured crucially in the rationale arguing for the legalization of same-sex marriage in the United States. In so doing, Iowa's legalization narrative highlights the importance of the American "heartland," and the "traditional" values historically associated with it, to this allegory, and to the achievement of the American promise of full equality for all. Whereas California (which I discussed in the last chapter) is represented as the leading edge of change, Iowa is typically seen as stable, slow to change, and "traditional"—the epitome of middle America.

Each side in the "for or against" tussle of Iowa politics claims the high ground as the bearers of the legacy of the civil rights movement, and, thus, of American equality. Race is overtly present in public discussions of freedom, equality, and citizenship that narrate racial discrimination as part of the past, yet it is also covertly present in the connections between public law and social equality in the United States. Indeed, as my discussion of public responses to the legalization of same-sex marriage in Iowa shows, both objections to and celebrations of the decision were grounded in a narrative of American freedom and race.

Varnum v. Brien: The Case

The status of same-sex marriage in Iowa was a popular topic in our interviews. Some people had a hard time believing legalization could happen in Iowa. Others were hopeful and followed news and policy debates voraciously. Rae, an African American single mother of two living in Des Moines, was among the latter group. She was excited to talk about the details of the case with us; she had worked for Lambda Legal prior to our interview and was deeply engaged in the Iowa same-sex marriage battle. She began the story with a chuckle:

> RAE: Oddly enough, when Jasmine and I were together, Lambda came and interviewed us. [Melanie and I start laughing] They interviewed you too? [She laughs]
> SANDI: [We nod] We had just had the kids and we didn't remember to sign the papers and send them back!
> RAE: Yeah, that was right around the time we had Jack too. That's so funny.

In 2004 Lambda Legal conducted interviews with prospective plaintiffs in the lawsuit. Our lawyer in the YMCA case was one of the most active organizers of the marriage movement in Iowa, and she urged us to participate. For various reasons—we were too busy parenting infant twins to think about it, and Rae and Jasmine broke up—neither couple partici-pated; I am not sure at what point which disengaged from the process. Had either one of us pursued it, I do not know if we would have been chosen as plaintiffs. I do think it is striking that we are both interra-cial couples, and the six couples that ultimately participated were white. Reproductive justice scholar Melissa Murray writes:

> As some scholars have acknowledged, those selected to front marriage equality lawsuits are carefully selected in an effort to emphasize certain traits and downplay others. By and large, the plaintiffs in these lawsuits are in "long term, committed, marriage-like relationships in which they are raising children." The selection of these "model" plaintiffs is at once an effort to normalize the claim for same-sex marriage—to underscore that same-sex couples are just like the opposite-sex couples permitted to legalize their relationships as marriage—and an attempt to amplify the injustice of their exclusion from civil marriage. (2012b, 422–23)

As Murray notes, sameness was an explicit strategy. If it could be dem-onstrated that these couples were "just like" opposite-sex couples, discrimination would be clear. Six white lesbian and gay couples, organized and screened by Lambda Legal, entered the Polk County Recorder's Office in 2005 in Des Moines, the state capital. When they were denied marriage licenses, Lambda Legal filed suit against county clerk Timothy Brien.

The petition for declaratory judgment, introduced by Lambda Legal on behalf of twelve lesbian and gay Iowans and three of their children, was distinctive for the inclusion of children as plaintiffs in a same-sex marriage case. *Varnum v. Brien* argued that prohibiting same-sex mar-riage violated the plaintiffs' rights to equal protection under the law, emphasizing that "without access to this unique and extraordinarily sig-nificant legal and social institution" same-sex couples were effectively rendered "second-class citizens" (2007). This was not a new legal strat-egy. The arguments for equal protection and due process for gay and lesbian adults had been made in lawsuits challenging marriage laws in other states, but the introduction of children as petitioners was unique. This inclusion was the next step in the reliance on children's issues that began in the Vermont and Massachusetts cases. *Varnum* stated: "Because their parents cannot marry, Minor Plaintiffs are subjected to the historical stigma of 'illegitimacy' or 'bastardy' which, though of diminished social and legal force, is still a status widely considered undesirable. Minor Plaintiffs also experience the effects of stigma directed at them and their parents because of how their parents are treated unequally by the government as a result of their parents' sexual orientation. The Minor Plaintiffs would benefit from having even the threat of such stigma removed from their lives" (*Varnum v. Brien* Motion for Summary Judgment, 2006, 7). The citizenship rights of children depend upon the rights accorded their parents, a recognition that, in my view, should serve as an important bridge to the experiences of other children whose parents do not fit the heteronormative marriage mandate. This makes the inequality of regulating rights through marriage apparent by emphasizing the tenuous nature of citizenship when it depends upon unstable relationships between families of different kinds and the state.

As I have discussed, the illegitimacy-as-injury argument implicitly relies on sociopolitical narratives about unfit single mothers to make the case that not being allowed to marry puts the children of same-sex couples in the same injurious category as children of people that "choose" not to marry. These racially inscribed stories about illegitimacy and bad choices causing poverty and social chaos function as valuable currency in policy discussions, where such narratives are framed as a counterpoint to liberal arguments celebrating heteronormative families.

This narrative of illegitimacy fundamentally denigrates the lives of children born and raised outside of patriarchal nuclear families. Several important beliefs undergird it—first, that marriage is the best family form for raising children, and that people who can get married but choose not to are deviant; second, that adequate income is a prerequisite for becoming a parent; and, third, that families of color are fragile or broken, leading to children's instability and inadequate socialization. None of these explanations accounts for structural inequality based on race and gender. In contrast to these images of mothers of color, "[white] lesbians with capital are positioned as the idealized inhabitants of an increasingly acceptable and assimilated same-sex version of the heteronormative nuclear family, one in which 'financial protection' is inextricably bound together with political citizenship and (a racialized) social belonging as the prerequisites for queer family and kinship" (Eng 2010,

101). Whiteness and middle-class stability override the deviance of homosexuality in the case of white lesbians. A long history of representations of white mothers as contrasted with mothers of color provides the qualifications for inclusion in the national imaginary of family legitimacy. The structure of the illegitimacy as harm argument is essentially identical to that of sociopolitical allegories about adoption: as stories about the colorblind imperative to privatize care for dependents. This neoliberal approach to family, rights, and race magnifies inequality for families outside marriage, by determining "fitness" through marriage and membership in the middle class. When we look at the illegitimacy-as-harm argument in this context, its investment in the reproduction of middle-class whiteness is clear.

"Dykes of the Roundtable" and "One White Iowa"

By 2009 Melanie and I had conducted interviews with lesbian mothers in Iowa, Minnesota, Michigan, California, New Mexico, and Massachusetts. We had conducted several in Des Moines, but most of our Iowa interviews had been conducted on a 2006 research trip to Iowa City (a two-and-a-half-hour drive from Des Moines). We were particularly interested in interviewing queer mothers of color in Iowa, which had not been easy. Frankly, it was both a research challenge and a social challenge. Though we had at that point lived in Des Moines for seven years, we had yet to meet many queers of color and continued to feel isolated as an interracial queer couple with biracial children. In early March, Sandy Volpalka, founding director of the nonprofit Equality Iowa, invited us to a pizza dinner at the Hotel Fort Des Moines with queer Black activist Mandy Carter, whom the organization had brought from North Carolina for a series of events. When we arrived in the John Edwards Suite, we were pleased to meet Mandy—a warm, engaging, and motivating activist—as well as a handful of interracial lesbian couples.[1]

The evening was like none other we had ever experienced. In this group of lesbians committed to antiracist community work, excitement grew as we sat around a large round table making jokes about how many presidential campaign plans had been hatched here, and speculating optimistically about the forthcoming Iowa Supreme Court decision. The group discussed the shared issue of queer-of-color "invisibility" in Iowa.

Mandy Carter's visit was part of the launch of a new LGBTQ community center, sponsored and run by Equality Iowa; that evening we all committed to working with it, and jokingly named ourselves the "Dykes of the Roundtable." Thus began my in-depth participant observation with a growing number of other queers working to establish an organization that served the needs of the most underserved in the Des Moines LGBTQ community. As I will discuss, the perspectives and experiences of the women in this group articulated an oppositional narrative to the two most dominant stories about same-sex marriage in Iowa.

When marriage was legalized in Iowa a few months later, these were the people with whom we celebrated, and with whom we discussed the public representation of queer Iowans. While all of the women— including me and Melanie—were thrilled with the Court's decision, we were simultaneously critical of the heteronormative white middle-class ideal the law reproduced. These women, mostly mothers, were, as one would expect, very critical of the conservative narrative about families headed by lesbians and gays. However, it was not only the conservative discourse that seemed to ignore the very existence of lesbians of color.

One Iowa is a nonprofit organization that was founded as a pro–same-sex marriage organization in 2006, following the filing of the *Varnum v. Brien* lawsuit. Its mission, it says, "for full equality includes educating Iowans about why marriage matters to gay and lesbian couples, ensuring that communities are safe for LGBTQ youth, reaching out to communities of faith, addressing concerns about Iowa's aging and elder LGBT populations and improving access to resources for transgender Iowans." Like similar organizations around the country, One Iowa's framework for social equality focuses on marriage equality as the means through which the LGBTQ community can achieve their full civil rights. As I have discussed, US liberal public narratives have largely emphasized the right to marry, rather than the right of citizens to a range of family protections reserved for married heterosexual couples. Though the most pervasive public dialogues are framed through the question of whether or not same-sex couples should be allowed to marry, this debate doesn't fully represent the range of concerns in queer communities. Indeed, it does not fully represent the range of life experiences in "LGBT populations" in Iowa, either. One Iowa specifically highlights "couples, youth, communities of faith, elderly people, and transgender Iowans."

At first glance, this may seem inclusive, but the mission statement of another nonprofit, Equality Iowa, reveals a stark contrast. Equality Iowa was created to fill a perceived gap in public recognition of the range of diversity within Iowa's LGBTQ communities. Its mission statement focuses on the "most underserved of Iowa's queer population," including—like One Iowa—youth, aging and elderly people, and trans* people. Unlike One Iowa, however, their mission also focused on queer communities of color, people experiencing poverty, and people with disabilities. The women involved in Equality Iowa critiqued One Iowa on the basis of its self-presentation as narratively colorblind when it was substantively white. In 2009, when same-sex marriage was legalized, the entire board of directors and office staff of the organization was white. While the organization seemed determined to represent "One" all-encompassing community of queers in Iowa, to the lesbians of color who were not substantively or representationally included, it looked more like what some called "One White Iowa." This was not unique to the state, but part of a national pattern in organizations working for "marriage equality." Jane Ward explains: "By some accounts it has been this pervasive focus on diversity that represents the hypocrisy of lesbian and gay politics, given the sharp contrast between queer diversity rhetoric and the predominantly white and middle-class leadership of the movement" (2008a, 5). Such critiques of the liberal LGBT marriage movement as racially exclusionary and normative amplify those raised by African American, Latinx, Asian American, and Indigenous queers. Queer of color theorist Roderick Ferguson's analysis contextualizes this set of local stories in twenty-first-century politics of race, gender, and sexuality: "The appeal to gender and sexual normativity by gays and lesbians in this moment, inevitably, operates as a mode of state identification that promotes racial exclusion. Gay rights has become a site of racial exclusion and privilege defined by the rights to marriage, hate crime protection, and military inclusion" (2005, 61). His analysis registers the links between colorblindness and the regulation of various social differences.

The Decision: "The *Heartland* Proves Again to Be Fitting of Its Name"

On the morning of April 3, 2009, One Iowa and Lambda Legal held a press conference at the Hotel Fort Des Moines to announce the Iowa Supreme Court decision legalizing same-sex marriage. One Iowa's executive director Carolyn Jennison welcomed the audience: "I want to begin by saying how great it is to be an Iowan. The *heartland* proves again to be fitting of its name." Part of the impact of the decision and the public response to it is bound up in the representation of Iowa as the heartland of America: if it could happen here, surely it could happen anywhere. As Lambda Legal lawyer Camilla Taylor explained: "This is a beautiful, powerful decision. It will be read everywhere. It will have great impact even outside the state of Iowa. It will have a transformative effect on the nation."

The day the decision was announced, news outlets and social media reacted with pride, disdain, and *surprise*. Facebook statuses and blog sites abounded with observations tantamount to, "Same-sex marriage is legal in Iowa, the sun has risen, and the sky hasn't fallen." Such pronouncements were, in part, responses to the catastrophizing conservative rhetoric against same-sex marriage that predicted the demise of traditional marriage and the end of social order in the United States. The legalization of same-sex marriage in Iowa extended a handful of rights and protections previously denied same-sex couples and their families at the state level, although these marriages were not recognized as legitimate by the federal government until 2015. While civilization did not collapse, neither, I argue, did the structure of inequality.

Immediately following the press conference, Dawn BarbouRoske, one of the plaintiffs in the *Varnum v. Brien* case, explained to us, along with a small group of reporters:

> DAWN: It's great to know that the justices looking at the laws, looking at our constitution, came up with the same point of view—that we were being discriminated against; that we are a loving caring family. We've been together for eighteen and a half years. We've got two beautiful, intelligent and strong girls. And you know, the fact that they all could see that—it shows respect for our family and all of Iowa families, and we're just elated.

Her emphasis on the justices seeing and respecting her family and other queer families in Iowa suggests the importance of the social and cultural recognition that accompanies legal recognition. Her family felt legible as a family and legitimate as citizens.

I began this chapter with the words of Nancy, one of the dozen or so speakers at the celebration rally that night organized by One Iowa. Other speakers were from One Iowa leadership, as well as a local politician and people who represented other (non–LGBT-focused) social justice organizations in Iowa. Only one speaker was of color: Rudy Simms, director of the Des Moines Human Rights Commission, who is a heterosexually married African American man. No women of color stood on the stage.

The parade of speakers praised the decision, challenging representations of Iowans as conservative corn and pig farmers in a flyover state. Jokes about Iowa being more progressive than California and New York (two coastal states where same-sex marriage was not legal at the time) seemed to suggest that a significant corner had been turned—legally, symbolically, and practically—regarding equality for gay and lesbian couples. The crowd cheered, clad in mixtures of rainbows and American flags, carrying signs declaring the end of second-class citizenship. People were smiling and hugging. The air was charged with possibilities for change. It felt like a brand-new day as Iowa became the first state in the Midwest to legalize same-sex marriage.

In his celebratory comments at the rally, Brad Clark, campaign director for One Iowa, located the decision to overturn the state ban on same-sex marriage in the context of Iowa's history of civil rights rulings:

Iowa has *always* been a leader in civil rights. In 1839 the Iowa Supreme Court rejected slavery in a decision that found that a slave named Ralph became *free* when he stepped on Iowa soil, twenty-six years before the end of the civil rights [sic]—before the end of the Civil War decided the issue. In 1868 the Iowa Supreme Court ruled that racially segregated separate-but-equal schools had no place in Iowa, eighty-five years before the US Supreme Court reached this decision. In 1869 the first female lawyer in any state was admitted to the bar in Iowa. In the case of recognizing loving relationships between two adults, the Iowa Supreme Court is once again taking a leadership position on civil rights. Today we congratulate the thousands of Iowans who now can express their love for each other and have it recognized by our laws.

This speech narrates a genealogical allegory about equality in Iowa and in the United States. Clark counters the surprise expressed that day in national media about the "progressiveness" of the court's decision with a story about how Iowa has always been a beacon of equality. In 1839 "a slave named Ralph became free when he stepped on Iowa soil." Children of different races have been legally attending school together there since 1868. The first female lawyer in the United States was admitted to the bar in Iowa in 1869. This history figures the legalization of same-sex marriage as the capstone of civil rights in Iowa. Freedom is envisioned through African American male emancipation; liberty is personified in the education and employment of white women; equality is narrated as children of different races learning and playing together.

Same-sex marriage is represented in public dialogues on both liberal and conservative sides as a white issue, yet race serves a crucial function in each version of the narrative. This progress-of-the-nation story rests on our willing suspension of disbelief that racial inequality was eliminated by the civil rights movement, but so does the decline-of-the-family-and-nation story. Like the liberal version of history shared at the Des Moines celebration rally, the conservative version posits a United States in which racial inequality has been overcome. Political scientists Weaver and Lerman explain this common narrative maneuver: "In this telling, the nation's antidemocratic periods are historical pitfalls overcome in the forward march toward democratic inclusion. Political struggles for equality—to end slavery, enfranchise blacks, extend the vote to women, and secure civil rights—progressively built on one another over time to bring the country's practice of democracy into line with its promise" (2014, 5). Both stories celebrate the end of racism and inequality due to the civil rights movement of the 1950s and 1960s. This progression toward the American Dream of freedom and equality for all was embraced and celebrated by marriage equality activists.

Race, Equality, and Choice: "For There *Is No Parallel!*"

In the days and weeks following the decision, the public debate escalated. The anti- side pushed for any and all legislative measures they could imagine to challenge the State Supreme Court ruling. The pro- side blocked the legal volleys and rhetorical grenades lobbed by conservatives. The week of the announcement brought organized protests on both sides of the State Capitol, each organization holding their own community political event and largely ignoring each other. While the One Iowa leadership visited a meeting of Congress, the Iowa Family Policy Center (IFPC), a conservative Christian organization, held a protest rally on the Capitol steps. The air was frigid, yet the sun bounced brightly off the Capitol's shiny copper dome against a clear blue sky. Chuck Hurley, director of IFPC, introduced the featured speaker, Reverend Keith Ratliff. As Hurley, who is a tall, thin, white man, introduced Ratliff, a shorter, roundish African American preacher, he playfully joked about what he had learned from the reverend about dressing appropriately for the occasion. He unbuttoned his winter coat to reveal a red three-piece suit—his appropriation of Black preacher garb. Ratliff joined him at the podium and embraced him, white and Black patriarchs legitimating each other for his constituency.

Reverend Ratliff of Des Moines's Maple Street Missionary Baptist Church, then-president of the Iowa-Nebraska chapter of the NAACP, was one of the most vocal opponents of the decision.[2] He delivered a fiery speech in the style of Southern Baptist sermons to a small, predominantly white crowd at a rally in front of the Iowa Statehouse: "We the people of Iowa want the opportunity to vote on this issue. For there are those in the gay community who say their movement is parallel to the African American civil rights struggle here in America. And speaking as one individual who is the grandson and son of the Civil Rights struggle, for the gay movement, in my individual humble opinion is *pimping* [beat], iiiis *using* [beat], iiiiiis *prostituting* [long beat] the African American struggle for their *own* purposes. [Crowd cheers] For there *is no parallel!*" Here, he effectively calls the "gay community" pimps and whores. In the lexicon of the Missionary Baptist cultural meaning system, the most egregious sins are tied to deviant sexuality. Through his choice of words, Reverend Ratliff has drawn an ideological box for his audience.

He also locates himself as the legitimate heir of Black patriarchy and masculinity through this genealogy of freedom and citizenship, which follows a long tradition of equating Black equality with African American *male* equality.[3] His moral authority is further bolstered by the central involvement of Black preachers in the civil rights movement. Black patriarchal church authority is constructed here as the moral arbiter of legitimate and moral marriage, as well as what behaviors should be legally protected. The reverend continues: "For in Christian love there is no parallel, in my humble opinion, to your movement and the African American struggle in this country. [Applause] It is an insult when you attempt to make such a comparison." The perceived insult to the African American civil rights struggle is grounded on static, immutable views of race, gender, and sexuality. In this view gays are white, Blacks are straight, and deviance is *chosen*.

Ratliff defines oppression through the experiences of African Americans, narratively foreclosing challenges to his perspective with both his preacherly fire and his rhetorical maneuvering:

> For the gay community, for the gay community, you have not gone through physical slavery. You haven't been sold as cattle [*sic*], or as property. You weren't considered at one time three-fifths of a person. You didn't go through Jim Crow. You didn't have and you don't have separate water fountains, separate bathrooms, separate schools or have to ride on the back of the bus. When was it illegal to teach gays to read and write? I haven't seen any signs that say straights to enter the front of the building and gays to enter the back of the building. I haven't seen segregated lunch counters based on straights and gays. You haven't been denied the right to vote. And I could go on and on.

It is difficult to challenge this kind of comparative logic. Within this framework "there is no parallel" not only because discrimination against gays looks different than the blatant oppression of Jim Crow racism, but also because, in his view, gays and lesbians have chosen a deviant lifestyle. His views of both oppression and equality parallel the legal concerns about equal protection at the center of the same-sex marriage debate.

Equal protection is granted to protected classes of citizens, and, historically, these legal decisions have depended on the concept of immutability. It is in this context that questions of what "causes" a person to "be gay" arise. This legal principle was a central point of contention in the *Varnum v. Brien* decision: the question at issue was whether or not the doctrine of equal protection applied to same-sex couples in Iowa. As the Iowa Supreme Court explains, "A human trait that defines a group is 'immutable' when the trait exists 'solely by the accident of birth,' or when the person with the trait has no ability to change it" (*Varnum v. Brien* 2009, 42). This is an important consideration for the Court because the question of whether or not a person can "change a characteristic that is used to justify different treatment" determines whether or not a person is protected under the Fourteenth Amendment. In this view people of color and women should not be discriminated against because they were born Black or female. The issue is what makes a person gay, and whether or not that aspect of identity is changeable. Within this legal framework, if a gay identity or lifestyle is chosen (i.e., cultural), then it is not protected. If it is inherent (i.e., biological), then such persons are members of a legally protected class. Immutability is to choice as nature is to nurture.

In a significant shift, the justices on the Iowa Supreme Court reframe the concept. They avert the nature-nurture controversy by redefining immutability from biologically grounded to "so central to a person's identity that it would be abhorrent for government to penalize a person for refusing to change [it]" (*Varnum v. Brien* 2009, 44). This is profoundly important. Moving beyond the nature versus nurture question in determining equal protection claims opens the door for white women to symbolically redeem LGBT families as normal. As Ferguson explains, "Liberal forms of whiteness use innocence, redemption, and cultural sensitivity as ideological covers" (2014, 1105).

The rallying cry among conservatives for saving innocent children from the evils of aberrant sexuality encompasses both the immoral behavior of homosexuals and unwed mothers. While the courts have decreed that children cannot be punished for the sins of their parents, conservatives have continually protested what they perceive as sexual and moral perversion, and the resulting breakdown of the family. Reverend Ratliff continues: "For my grandfather and father marched in the civil rights movement because of what our country was doing to the American Negro. For my grandfather and father were not marching so that two men and two women could sleep together in the same bed and call themselves husbands and wives." In this worldview, in which homosexuality is defined as deviance from the static moral/sexual/patriarchal law, deviating from the heterosexual norm takes one out of the equal protection loop; only "innocent" victims of oppression deserve recognition and protection from the state.

The Salvation of Magical Beings: Motherhood and Racial Innocence

While conservatives were up in arms over the Iowa court decision, liberals engaged in "colorblind" celebrations of equality in the heartland. One Iowa, who organized the activities in Des Moines, launched a campaign that included press releases, celebratory and public information videos, and public events. Equality Iowa participated in many of these and, in the months to come, would organize their own events, designed to fill the gaps we perceived in One Iowa's campaign concerning race, disability, poverty, and trans* identity.

The promotional material released by One Iowa celebrated family in the heartland through rainbowed images of same-sex weddings, cornfields, and smiling faces of parents and children. Women of color were distinctly absent. One Black gay man who lives in Des Moines was the solitary adult of color. The video he appears in included footage of the press conference and celebration rally, with shots of people holding celebratory signs. In my many viewings of this video, I was only able to identify one other nonwhite man, who appeared briefly, who may have been of Asian descent; all of the other adult faces were white. The Black lesbians involved in Equality Iowa were critical of the "heartland" video's lack of racial representation, and they framed this man's inclusion through the trope of the "magical Negro."[4] His image—with virtually no representation of Black women, or Indigenous, Asian, or Latinx adults of any gender—mirrors the conservative narrative recuperation of Black masculinity as a symbol for American equality represented by Reverend Ratliff.

It might be tempting to believe that lesbians of color were not represented because they do not exist in Des Moines, Iowa (like unicorns or witches, depending on whose version is being narrated). In Iowa, whiteness is pervasive and overwhelming. While not a large population, lesbians of color do exist and are visible if you know how to see them. Visibility is context-dependent, and the differences in how our family—a Black mom, a white mom with red hair, and biracial red-headed twins—is seen and treated in different locations and time frames, and by different people, has been instructive for us. We became more socially legible in Iowa after the *Varnum* decision.

Another set of "magical beings" represented in the One Iowa video were children of color adopted by white same-sex couples. These children can be considered in light of what Spike Lee has referred to as the "super-duper magical Negro" trope or what we might call "magical minorities," whose inclusion in this context serves as proxy for colorblind equality (Gonzalez 2001). Representations of children of color with white parents function narratively as signifiers of the resolution of social difference and inequality within the intimacy of family. Legitimate white motherhood is at the center of this classic tale. Mothers are perceived as the keepers of children's innocence, and, as historian Robin Bernstein reminds us, "This innocence was raced white" (Bernstein 2011, 3–4). Representations of white motherhood, rooted in nineteenth-century Victorian views of the ideal mother as the "angel in the house" who gently socializes children into productive future citizens, have been a fixture in these political debates. As such, the ideal white mother is almost always shadowed by the racialized trope of the illegitimate mother of color—the imagined threat to innocence.

The influence of these stories is evident in the ways that transracial families are seen and treated. Kimberly shares a social encounter that is typical for their family. Intrusive questions about racial identity, adoption status, gender identity, and even age, flag "difference" and convey messages about belonging and outsiderness.

KIMBERLY: *"What are they?"*
SANDI: They always phrase it that way!
KIMBERLY: [Giggling] I said, "They're kids!" Then I had another experience at the—because you know when you have a child of a different race you know, you're automatically pegged as different immediately. You don't pass the way you do, when like Mischa is off with Sheridan

from Russia, nobody thought Sheridan was anything but Mischa's child. You're such a magnet for questions when you have a child of a different race.

Racial difference outs adoption by challenging the "as if" construction of adoptive families purporting to mimic nature. This interaction highlights the ways that the comments of strangers can function as a way of policing family legitimacy.

If families are defined through sameness, then families embodying difference must be marked in order to resolve the tension. Mischa and Kimberly continue:

MISCHA: And any kind of question somebody wants to ask.
KIMBERLY: One time when Theo [who was adopted from Cambodia] was quite young, maybe eighteen months old, this woman rushed up to me and actually kind of put her arms around Theo and said, "*Oh, the poor thing! Is his mother dead?!*" I was completely . . . [laughter all around]

Such social interrogations enforce normative definitions of motherhood and family. Yet, more important, this interaction highlights the ways that identities and families are defined relationally. When she is with her partner, Mischa (who presents as butch), and their children, Kimberly and Mischa are often seen as "lesbian moms" and not always made to feel welcome. In this instance, Kim is made legible as a mother through this woman's deployment of the racialized narrative of white women saving brown orphans. "Oh, the poor thing! Is his mother dead?!" reflects sociopolitical assumptions that children adopted transnationally are orphans in need of salvation. An "orphan" is, for purposes of transnational adoption to the United States, defined more bureaucratically than literally, and the child's innocence is symbolically saved through the whitewashing of his adopted identity.

White mothers, too, are redeemed as legitimate in this narrative. As I argue throughout this book, sociopolitical narratives about mothers and children have been key to covert discussions about race in neoliberal policy debates. Feminist scholar Leifa Mayers explains:

238 | QUEER IN THE "HEARTLAND"

While conditions of precarity are overshadowed, discourses of the child's racialized vulnerability enable the constitution of the adoptive couple as the rescuers of "needy" children. Recent same-sex marriage debates have featured descriptions of lesbian and gay couples as most willing to adopt children with "special needs," including children of color and children living in poverty. Their deservingness is evidenced by the choice to rescue racially or physically "vulnerable" children from their communities and bring them into the stability of a two-parent family. Symbolic assimilation of queer parents and their adopted children, in turn, marks the nation's continued progress. (2016, 63)

In this familiar tale, the mythical white mother is venerated as the savior of the baby, yet the baby has also redeemed the mother. In the same-sex marriage debate, it was the story of vulnerable children needing to be saved by middle-class mothers that tipped the scales in arguments for legalization. The child is saved, the mother is redeemed, and the nation continues its progress toward the promise of equality for all.

Motherhood has been a rich repository for political debates about social problems throughout US history. As historian Monica Perales explains: "Motherhood is more than a private, intimate relationship; it is an important site wherein the very meanings of nation and citizenship are defined. Familial and gender relations served as models against and through which the United States imagined itself as a nation, thereby placing women and families at the center of nation building, class formation, and determining the boundaries of civic inclusion" (2012, 147). Transracial adoption narratives serve as the bridge over which white lesbian mothers are symbolically included in legitimate family and citizenship. In saving children, they are narratively redeemed from the sin of sexual deviance. As Bernstein makes clear, "Innocence was not a literal state of being unraced but was, rather, the performance of not-noticing, a performed claim of slipping beyond social categories" (2001, 6), which accomplishes the narrative work of justifying race-evasive family policies as race-neutral. This discussion of colorblindness articulates the experiences of many transracial adoptees: they are hypervisible, and the idea that race doesn't matter is engaged to mediate the racial tensions this incites. As Eng reminds us, "The emergence of queer liberalism depends upon the active management, repression, and subsuming of race" (2010, 17). This is evident in the shared language used to talk about transracial adoption and same-sex marriage. These representations of white legitimate families are deeply enmeshed in the justification of family laws and policies organizing family rights and protections through legal marriage.

Images of transracially adoptive families suggest a rainbow-hued narrative of the nation's future. This story of transracial adoptees as symbols of a colorblind future is not isolated to Iowa, nor to the marriage equality movement, but is part of a long tradition of US racial narratives of what I have referred to in other places as a gendered version of the "white man's burden" to civilize the "non-white other" (Patton 2000; Patton-Imani 2012). The glorification of white motherhood was infused with a settler-colonial mission to nurture, educate, and save the future of the nation. The narrative function of multiracial children as a signifier of a future, integrated world cannot be fully understood without attending to the politics of poverty, race, and gender that lead to circumstances under which birth mothers are unable or not allowed to keep and parent their children. Again, there are no women of color in this transracial story; their presence would make audible the unspoken way class and white privilege shapes adoptive family construction (whether queer or not), and challenge the myth that adopted children are orphans in need of salvation. One Iowa's video covertly narrates this erasure of mothers of color and salvation of brown babies by white women. As Mayers makes clear, "Same-sex couples are among those whose freedom has been written through the rescue of vulnerable children" (2016, 75).

License Day: Rights, Recognition, and Legitimacy

April 27, 2009, was the first day county recorder's offices in Iowa could legally issue marriage licenses to same-sex couples. The long hallway leading to the office of vital records was packed with a line of same-sex couples waiting for the official state document that would declare their unions legitimate. I spent the day there with my video camera and a stack of release forms, conducting short interviews with people about why they were there and what it meant to them, and I worked with members of Equality Iowa giving out flowers to all the couples obtaining marriage licenses. The State of Iowa requires a three-day wait between issuing a marriage license and allowing a marriage to be performed. Some couples there had already been granted judicial waivers of the waiting period, or had them granted that day. Several couples brought a clergy member to perform the ceremony on-site, while others had plans for weddings within the week. Some wore t-shirts; others wore tuxes. Couples were giddy with a newfound sense of social legitimacy.

"It's all about rights. It's about civil rights, *not* special rights," said a white, middle-aged woman named Marsha, who was wearing a baseball cap and a black t-shirt that said "GOT JESUS?" She was standing in line for a marriage license with her partner, Jody, who was wearing a royal-blue blouse and matching earrings. In her answer to my question of why she and her partner were there, she was very clear that the meaning of marriage for them was not only about affirming their commitment and gaining the state's rights it would provide them; it was also about social recognition of full civil rights for gays and lesbians. Her emphasis on "civil" rights rather than "special" rights is a direct response to conservative political rhetoric defining the demands of LGBTQ activists as special rights for minority groups and using that formulation to argue against legal remedies for systemic discrimination. James Dobson, founding director of Fundamentalist Christian organization Focus on the Family, articulates the boundaries of the conservative definition of "family" in *The Complete Marriage and Family Home Reference Guide*: "[The homosexual] agenda includes teaching pro-homosexual [*sic*] concepts in the public schools, redefining the family to represent 'any circle of people who love each other,' approval of homosexual adoption, *legitimizing* same-sex marriage, and *securing special rights* for those who identify themselves as gay [emphasis added]" (2000). In this view, families and individuals must conform to a strict definition of legitimacy in order to be eligible for the rights and protections of citizenship. Within this logistical framework, nonconforming individuals are, by definition, asking for special rights.

That day at the county recorder's office, couples not only talked about love and rights; children were discussed frequently as well. Shari and Eugenia, an interracial couple that live in Des Moines, were getting married at the end of the week. Eugenia explained, "This means everything to me. It is validation for us and for the world. I want [Shari] protected, to see her in the hospital if she's sick." She went on, emphasizing "the legalities, so many we haven't been afforded until now," and discussed the reaction of her fifteen-year-old daughter.

> EUGENIA: She hasn't seen me this happy in my life. This is validation for her that we are a family and she can count on that. She needs to know who will be in her life. Her dad hasn't been around much, and she always wanted more stability. And she appreciates us and what we are about. She is a huge part of it for me.

The stability of her child's life was an important factor in Eugenia's excitement about finally being able to marry her partner. Shelley and Melissa were the very first couple married that day in Polk County. They were granted a judicial waiver of the three-day waiting period on the grounds of the protection of their unborn child.

> MELISSA: Basically, we just said it would relieve stress for me, given that we're getting ready to roll into the third trimester, if we could be married. And three days doesn't seem like a long time, but honestly, it would really be an unpleasant experience if I suddenly went into labor in the next three days, which is highly unlikely. But [the judge] felt . . . that was just cause. So after she said we qualified for the waiver I started crying.

Their minister, also a lesbian, met them at the Polk County Recorder's Office and married them outside. Other couples there that day talked about how important it is to them that their children would grow up with married parents.

A Busload of Queers Getting Married

The advent of legal marriage in Iowa was exciting, and the joy at the public recognition of same-sex relationships was socially palpable. Like many of the people we talked with, our family felt "seen" in a way we had never been before in Iowa. The first week of legal same-sex marriage, I drove to Iowa City to videotape the collective weddings of a busload of same-sex couples from Kansas and Missouri. I conducted short interviews with most of the female couples and several of the male couples.

FIGURE 8.1. Shante and Stephanie, getting married, Iowa City, Iowa. Photo credit: Sandra Patton-Imani.

Jolie and Shanda, a white couple from Kansas City, Missouri, shared with me a romantic story of having been friends in childhood, losing touch, and falling in love when they met as adults.

> JOLIE: I think that the most important thing is that *we* recognize our relationship, and that—before Iowa's decision even came down we had made a decision to have a ceremony for our family and friends this fall, so I think it will be all the more meaningful to have a certificate to take with us to that ceremony.

While the symbolism of marriage and the excitement of social change made most people there feel giddy, Jolie, speaking also in her role as a state-level politician, reminded me of the limitations of focusing on marriage as the primary path to equality. In the following exchange, my excitement over marriage shaped my question in a particular way:

> JOLIE: I am a state senator for Kansas City.
> SANDI: So what are you doing to make marriage legal in Kans—I'm sorry—in Missouri?

JOLIE: What we are doing in Missouri right now is fighting for basic equality. We are fighting for nondiscrimination law that includes LGBT people, that provides we cannot be denied housing or fired just because we're gay. We are fighting for a safe schools act. We are fighting for domestic partner benefits and protection of those benefits. So, those are the battles we're fighting right now.

Caught up in the excitement of the day, in my question I fell into the marriage equality framework. Without hesitation, Jolie put me back on track, reminding me that state-level access to marriage for same-sex couples does not provide basic equal protection under the law. Like anyone else, I have internalized certain social meanings of love and marriage, and, in this instance, I experienced a sense of affirmation that overrode my intellectual understanding of the importance of exploring same-sex marriage laws in relation to other laws shaping the quality of life for LGBTQ people and families.

A. J., an African American mother of six living in St. Louis, Missouri, discussed the symbolic aspect of this legal recognition:

A.J.: For me it's more of a symbolic gesture, because I know once I leave Iowa and go back to Missouri it's as if it never happened. However, I didn't choose my mate for Missouri and I didn't get married for Missouri. So what Missouri thinks of my relationship really doesn't matter to me.

Her perspective on state differences was shaped by the fact that she had recently moved to Missouri from North Carolina, where she worked against the campaign for a state amendment defining marriage as between one woman and one man. "After that," she said, "Missouri is no problem." Like many of the couples I interviewed, she also discussed the importance of obtaining whatever legal recognition is available, so that when laws do change, their relationships will have been legally documented in some locale.

Christine explained why she and her partner Chris traveled hours north on a chartered bus full of same-sex couples to get married in Iowa, even though the marriage will not be recognized by their home state of Missouri:

> CHRISTINE: Today we are getting married in IOWA [slowly]. We are actually renewing our vows today. We were married in St. Louis three years ago, so today we are renewing our vows and adding a piece of paper to our collection. [Big smile]
> SANDI: So what does this mean to you?
> CHRISTINE: It means that America is finally trying to hold her head up and not down in shame, and being a country that is once again leading in human rights. And it's a support to our new president who is going to overturn the *Defense of Marriage Act*!

She and her wife, Chris, African American mothers living in St. Louis, Missouri, explained that they would be legally prepared when US laws recognize same-sex marriage. Yet it was also important to them in light of what the United States stands for—equality and human rights. Chris completes the circle by emphasizing how important this change is for the future their children will inhabit.

> CHRIS: It means change and hope. Um, I really look forward to what this nation can and I believe will become. Hopefully, when our children look back on this time they will really be baffled as to why they had such laws in place that didn't allow us to be legally married in all states.

In the debate around and response to the legalization of same-sex marriage, much of the rhetoric interwove the symbolism of love, marriage, and children with sociopolitical narratives celebrating American equality.

Conclusion

The legalization of same-sex marriage in Iowa was framed through competing narratives about the meanings of family and nation. Both conservative and liberal versions of these stories depend on the representation of queers as white. The perspectives of African American queer mothers in Iowa make evident the covert role of race and gender in the regulation of family legitimacy and recognition in contemporary US dialogues concerning same-sex marriage. Their stories are important for understanding the lived experiences of mothers who have been excluded from both popular and academic considerations of lesbians and their families. Yet perhaps a more important aspect of this intersectional recentering concerns the ways their stories make evident the larger, systemic role of race and reproduction in the legal and symbolic regulation of equality and American citizenship.

SAME-SEX MARRIAGE, 2009–2015

April 2009   Vermont legislature legalizes same-sex marriage

May 2009   Maine governor signs bill legalizing same-sex marriage

June 2009   New Hampshire legalizes same-sex marriages

November 2009   Maine voters repeal state's law allowing same-sex marriage

July 2010   Argentina becomes first country in Latin America to legalize same-sex marriage

June 2011   New York legalizes same-sex marriage

February 2012   US Ninth Circuit Court of Appeals rules California Proposition 8 unconstitutional

February 2012   State of Washington legalizes same-sex marriage

March 2012   Maryland legalizes same-sex marriage

May 2013   Rhode Island becomes tenth US state to legalize same-sex marriage

May 2013   Delaware becomes eleventh US State to legalize same-sex marriage

May 2013   Minnesota becomes twelfth US State to legalize same-sex marriage

June 2013   US Supreme Court finds key part of the Defense of Marriage Act (DOMA) unconstitutional

September 2013   New Jersey becomes fourteenth state to legalize same-sex marriage

November 2013   Hawaii legalizes same-sex marriage

November 2013   Illinois legalizes same-sex marriage

December 2013   New Mexico legalizes same-sex marriage

December 2013   Utah's same-sex marriage ban ruled unconstitutional by federal judge

January 2014   Nigeria bans same-sex marriage

May 2014   Oregon becomes eighteenth state to legalize same-sex marriage

May 2014   Pennsylvania becomes nineteenth state to legalize same-sex marriage

October 2014   US Supreme Court clears way for same-sex marriage in five states

November 2014   Kansas becomes thirty-third state to legalize same-sex marriage

November 2014   South Carolina becomes thirty-fifth state to legalize same-sex marriage

May 2015   Ireland becomes first country to legalize same-sex marriage by popular vote

June 2015   US Supreme Court makes same-sex marriage legal in all 50 US states

Adapted from https://gaymarriage.procon.org

Conclusion

Grafted Trees and Other Allegories, 2015–

In this book I argue that the legalization of same-sex marriage both expanded marriage rights and benefits to same-sex couples, and further entrenched patriarchal structures of inequality. *Obergefell v. Hodges* (2015) enacts legal and social changes that affect LGBTQ family lives, both practically and symbolically. Yet we must also be clear that, contrary to celebratory media narratives, legalizing same-sex marriage does not signal full equality for queer folks. The structures of patriarchal white supremacy and capitalist inequality remain intact in the United States. The same-sex marriage debate and the trajectory of progress from prohibition to inclusion that *Obergefell v. Hodges* purportedly represents fits neatly into the traditional patriarchal framework for legitimate family trees. Nothing about the structure and integrity of patriarchy is challenged by the inclusion of same-sex couples. What counts as "legitimate" constitutes a narrow slice of family experiences in the United States, and this ideal has been used strategically throughout history to justify discrimination against people and families outside that norm. At the same time, this "traditional" family is represented as if it were grounded in biology and genetics. The representation of family trees as natural obscures attention to power relations. Beneath the discourse highlighting biology and genetics is a concern with legitimacy.

The legal changes regulating same-sex marriage and adoption that occurred in the United States at local, state, and federal levels between 1991 and 2015 were momentous and, without a doubt, changed the lived experience of family and citizenship for same-sex couples and their children. In this book I have sought to understand how these legal changes came about and what they mean. The most basic answer to these questions is: it depends whom you ask. As I have demonstrated, the lived experience of family-making and citizenship in this era varied depending on interactions between and among geographic location, race, gender, sexuality, and socioeconomic status. The reproductive stratification of mothers in different social locations in this era did not disappear when same-sex marriage was federally legalized in 2015.

The genealogy of illegitimacy I have presented in this book makes evident the complex power relations shaping reproduction and kinship in the United States. No single law or area of policy regulates the lived experience of family-making. The stratified reproduction experienced by the mothers we interviewed was constructed and regulated by the intersection of laws regulating marriage, adoption, fertility, domestic partnerships, civil unions, housing, employment, education, public accommodation, and immigration. Considering the ways that same-sex marriage laws interact with other public policies makes clear that a single law including same-sex couples in the social institution of marriage could never ensure equality for all LGBTQ folks.

As I have suggested, the structure of traditional family trees can be read as allegories about legitimate kinship. Traditional family trees are envisioned as solitary, patriarchal structures, legitimating all in their branches. In contrast, grafted trees are intersectional, celebrating and nurturing connections between redwoods, bamboo, oaks, madrone. This story emphasizes care, affiliation, and culture alongside biology, genetics, and law in understanding kinship. The cultivation required to graft a new shoot on to an old tree suggests the importance of context, whether soil and sun or law and society. The understory matters. Perhaps most important for this discussion, stories about grafted trees make power relations visible, allowing us to see whose stories are excised from legitimate history, and how that sleight-of-hand is accomplished.

Historian Saidya Hartman speaks about the process of making meaning of scattered and partial stories: "If you listen closely, you can hear the whole world in a bent note, a throwaway lyric, a singular thread of the collective utterance" (2019, 345). Throughout this book I have sought to listen closely and to find the world in each narrative I have heard about queer family-making at the turn of the twenty-first century. Some "notes" are the voices of the people that shared their family-making stories with us. Others are labeled "news" and broadcast widely. Still more lyrics about family-making are deeply embedded in debates between legislators in the US congressional record and the resulting laws. Each thread of discourse is partial, relational, and shaped by power. A central tenet of allegory—like that of ethnography—is that stories are always grounded in specific historical and cultural moments. The goal of an allegory is not "objective representation," but, rather, critical interrogation of connections between the specificity of any life story, the larger narratives available for making sense of families and lives, and the power relations shaping the contours of our experiences in ways we are often oblivious to. While the legalization of same-sex marriage and adoption has provided avenues toward equality for some couples, structural and economic barriers have meant that others—especially queer women of color with fewer financial resources—are not, in practice, able to avail themselves of the supports necessary to create and sustain their families. The family-making stories of the Indigenous, African American, Latina, Asian American, and white queer mothers we interviewed demonstrate that, in fact, using legal marriage as a strategy for equality and full citizenship for queer folks deepens and magnifies social inequalities for the most vulnerable families—queer and otherwise.

In this conclusion I focus on three principles outlined in *Obergefell v. Hodges*, to discuss how this research contributes to an understanding of the way same-sex marriage was legalized and what it may mean for different families. I explore three allegories—each a story exploring contested meanings of the legalization of same-sex marriage in the United States. In the first section I take up the Court's principle that marriage is important because it safeguards children and families, and I consider adoption allegorically in order to critically explore how sociopolitical narratives about innocent children served to both argue for the rights of same-sex couples to create legitimate families and to further reinforce the marginalization of unmarried women of color of all sexualities. The second allegory explores the emphasis on same-sex marriage as the "keystone of the nation's social order" (*Obergefell v. Hodges* 2015, 4). I discuss the ways that *Obergefell v. Hodges* entrenches marriage in the US Constitution as the ideal family form and how this affects queer families in different social locations. The third and final allegory explores the limitations of the choice to marry as a measure of LGBTQ equality. I consider same-sex marriage as compulsory in light of the nullification of civil unions and domestic partnership laws.

Grafting Family Trees: Adoption as Allegory

> KELLY: My biggest concern is—and it's been a concern for me all
> along—is how he's going to be treated and how much more difficult
> his life may be as a result. And with conservative backlash that's
> happening right now, that makes it even scarier, how he's gonna be
> treated. I want him to have equal treatment. And I think it won't
> start—the first time I think it will be a problem will be kindergarten.
> In kindergarten they do a *family tree* and he has to be *out* just like we
> have to be *out*.

Kelly's worries about how her child will be treated in school when he
draws a family tree with two moms and no dad echo those of many of
the mothers we interviewed. The driving question here is how to protect
their child from the stigma of having same-sex parents in a society that
celebrates heteronormative, biologically constituted families as normal
and natural. Her concerns speak to the questions raised in the children's books *Heather Has Two Mommies* (1989, 1990) and *Molly's Family*
(2004). One of the questions pulsing beneath the surface of this public
debate is how to make sense of family relationships that are not codified as legitimate by "blood" or law. This concern is at the core of the
illegitimacy-as-harm argument that was so important to the success of
the "marriage equality" movement. Marriage legitimizes familial relationships, facilitates national belonging, and thus "safeguards children
and families" (SCOTUS 2015, 4).

In *Obergefell*, the Court builds on the illegitimacy as injury argument
developed in Vermont, Massachusetts, and Iowa cases, emphasizing
the humiliation and harm that accompanies illegitimacy: "Without the
recognition, stability, and predictability marriage offers, their children
suffer the stigma of knowing their families are somehow lesser. They
also suffer the significant material costs of being raised by unmarried
parents, relegated through no fault of their own to a more difficult and
uncertain family life. The marriage laws at issue here thus harm and hu-
miliate the children of same-sex couples" (2015, 15). It is no wonder that
these children experience humiliation, given the language used to talk
about them and their mothers in policy and news media. The decision
makes clear that children whose parents cannot marry—as opposed to

those who can but choose not to—unjustly suffer the harms of stigma, humiliation, and "more difficult and uncertain family life." For which children is such suffering justified? Which families does the Supreme Court see as "lesser"?

Feminist scholar Leifa Mayers explains that people arguing for the legalization of same-sex marriage "advocate on behalf of two sets of vulnerable children—those who are currently experiencing stigmatization and psychological harm derived from 'illegitimate' status and who would benefit from increased 'stability' if their parents were allowed to marry, and those who have been or will be rescued by same-sex couples—in asserting the superiority of two parents" (2016, 76). The logic of this argument depends on views of unfit illegitimate mothers whose bad choices and culture of poverty have supposedly endangered their children. The racialization of illegitimacy is central to this narrative function. Legitimation into a "fit" family—figured as white, two-parent, and middle-class—is represented as salvation from social stigma and racial and economic harm. This is the traditional script of legitimate family trees. Critical legal scholar Melissa Murray argues that

> the denigration of non-normative family forms is especially concerning because it indicates a lost opportunity for building strong coalitions between the LGBT rights movement and those who historically have been marginalized, whether because of gender, race, ethnicity, or sexual orientation. As history attests, racial minorities and sexual minorities have, at one time or another, been denied legal recognition as families. The danger of the marriage equality movement's uncritical embrace of the illegitimacy as injury argument is that it implicitly endorses the marginalization of outlaw families, even as it fights for the right to be in-laws. (2012b, 435)

Let us be clear: this argument for inclusion and protection for families headed by same-sex couples depends upon the exclusion of family structures that do not conform. Rather than challenge the structure of a system that only confers legitimate citizenship on children of married parents, the legalization of same-sex marriage stretches the definition of legitimacy. Abolishing the concept of legitimacy would do far more for a greater number of children in the United States than legalizing same-sex marriage does.

As I have suggested throughout this book, adoption serves as a useful allegory for understanding this era of family change. Tales of the salvation of orphans obscure the power relations organizing the systemic transfer of children and disguise the economic disparities that drive the industry and enforce stratified reproduction at the levels of lived experience and policy and law. How do such narratives as the orphan-rescue myth support neoliberal political agendas? Adoption operates on the mythical split between the economic public realm and the caring family realm, just as neoliberal economic agendas do. Lisa Duggan explains: "The most successful ruse of neoliberal dominance in both global and domestic affairs is the definition of *economic* policy as primarily a matter of neutral, technical expertise. This expertise is then presented as separate from *politics* and *culture*, and not properly subject to specifically political accountability or cultural critique" (2003, xiv). Adoption can be read as allegorical of this mythical bifurcation. Economic inequalities and the coercive race-gender policing that drive the market in babies are hidden by ideological tales of redemption from the horrors of poverty. Stories about babies being destined to become part of new families hide the enormous sums of money required to adopt transnationally. They obfuscate the global reality that being unmarried and living in poverty are the primary factors shaping whether or not mothers are able to care for their children. And they obscure the fact that economic resources and assimilation to the ideal family structure determine who adopts and raises these children (Raleigh 2018).

Each of the various characters in this allegory speak to how they are positioned in relation to the state. Adoptive mothers (typically figured as white) represent a legitimating force in which vulnerable children (often represented as of color) can be socialized into the kind of productive citizens the nation needs to ensure a successful future. Birth mothers, of course, are absent, and this space is often narratively filled with images of unfit women of color whose lack of capacity to properly socialize their children narratively represents conservative fears for the future of the nation. Finally, transracial adoption stories in particular function as a means of hiding racial inequality in plain sight through a celebration of racial harmony. Together, these pervasive narratives—which were crucial in the legalization and symbolic acceptance of same-sex marriage—camouflage the forces of capitalism, patriarchy, and white supremacy.

Literary scholar Cynthia Callahan's research demonstrates that the use of transracial adoption as a literary trope functions as a means of addressing larger social concerns about such issues as "multiracial identity, mixed-race families, social change following the civil rights movement, tribal autonomy, and immigrant identities" (2011, 25). Transracial adoption also functions this way in sociopolitical allegories. Eng asks, "What kind of work is the transnational adoptee performing for the family and the nation?" (2010, 108). This story, as I demonstrate throughout this book, has done a tremendous amount of work on behalf of both liberal *and* conservative sides of this decades-long debate about American families.

The meanings of transracial adoption in the United States have shifted over time, yet it has remained a rich repository for sociopolitical tensions about family, race, gender, and citizenship. Literary scholar Mark C. Jerng's work demonstrates that "transracial adoption appears most prominently in literature, public discourse, and social practices during precisely some of these large-scale national traumas focused on the formation of its citizenry and the question of national and racial belonging: Native American removal; slavery and emancipation; the height of Jim Crow/segregation; and the Korean and Vietnam wars" (2010, xii). These social dialogues articulate more than racial politics; significantly, each of these "large-scale national traumas" is addressed through issues of reproductive stratification as well. The celebration of transracial adoption as a colorblind ideal of family at the turn of the twenty-first century deflects attention from the ways the bodies of mothers and children are regulated through family and reproductive politics.

Transracial adoption functions, as Eng points out, as a "contemporary mode of forgetting race" (2010, 95). Indeed, adult transracial adoptees are critical of the denial of race in the colorblind socialization that many of them experience. Yet the forgetting of race is also quite literal in regards to the absence and denial of information about birth parents, erasures that are cemented through sealed adoption records. Thus, we see how the invisibility of mothers of color in transracial adoption narratives functions allegorically for the erasure of women of color in the same-sex marriage debates. Adoption narratives can also be read as an allegory for complex relationships between families and the government. Adoption is figured as an ideal tool for neoliberal privatization:

responsible married citizens assume full responsibility for children who would otherwise drain public resources through welfare, foster care, homeless shelters, Medicaid, and other governmental supports. As Eng states, "Under the banner of freedom and progress, queer liberalism thus becomes linked to a politics of good citizenship, the conjugal marital couple, and the heteronormative family" (2010, 25). This framework for reproducing heteronormative two-parent families is deeply embedded in the legalization of same-sex marriage. The erasure of mothers of color, the elevation of white mothers, and the representation of transracial adoptees and multiracial children as symbols of equality function together in this discourse to represent the legalization of same-sex marriage as the achievement of equality for LGBT people. In a framework defining family through sameness, transracial adoption is a difference that is symbolically mediated through colorblindness in order to resolve social tensions about race, gender, and class. Callahan argues that transracial adoption "operates as an expansive metaphor through which authors attempt to define the parameters of authentic belonging on the level of family, race, and nation" (2011, 16). In the patriarchal family tree, erasure of difference is required for belonging.

Allegories of grafted trees provide a more expansive vision of belonging than traditional family trees organized through legitimacy. Grafted trees are complex, hybrid, and partial templates for family relationships and structure. The family-making stories of the mothers and children we interviewed ask us to reimagine the ways we think about kinship and belonging. Their family ties are not based solely in heterosexual relationships, biological ties, nor law. These relationships also challenge myths of sexual and racial purity. Grafted trees reproduce outside of what we think of as "normal" propagation. Indeed, the grafting of a tree requires human intervention to facilitate reproduction. Social workers, lawyers, and medical professionals provide that intervention for same-sex parents, operating in compliance with policies and laws regulating adoption and reproductive technologies. Yet this applies to all families, not just those shaped by adoption. The power relations operating in adoption are more obvious, but all families are constructed and regulated through interaction with sociopolitical allegories, public policies, and laws. The traditional family tree template has never represented the only kind of family.

The legalization of same-sex marriage is not a simple tale of progress in the twenty-first century. It isn't that we used to have traditional families and now they are endangered, as conservatives often emphasize. Families have *always* had a broad range of structures, and tensions between social definitions of legitimacy and the experiences of actual families necessitate navigation and negotiation of conflicting and contradictory meanings at multiple levels of society. The grafting of this multiracial assemblage of queer family-making stories asserts a new kind of legibility and pushes us to think about kinship as a means for coalition between everyone defined as illegitimate.

Rainbows and American Flags: "Keystone of the Nation's Social Order"

The June 2015 *Obergefell v. Hodges* Supreme Court decision overturned the Defense of Marriage Act and made same-sex marriage legal in the United States.[1] Celebrations erupted all over the country. The decision was broadly hailed as the achievement of equality LGBT folks had been working for. Legal scholar Kenji Yoshino suggests *Obergefell v. Hodges* "achieved canonical status even as Justice Kennedy read the result from the bench" (2015, 147). Legal scholars agree that it was a momentous decision. Marc Spindelman explains: "The US Supreme Court's announcement in *Obergefell v. Hodges*—that the US Constitution promises marriage equality for same-sex couples—has quickly and broadly swept the nation as a powerful symbol of social progress: of justice, of liberty and equality, of dignity, of freedom, delivered" (2016, 1).

Rainbows and American flags were everywhere. "Love wins!" was the pervasive sentiment in news reports of celebrations in cities all over the country.[2] Disneyland bathed its iconic castle in rainbow lights. Companies including American Airlines, Kellogg's, AT&T, Jello, and Snickers made rainbow versions of their logos in celebration (Bogage 2015). The White House was lit up with rainbow colors, and President Obama called the decision "a victory for America" (Korte 2015). The Court, however, did more than extend marriage rights to same-sex couples. In reverential tones, the decision enshrined marriage in the US Constitution as the most beneficial family structure to individuals, children, and the nation. As Melissa Murray writes,

"From start to finish, the majority opinion in *Obergefell* reads like a love letter to marriage" (2016a, 1212).

This glorification of marriage was linked to the maintenance of social order: "This Court's cases and the Nation's traditions make clear that marriage is a keystone of the Nation's social order" (*Obergefell v. Hodges* 2015, 4). As I have discussed, this view of "social order" was linked to the legitimation of children and families through the promotion of marriage, and it functioned as code for a particular vision of society that supports the status quo. Legitimacy was the backbone of this social vision. Yet this sentiment is remarkably similar to the language used to prohibit same-sex marriage in the 1996 Defense of Marriage Act. That discourse, too, focused on promoting marriage and two-parent families in order to foster social order and stem broad social problems. In 1996 conservative commentator William Bennett's view of traditional marriage and family as "an institution that is the keystone in the arch of civilization" was widely shared by conservatives (Bennett 1996, A19; Judiciary Committee Report 1996, 18).

In the 1990s conservatives held marriage as a sacred institution from which LGBT couples must be barred. In 2015 marriage was so sacrosanct that the US Supreme Court mandated the inclusion of same-sex couples. The Court states: "It is demeaning to lock same-sex couples out of a central institution of the Nation's society, for they too may aspire to the transcendent purposes of marriage. The limitation of marriage to opposite-sex couples may long have seemed natural and just, but its inconsistency with the central meaning of the fundamental right to marry is not manifest" (*Obergefell v. Hodges* 2015, 4). How is it that a law *including* same-sex couples in legal marriage can be justified using the same language that two decades prior was used to *exclude* gays and lesbians from marriage? While a broader range of couples are now included in the institution, the determinants of family legitimacy have not changed. As I have argued, legalization provides new rights to same-sex couples, yet at the same time the ruling cements legal marriage and patriarchal legitimacy as the only basis on which those rights are allocated. Legitimacy remains the spine of state recognition.

Entrenching marriage as the normative family structure in the United States was not the only way same-sex marriage could have been legalized. While same-sex couples now have access to marriage, queers still experience discrimination on other fronts that marriage does not address, including housing and employment. Legal scholar Kristin Haule explains that if the Court had established the basis for same-sex marriage by holding that homosexuals are a protected class, then other inequalities like housing and employment could also have been addressed. This strategy could have protected the rights of gays and lesbians without entrenching patriarchal marriage as the vehicle for accessing rights. She argues, "By determining that discrimination on the basis of sexual orientation runs afoul of the Equal Protection Clause, then any law, which discriminates on that basis, would be subject to strict scrutiny, and more often than not, invalidated" (2016, 5). Such a ruling would have legalized same-sex marriage, but it could also have been used to mitigate other forms of discrimination. Instead, the Court chose a profoundly conservative way of legalizing same-sex marriage that solidified marriage as the path to family legitimacy.

When we consider same-sex marriage in the context of other policy issues, the larger economic and political imperatives driving these changes become evident. As Laura Briggs's astute analysis reminds us: "It couldn't be clearer than that: the purpose of gay marriage is to privatize dependency. A generation earlier, custody was being denied to lesbians and gay men because sodomy laws made them criminals; now, in a stunning reversal, gay folks were being made respectable because having children made them citizens" (2017, 181). Beneath public exclamations that "love wins" there are economic imperatives going in both directions. Governmental privatization removed the social safety net for low-income and middle-class families by dismantling the social welfare system.

The push for same-sex marriage is deeply implicated in the context of dwindling social support for vulnerable families in the 1990s. As I have discussed, the mothers we spoke with had conflicting perspectives on same-sex marriage. Many critiqued it as a patriarchal institution they had no interest in while simultaneously feeling the need for legitimation of family relationships. According to Briggs, "Family ties—of a particularly matrimonial sort—were not only the only way to get health insurance or pensions. But also to visit your dying lover in the hospital, hang on to custody or visitation of your kids, or stay in relation to the people you love in the event of illness or serious disability. After forty years of changes in the workplace and government, the critical necessity of family to support dependency was the new normal, and the push for same-sex marriage revealed exactly how limited our concept of family and household had become" (2017, 17). As Briggs makes clear, the need for family care was a response to structural changes in the economy. These legislative changes were justified through narratives about the dangers of nonnormative families. While some of the families we interviewed were excited to gain a sense of the social legitimation and access to social resources that came with same-sex marriage, for other couples the benefits were more symbolic than practical. The differences in how families experience legalization is shaped by complex intersections of class, gender, race, religion, tribal identity, and ethnicity.

Academic and mainstream discussions of the meaning of same-sex marriage were largely organized through questions of whether or not marriage is assimilative or resistant. The life stories of the mothers I have drawn on demonstrate that these categories are too simple to explain the complexities of navigating family-making in a policy and law context of stratified reproduction. How does the legalization of same-sex marriage shape the family lives of queer mothers? The answer varies, depending on who the families are and where they live. Sociologist Mignon Moore discusses the ways her own her two-moms-and-two-kids African American family has benefited from the legalization of same-sex marriage. Her discussion of bringing her family to the conservative Black Pentecostal church she was raised in challenges the assimilation versus resistance tension that has characterized academic and activist conversations:

> While scholars may theorize our church participation as an attempt to conform to societal standards of heterosexuality, our presence and involvement is in no way experienced by us as an attempt to conform. I am sure the parishioners do not see us as conforming. When I sit in the pew and a visiting minister gives a sermon, I hold my breath waiting to hear something homophobic. I believe the visible participation of our little LGBT-parent family in this storefront Holiness church in Queens, New York, is radical, even revolutionary behavior. Every time we walk through those doors, I am making myself vulnerable while I silently bring my full self to the altar. Those who say this is conformist have not experienced this type of participation in conservative institutions. (2019, 77)

What counts as resistance or assimilation is context-dependent. When Moore's family interacts with other parishioners they push boundaries of legitimacy and belonging. She sees "the marriage-equality movement as a vehicle through which people, particularly people of color, could begin to talk about LGBTQ issues with their family members and individuals in their racial and ethnic and cultural communities" (74). Like other middle-class families, many of the benefits Moore's family experiences are grounded in economic privilege. Her family embodies a different sort of resistance while navigating the predominantly white private school system of New York City. Their economic privilege opens doors that have often been closed to African American families, and they experience a sense of resistance as they interact in these privileged spaces as well. Moore acknowledges that other families experience this legal and social recognition differently, but she explains that the change "offered something important" to her family and others "for the way they wanted to live and be in the world" (74–75).

For Ronnie and Yvonne, who live on the Navajo Reservation in Tsaile, Arizona, life has not changed much since the legalization of same-sex marriage in the United States. The Diné Marriage Act of 2005 remains in effect. They could be legally married in any US city, but that union would not be recognized by Diné Sovereign law, which governs rights, privileges, and protections for families and individuals living on the reservation. Ronnie and Yvonne's relationship is not recognized, nor does Ronnie have parental rights to their son. For Indigenous peoples the contradictions between laws in different jurisdictions have been a persistent issue. On the face of it, legalizing same-sex marriage can function in positive ways for queer families, yet the complexity of the understory of the contradictory laws at international, state, and local levels emphasizes that its protection is only partial. If you look at marriage by itself it makes sense, but when you consider it as enmeshed in other policy and legal contexts the fissures in the veneer of equality become apparent. Yvonne and Ronnie have the choice to be legally married, yet that option means very little on the reservation, where they live and work. For them, this contradiction between laws at different levels of government regulating their family legitimacy has not significantly changed. While this is literally the case regarding same-sex marriage for Ronnie and Yvonne, an allegorical reading points us toward the recognition that what same-sex marriage means for any particular family is fundamentally shaped by their location in the larger context of politics, law, and policy. Being able to legally marry does not address other inequities, such as discrimination in employment, housing, and education.

As I demonstrate throughout this book, contradictory family laws and policies at various levels were a primary factor maintaining stratification among queer mothers of different races, ethnicities, tribal identities, and socioeconomic circumstances between 1991 and 2015. That stratification remains, even after same-sex marriage has become legal at the federal level, and is made evident by stories like Ronnie and Yvonne's. Asian American Studies scholar Glenn Magpantay discusses queer Asian Pacific American views on same-sex marriage: "LGBT APAs cannot spend valuable time and energy to support a right in which they cannot avail the benefits. Other issues are more pressing, namely immigrants' rights, media defamation and visibility, and racial intolerance. The lives of LGBT APAs involve a complex web of issues arising from being sexual, racial/ethnic, language, gender, immigrant, and economic minorities" (2006, 112). Looking at tensions between laws regulating other forms of discrimination—such as housing, employment, health care, education, and immigration for LGBTQ populations—demonstrates the importance of considering how the choices provided by one law (to be legally married) might be circumscribed by laws permitting oppression in other realms.

Compulsory Marriage and the Illusion of Choice

On June 12, 2016, a deadly mass shooting took the lives of forty-nine people on Latin Night at a gay nightclub in Orlando, Florida. It was the forty-ninth anniversary of the US Supreme Court decision in *Loving v. Virginia* that overturned antimiscegenation laws. It was also the day of the annual Pride Festival in Des Moines. People gathering for the parade that Sunday morning looked to each other for confirmation of our survival and resilience. We had all likely woken to the horrific news of the Pulse nightclub shooting. Though it was just midday, the temperature was already in the nineties. The air was heavy with humidity and sorrow. There was a powerful tension between our celebratory rainbow flags, balloons and apparel, and the tenuous hold we seemed to have on our own safety. But we were here, gathering together to affirm our common humanity.

Just before the parade began, three drag queens in resplendent rainbowed attire turned on the mic and asked the crowd, "Who wants a wedding?!" The crowd cheered as our family, friends, and wedding officiant stood in front of the announcers. We (reluctantly) got legally married with our twelve-year-old twins standing next to us, in front of the Pride crowd in Des Moines. This intersection of events speaks strongly to the concerns at the heart of this book.

When same-sex marriage was legalized in Iowa in 2009, Lambda Legal advised couples that had been married in other states to basically "act married." The Iowa decision was not clear on how the state would recognize same-sex marriages and civil unions from other states. Lambda Legal was invested in having the state recognize all unions, wherever performed. We were pleased to hear this. Couples around us were quickly heading to chapels and courthouses, many fearing that the law would be overturned. We didn't feel the need to get married again; we assumed that our civil union would be recognized by the State of Iowa, and, after 2015, by the federal government.

In late spring of 2016, I noticed a deduction from my paycheck that I had never seen before. I looked at previous pay stubs and saw that $337 was being deducted each month through something called "imputed income insurance." I contacted the human relations department at my university and was told this imputed income was a federal tax on my health insurance benefits for my "partner." I explained that we were married and should not be taxed on these benefits. As it turns out, *Obergefell v. Hodges* was explicit about what previous unions would be recognized, and civil unions were not. When Vermont legalized same-sex marriage in 2009, they did not convert previously granted civil unions into marriages, unlike many other states. In the eyes of the US government, we were still not legitimately married. We were told that the only way to stop $337 from being deducted from my paycheck each month was to get legally married. At this point we had been what we considered legally wed for sixteen years. We did not want another wedding, and we were angry that these financial issues compelled us to do it again. We decided that if we had to do it we might as well have a little fun and get married at the upcoming Des Moines Pride Festival.

We planned it in less than a week. We posted the following on Facebook:

We are getting legally married this Sunday at 12:30 at the Pride Parade Stage at 5ᵗʰ and Locust! Friends, please join us in our celebration of love and our protest of compulsory matrimony! We have been married for 16 years (Civil Union in Vermont), but we recently learned that *Obergefell v. Hodges* 2015 does not recognize civil unions as marriage. The financial consequences force us to get married again, for the federal government and all the other neoliberal entities regulating legitimate citizenship.

Thank you to friends Amy Letter and Eugenia Kutsch-Stanton for their help in arranging this! And thanks to our friend Beth Younger for officiating and promising to include a feminist analysis of patriarchal marriage in the ceremony!

Our post was "loved" and "liked" vigorously and sprinkled with comments about who could attend and who could not. One person took issue with our assertion that this was compulsory matrimony.

> MARLA: This is not compulsory. Civil unions were never meant to be civil marriage. They were designed to prevent us as a people from civil marriage equality and to enforce our second-class status. If it is to your advantage to have a civil marriage, great—exercise your choice to do so. I will celebrate that we as a people now have that choice. Besides, a ceremonial party celebrating your love sounds fabulous!

This writer echoes the *Obergefell* decision embracing choice as liberty: "The first premise of this Court's relevant precedents is that the right to personal choice regarding marriage is inherent in the concept of individual autonomy. This abiding connection between marriage and liberty is why *Loving* invalidated interracial marriage bans under the Due Process Clause" (SCOTUS 2015, 3). Equating choice with equality only makes sense when removed from socioeconomic and political context. We were effectively coerced into getting married by the financial penalties for not doing so.

The day we were married also happened to be the forty-ninth anniversary of the US Supreme Court decision in *Loving v. Virginia* (1967) that legalized interracial marriage. We had not realized it until our officiant mentioned it in her comments. As an interracial couple with bi-

FIGURE C.1. Sandi, Melanie, and kids, getting married. Photo credit: Brian Spears.

racial children we could not help but acknowledge that both *Loving* and *Obergefell* made the legality of our marriage possible. However, the connection with *Loving* narratively deploys the trope of colorblind American progress toward the promise of full equality for all citizens that had not borne out in our lives. The circumstances of our marriage(s) and our family life challenge any simplistic embrace of equality based on race, gender, class, or sexuality. This symbolic recognition felt hollow in the context of both the coercive quality of the marriage, and the massacre in Florida early that morning.

Murray argues that *Obergefell* must be understood "as an effort to further entrench marriage's primacy and foreclose opportunities to establish and protect nonmarital alternatives" (2016a, 1239). Indeed, following this decision, protections for nonmarried couples have diminished. As Murray explains, *Obergefell* "promotes marriage-and only marriage-as the normative ideal for intimate life" (1240). Her research demonstrates that this decision goes beyond "favoring marriage over potential alternatives" to invalidate what she refers to as "non-marital equality" (1240). This is what happened with our civil union: if you *can* get married, apparently, you *must* get married. As legal scholar Katherine Franke's work demonstrates, the rights gained are accompanied by expectations that people will conform to "traditional" understandings of marriage. This "can have the unintended consequence of making the lives of lesbians and gay people who aren't in traditional relationships more precarious, not less" (2015, 13). Resistance to marriage comes at a quite literal cost.

As *Obergefell* enshrines marriage, it entrenches "the fundamental *inequality* of other relationships and kinship forms" (Murray 2016a, 1210). And with this decision, we seem to be back to the questions raised in our YMCA case. As I have discussed, the YMCA of Greater Des Moines was required to change their definition of "family" from one based on legal marriage to one based on household. In 2007, when that ruling was made, we were prohibited from marrying each other; our civil union did not count. Here we were again. This was not a triumphant "love wins" story. The love in our family had been "winning" for years—*that is how we survive*. This was about a governmental regulation that was required for us to access all the rights and protections available to us. If this had been about love, we would not have been compelled to get married again. Governmental sanctions prevailed. In getting married, we were not celebrating the new inclusivity of same-sex marriage—we were protesting it, while simultaneously engaging in a compulsory performance of citizenship. Although we gained some rights by doing so, on that same day we were reminded that threats of hatred and violence against queer folks, particularly those of color, are very real and ever-present. The colorblind neoliberal politics of *Loving* and *Obergefell* cannot save us from hatred.

Mass killings are horrific and far too common. Yet hatred, violence, and fear of difference manifest in less explicit ways as well. Part of the story of living in Iowa has been a struggle dealing with covert animosity and aversion expressed in race-evasive heteronormative guise. What does veiled hatred look like? Sometimes it looks like someone who just cares about following rules or maintaining respectability. The mothers we interviewed talked about "that feeling" they often get when they introduce their families or enter certain spaces. We feel the gaze of strangers in regular gestures of dismissiveness. On a consistent basis we must question the motives for people's behavior. Did that person scowl at me because I am queer or because he had a bad day? Was that cold shoulder about race? I have tried to lean toward the benefit-of-the-doubt side, clinging to the belief that the our family was not the source of social ire. I wanted to believe the university was the open-minded place it was supposed to be. Yet, while people publicly articulated their support for marriage equality, some still cringed inside when I introduced my Black "wife." People thought of us as too "intense," too "radical." We called too much attention to difference and inequality as we encountered it. We didn't blend in.

When we were discriminated against or bad things happened to us, the social institutions charged with protecting us failed to adequately do so. In her poem "A Litany for Survival," Audre Lorde reminds us that some of us "were never meant to survive." Our years in Iowa have taught us that we are not the people the system intends to protect and nurture. Not all of us can "indulge the passing dreams of choice" (1978, 255). Or perhaps, in this instance, it is more accurate to say that none of us has the capacity for choice that the American Dream supposedly provides. Some have more access than others. Survival in this context is about living a meaningful, safe, and legally recognized life, family, identity. The system was not set up to nurture those of us whose lives and families are defined as illegitimate. The power of the norm has profound consequences. The costs of hate and inequality are complicated, hidden in plain sight and disacknowledged by sociopolitical narratives about equality and choice. The writing of this book has been part of a survival strategy for facing an onslaught of social stressors of a magnitude neither I nor my family could have imagined. *There are pieces left out of this story.*

Following the November 2016 presidential election, hatred has been provided a green light by the tweeter-in-chief. In November 2018 the FBI released statistics indicating hate crimes had significantly increased in the United States for the third year in a row: "Of the more than 7,100 hate crimes reported last year, nearly three out of five were motivated by race and ethnicity, according to the annual report. Religion and sexual orientation were the other two primary motivators [emphasis original]" (Eligon 2018). If we ever thought that same-sex marriage would bring equality to LGBTQ people, surely the conservative backlash of recent years has made horrifically clear that people and families outside the narrowly defined category of "normal" (queer or not) are under assault. Virulent white supremacy, misogyny, homophobia, and xenophobia threaten lives. Fallout is heavy among the most vulnerable people.

Governmental forces continue to make clear that rich straight white American male citizens are the people the state values most, and laws and policies reproducing their wealth and privilege with impunity are relentlessly pushed forward. The onslaught of oppression is torrential.

What can we do? There is no easy solution to this complex system of stratified reproduction and citizenship. I have assembled a broad range of competing and complementary stories about kinship that point toward fissures in legal and policy protections for vulnerable families that are routinely obscured by racialized and gendered sociopolitical narratives. The history I have assembled here shows us how different realms of policy and law interact in profoundly complex ways to hide the presence of power relations while simultaneously regulating our lives. If we are to understand how to address these inequalities, we need to understand the ways they work. I would like to be able to provide a policy suggestion or plan to fix the problems these stories identify, but that would likely require another book. There are activists, organizers, lawyers, and policy and legal scholars who will continue to map out legal paths toward social justice through a multitude of channels. Legal changes are necessary, but not sufficient. There are no simple fixes. White supremacy, patriarchy, compulsory heterosexuality, and economic inequality are built into the structure of US society, even while their existence is denied.

Given that, there are some points we might consider as we move forward. Broadening the lens through which we consider questions of family legitimacy provides a more comprehensive perspective on the ways that power functions. Learning how to see and hear inequality and oppression behind sentimental family narratives and nationalist proclamations of equality is crucial. Part of the lesson of the history I have assembled here is that we cannot trust mainstream sociopolitical allegories to accurately convey the ways that oppression and privilege are structured and maintained. This is not just about "fake news." Every story is shaped by power, and it is crucial that we learn to recognize the complex ways race, gender, sexuality, and class function as signifiers of legitimacy and human worth in this capitalist system. How will we form and sustain coalitions for social change if we cannot comprehend how people in varying social locations experience the world and how their experiences are shaped by power inequalities? Social change demands vigilance and sustained effort on multiple fronts.

Conclusion: Grafted Trees and Radical Roots

As I write, I look outside at a stand of trees in my neighbor's yard, thinking about the patterns they make against the sky in the frame of my window. I cannot tell which branches belong to which trees. They crisscross, making intricate configurations of elegant irregularity. Some spaces are filled with sky, some with the lattice work of tiny branches. There are trees that stand almost straight, and others that bend toward the land, point to the sky, or spiral into the collective airspace. The story is never just about one tree. The integrity of a narrative requires attention to the context of land and space and air and resources they share. The understory matters.

Perhaps I have spent more of my life thinking about trees and roots than most people. My yearning to belong to a family tree that feels like mine has haunted me like the ache of phantom limb. Redwood trees shaped the landscape of my childhood. I grew up in California with a western horizon defined by the Santa Cruz Mountains, and I spent time in those forests whenever I could. Redwoods are distinctive not only for their majestic size and longevity; their root system is unique. One might think such enormous trees would require deep tap roots for stability, but the roots of redwoods are relatively shallow. They expand laterally. It is the interconnectedness of the root systems of all the redwood trees in a forest space that keeps them from toppling in fierce storms. They hold each other up. All the trees are nourished through a common root system. And when a great tree falls it keeps on growing, functioning as a rhizome, producing new shoots.

Queer of color theorist Jafari S. Allen pushes past mainstream representations of "roots" to suggest a "rhizomatic conceptualization of relations, space, and time." Traditional family trees represent linear and lineal time, providing a framework for understanding where individuals are situated in mainstream versions of history. Rhizomes disrupt genealogies organized through patriarchy and white supremacy: "In this time, one can project imaginations into the future and cut into the past—all in the pursuit of an elaborated *litany for thriving*. In this space, desires and socialities claim family and children not merely from biological or legal means but also by a process of nurture and nourishment [emphasis added]" (2016, 28). Rhizomes, like grafted trees, reproduce and develop laterally, growing beyond the primary root and trunk structure to create connective tissue between seemingly separate trees. Allen continues: "The Black/queer rhizome is generative, as it inspires connection beyond a staid, linear genealogy; it rejects old teleologies of heternormative natural 'progress' from a single root or (family tree). Feel here the ineluctable association and relatedness with 'intersectionality'" (29). This matrix of connections speaks to the ways that all of us outside of "legitimate" families are regulated and judged against the same constructed ideal of white, middle-class heteronormativity, yet in different ways. We need to foster connections between people and families positioned as outsiders.

The subtle and dramatic contrasts in the life stories of the mothers and children we interviewed shed light on the ways that family-making is stratified both between lesbians and straight women, and among lesbians. Exploring differences between and similarities among queer mothers makes evident the complex ways that gender, race, and sexuality are experienced and constructed differently for mothers in various social locations, as well as the ways that stratifications of motherhood are reproduced through genealogical templates for family legitimacy. At every level, there are tensions. Coalitional politics involves tackling deeply hazardous questions, like who counts as a legitimate mother. Native Studies scholar Kim Tallbear articulates the stakes in political debates about legitimate kinship: "In short, white bodies and white families in spaces of safety have been propagated in intimate co-constitution with the culling of black, red, and brown bodies and the wastelanding of their spaces. Who gets to have babies, and who does not? Whose babies get to live? Whose do not? Whose relatives, including other-than-humans, will thrive and whose will be laid to waste?" (2018, 147). These are not just academic questions. A politics of coalition requires us to rethink the ways we have been taught to think about equality and justice and whose lives matter. I am not embracing an emphasis on being an "ally"; that would suggest that I am engaging in someone else's political struggle. I strive to be a coconspirator. We need to learn the lessons of intersectional feminism—that unless the most vulnerable among us are free, none of us are.

The allegories assembled here help us see how the lives of some mothers are systematically denigrated while others are exalted. We see how narrow versions of history are supported and reproduced through the absence of a full range of voices, experiences, and stories. Denial and erasure are not productive survival skills for coping with contradictions at the personal level, nor are they sufficient ideological responses to social tensions. Conflicts and contradictions between personal experiences, family law, and political narratives shape how people understand the ways families relate to other families, whether perceived as similar or different. I return here to Cathy Cohen's call for a "politics where the *non-normative* and *marginal* position of punks, bulldaggers, and welfare queens, for example, is the basis for progressive transformative coalition work" (1997, 438). The lived experiences of these families challenge any neat division between social classifications of people. We overlap, we intersect, our lives are not defined solely by governmentally defined categories. Yet recognizing our connections can be difficult in the face of relational inequality that pits people against each other.

These politics are grounded in solidarity and intersectionality, not sameness. Rhetorical scholar Karma Chavez suggests: "'Queerness' is a coalitional term, a term that always implies an intermeshed understanding of identity, subjectivity, power, and politics located on the dirt and concrete where people live, work, and play." "Illegitimacy," too, is a coalitional term. It is defined by what it is not: legitimate. Families in various social locations are represented as outside mainstream or traditional families through a range of laws and policies focused on family and reproduction. The mothers we interviewed juggle multiple identities, and their lives are shaped by myriad relations of power. Experiences differ, yet we all live outside social definitions of legitimacy in some way. We are "punks, bulldaggers, and welfare queens," mothers who have immigrated without documentation, birth mothers whose children were removed by the state, mothers with no health insurance, incarcerated mothers, Indigenous queer mothers who are prohibited from adopting their children by patriarchal tribal laws. The meeting grounds for coalition-building is "on the dirt and concrete where people live, work, and play" (2012, 7). Coalitional politics often requires getting dirty.

The complex power relations imbricated in social uses of legitimacy are deeply embroiled in the race-gender politics of neoliberalism. Tales of marriage equality supersede attention to systemic discrimination in employment, housing, health care, and law enforcement. Narratives of orphan salvation obscure the power relations driving the transnational traffic in children. Our family tree stories are always already enmeshed in societal regulations designed to maintain social order. As Amy L. Hequembourg reminds us, "Lesbian mothers are never merely assimilationists or resistors" (2007, 173). We cannot help but participate in the system in which we live, even as we may critique the terms of belonging to it. Feminist theorist Donna Haraway explores questions of kinship and mutual survival: "Kin is a wild category that all sorts of people do their best to domesticate. Making kin as oddkin rather than, or at least in addition to, godkin and genealogical and biogenetic family troubles important matters, like to whom one is actually responsible. Who lives and who dies, and how, in this kinship rather than that one? What shape is this kinship, where and whom do its lines connect and disconnect, and so what? What must be cut and what must be tied if multispecies flourishing on earth, including human and other-than-human beings in kinship, are to have a chance?" (2016, 2). Haraway asks how we envision a future through stories that reach beyond the familiar. "What must be cut and what must be tied" to bring us to a future in which we can all thrive? Grafting is about cutting and tying to make new affiliations and coalitions. The lines of connection and disconnection are woven through stories about holidays and songs and birthdays and counting games and family crises and social movements. These affective connections are about raising children to both survive in the current world and build a future in which they can thrive. We must navigate these tensions in our everyday lives. There is no pure resistance, nor assimilation.

According to Allen, "Looking beyond 'survival' that was *never meant for us*, toward societal transformation and thriving, will require shifting the narratives we have rehearsed, toward a future in which we are indeed, 'fluent in each other's histories' and conversant in each other's imaginations [emphasis original]" (31). Intersectionality pushes us toward coalition. As Allen suggests, drawing on Elizabeth Alexander, we need to acquire fluency beyond the languages and stories with which we are familiar. When we consider the histories of race, reproduction, and class in this county, it is clear that families defined outside legitimacy have always found ways of surviving and navigating oppression wrought by white supremacy, patriarchal violence, and settler colonialism. We need to learn histories and cultural meaning systems beyond those we have been taught are our own, so that a broader range of people become legible to each other. How will we ever work together in coalition for a more socially just world if we cannot see or hear each other's life stories? If we cannot learn to be aware and critical of the ways that power hides its presence and pits people against each other? If we cannot look at lives different from our own with respect? If we cannot enter the room with a sense of humility and an openness to learning from other people? We do not need to share the same political perspectives and investments. But we do need to respect the different needs and commitments of other folks defined outside state legitimacy. We need, like redwood trees, *to hold each other up in the storm.*

ACKNOWLEDGMENTS

The writing of this book has been part of my life for so long it is difficult to account for everyone who helped shape it. I am deeply grateful to the families that shared their life stories with us. Their generosity of spirit was woven into their narratives and shared along with family dinners, lots of laughter, a few shows put on by kids, and the ever-present roar of children playing. The research and writing of this book have encompassed our children's entire lives, and while they were not always thrilled that Mommy and Mama had to sit down with the camera and listen to grown-ups talk again, they made friends and took in experiences they likely would not have without this project. These years have also been difficult in many ways, as is evidenced by the number of surgeons and oncologists I should thank here, along with the colleagues and friends that organized meals for us during several long-term medical emergencies. Our interactions with the families that participated in this research were truly sustaining for our us as we visited Pride celebrations and Family Week events in various cities over the course of several years.

I am grateful to Mignon Moore, two anonymous reviewers, and Melanie Patton-Imani for reading the entire manuscript (more than once in some cases), and for providing feedback that shaped this project in important ways. My editor, Jennifer Hammer, was committed to this book from the beginning, and her thoughtful choice of reviewers, along with her own comments, shaped the project in immeasurable ways. I thank the following people that provided feedback on individual chapters: Rickie Solinger, Renee Cramer, Yasmina Madden, Godfried Asante, Maura Strassberg, Daria Trentini, Nate Holdren, En Li, Brian Adams-Thies, and Christina Hanhardt. I am grateful for the support and feedback of the Faculty Writing Group at Drake University, who helped me think through revisions on several chapters. I am particularly grateful to my former colleague Lourdes Gutierrez-Najera, who was my Friday writing buddy while I was working out the structure of the book. Her insight and thoughtful feedback on several chapters undoubtedly improved the book. This project could not have been completed without the invaluable administrative support of Sofia Turnbull. My colleagues in the Department for the Study of Culture and Society at Drake University provided support and feedback as this work developed. I am grateful for research funding from the Williams Institute, Humanities Iowa, Drake University Humanities Center, Drake University Provost's Office, and Drake University College of Arts and Sciences.

My family has lived this book. Melanie and our children were part of each step of the research process, and they have survived the stresses of writing with grace. I would not have been able to do this without the love, support, intellectual feedback, encouragement, care, and feeding provided by my soulmate, Melanie Patton-Imani. Our children, too, sustained me, distracted me, and provided me with the love, laughter, and levity I needed.

NOTES

INTRODUCTION

1 The YMCAs in the twin cities had long had inclusive family policies, reflecting a long history of LGBTQ inclusiveness. Part of the profound culture shock we experienced when we moved from St. Paul to Des Moines was grounded in the contrasts between the relative open-mindedness of the twin cities over the more narrow views in Iowa. The family membership policy had been an issue in Des Moines even prior to our case, but there had never been enough legal or financial leverage to get it changed. What ultimately pushed our case over the edge was the threat of one Des Moines City councilperson of withholding city funding from the Y until they made their policy more inclusive.

2 See Kath Weston's classic ethnographic research on LGBT family formation, *Families We Choose* (1991).

3 The mothers we interviewed defined their sexual identities in a variety of ways. Many called themselves lesbians because they had an exclusive attraction to women. Others defined themselves as bisexual. People interchangeably used terms like "lesbian," "gay," "LGBTQ," and "queer." These definitions are fluid and contextual. Throughout the book, I do my best to honor the language employed by each mother, though there was often slippage between these labels. "Queer" is a term that is used in a variety of ways in the contemporary United States, depending on political context. While sometimes used to signify all gays and lesbians, it is more often engaged as a criticism of identity categories like "lesbian" and "gay." In the early years of the twenty-first century the term "queer" explicitly entered the public debate over the legalization of same-sex marriage through leftist critiques of heteronormativity and assimilation. I use the term in its historic specificity, but I also draw on the work of queer theorists to hone a definition of *queerness through illegitimacy*—everyone outside the heterosexual nuclear family norm is positioned as illegitimate citizens, and, in my view, this provides opportunities for coalition-building.

4 The research was organized and designed in order to maximize the diversity of experiences among mothers by conducting interviews in states with contrasting laws regulating same-sex marriage and adoption. Interviewees were located through a range of sources, including online contact with LGBTQ organizations, women's and gender studies departments, word-of-mouth, and casual conversations at LGBTQ-focused events. For example, we conducted short interviews

at every Pride celebration we attended. We set up appointments for in-depth interviews with as many people as possible. Finding white lesbians was relatively easy, while finding queer moms of color was more of a challenge, depending on geographic location.

5 Public dialogues about LGBTQ families have primarily focused on questions of sexual orientation. Very little attention has been paid to the ways that race, gender, and socioeconomic status affect the lived experience of citizenship for queers, or the public representation of this issue. Queer of color critiques have emphasized the importance of critically considering the ways that race in particular shapes both lived experience of queerness and public representations and discussions of it. See Cohen 1997; Somerville 2000; Ferguson 2003, 2005, 2016, 2108; Eng 2003, 2010; and Allen 2016. Feminist research has emphasized the ways that gender, race, and socioeconomic status intersect with sexual orientation to shape family and reproduction. See Dill 1988; Crenshaw 1989; Baca Zinn 1990; Higginbotham 1992; Glenn 1994 Roberts 1997; Solinger 2001, 2005; Ross 2002, 2006; Mamo 2007; and Gutierrez 2009. Reproductive justice and feminist analyses emphasize interactions between gender, sexuality, race, class, and power to account for the multiple ways that reproduction and family are embroiled in larger concerns about "social problems" and citizenship. Queer of color critique excavates the ways that race and queer people of color challenge mainstream understandings of family, gender, class, and sexuality, as well as queer theory, for its lack of attention to race. Reproductive justice analysis critiques feminist approaches to gender, family, reproduction, sexuality, and class in terms of race. I draw these critiques together to explore racialized sexuality in socioeconomic and political context.

6 As I demonstrate in later chapters, the public debate about same-sex marriage drew directly on analogies with *Loving v. Virginia*, the 1967 US Supreme Court decision overturning all bans on interracial marriage. Indeed, *Loving* served as a legal precedent in numerous same-sex marriage cases at both state and federal levels through an emphasis on equal protection and due process. David Eng makes clear that this decision marked a shift: "In the legal domain of family and kinship, we are said to have formally entered a colorblind society with the 1967 Supreme Court decision *Loving v. Virginia*, in which the Court struck down as unconstitutional Virginia's anti-miscegenation statute prohibiting marriages between whites and blacks" (2010, 4).

7 This set of questions emerged from queer and feminist critics, as I will discuss in later chapters, but the mainstream news media and policy debates continued to entrench the "common sense" of distributing rights via marriage.

8 Sommerville 2000; Duggan 2003; Kimport 2012.

9 I put these terms in quotes to signal the ideological nature of each, and to highlight that these are not words I would use, if they were not part of the historical record and the lexicon of popular understanding in the contemporary U.S. In addition, the term "colorblindness" is particularly offensive, not only in terms of the

denial of systemic racial oppression, but in the unproblematic use of "blindness" (a disability) as a metaphor.

10 Roberts 1997; Solinger 2001.

11 Sommerville 2000; Ward 2008; Kearl 2015.

12 See Polikoff 2008; and Conrad 2014.

13 The liberal view of marriage as a path to LGBT equality is articulated by: A. Sullivan 1997; Calhoun 2000; Eskridge 2002; Wolfson 2004; Rauch 2004; and Josephson 2005. The leftist critique has been articulated by: Ettelbrick 1992; Walters 2001; Valverde 2006; Ghaziani 2011; and Bernstein and Taylor 2013.

14 See Dill 1988; Baca Zinn 1990; Higginbotham 1992; Roberts 1997; Solinger 2001; Gutierrez 2009; Glenn 1994; Ross 2006; Dill and Zambrana 2009; and Briggs 2012.

15 Most of the names used in the book are real names, though I chose pseudonyms for a number of mothers with the same first name for clarity.

16 See Eng's (2003, 2010) discussion of this tension in Deann Borshay Liem's autobiographical documentary *First Person, Plural*.

17 The term was first introduced by Shelley Colen (1995) in Ginsburg and Rapp's important 1995 anthology *Conceiving the New World Order: The Global Politics of Reproduction*.

18 Anagnost 2000; Solinger 2001; Roberts 2002; Eng 2003; Volkman 2005, 2010; Briggs 2012; Ynvesson 2002, 2005, 2010; Haslanger and Witt 2005; Dorow 2006.

19 See Rivers 2015.

20 We interchangeably use "partner," "spouse," and "wife," depending on the moment and the context. Frankly, I began using "wife" to jar my mother's consciousness shortly after Melanie and I were "civilly unified." The reclaimed resistant quality was appealing, and it became a habit.

21 See Butler 1990 on performativity; and Xhonneus, 2016.

CHAPTER 1. FAMILY-MAKING AND CITIZENSHIP

1 See Wolfson 2004.

2 I put "American" in quotation marks for two reasons. First, I want to highlight the fact that the United States is but one country in North America. To call it "America" serves to erase all the other countries in North and South America. Second, I highlight this usage as a way of linking it to ideologies about family, citizenship, and nation.

3 See sociologist John Skrentney's work for an in-depth analysis of the narrative of social progress grounded in the civil rights movement.

4 *SisterSong* was founded in 1994 as a coalition of women of color joining concerns about reproductive policy and health with a critical race, gender, and poverty analysis. By emphasizing an intersectional approach to reproduction and gender, they reframed the activist and research conversation about reproductive politics. Including the voices of women of color expanded the terms of discussion beyond gender to also include race, sexuality, disability, and poverty, providing a more

comprehensive view of what constitutes reproductive politics and moving beyond the narrowly defined politics of the right to terminate a pregnancy to include attention to the right to bear and raise the children you conceive. Emphasizing the right to parent facilitates a broadening of analytical attention beyond abortion to include all aspects of family-making, and expanding beyond a politics that has largely focused on the needs of white middle-class straight women. This expansion allows for the inclusion of lesbian mothers. As Mamo and Alston-Stepnitz suggest, it is "surprisingly contentious" to maintain the inclusion of LGBTQ parenting as "part of reproductive justice" (2015, 521). Listening to the voices of women of color, women experiencing poverty, and women with disabilities points us particularly to issues of forced sterilization and eugenics. See Roberts 1997; Briggs 1998; Ross 2006; and Goodrow 2019.

5 Katie L. Acosta found in her research with Latina lesbian mothers that reconciling their childhood socialization in the church with their identities as lesbians was difficult. She noted that the ability to embrace contradiction was central to their process of negotiating between "loving God and loving other women" (2013, 39).

6 I have used italics in interview excerpts to indicate tone of voice and emphasis in how my interviewees narrate their life stories.

7 I use "Latinx" to refer to all genders, and "Latina" to refer to Latinx women.

8 The VA "survivor's benefit" applies to stepchildren of married parents, but because Tina and Cass were unable to legally marry, Cass's relationship with them was not recognized until she adopted them.

9 "Narratives of institutional identities in public policy therefore construct social boundaries, objectified forms of social differences creating unequal access to and unequal distribution of social resources and opportunities" (Loseke 2007, 669).

10 See Patton 2000.

11 Kimport 2013a found a "parent gap" between same-sex couples seeking marriage and those not concerned with legalization.

12 See Duggan 2003 for a critical discussion of heteronormativity and homonormativity.

13 Hequembourg suggests that even important work like that of Lewin 1993 and Stacey and Biblarz 2001 is limited by an unquestioning adherence to this framework.

14 See Conrad 2014.

15 Mink 1999; Solinger 2001.

CHAPTER 2. REPRODUCTIVE ALLEGORIES

1 "Help: Non-Traditional Families," WikiTree: Where Genealogists Collaborate, https://www.wikitree.com/wiki/Help:Non-Traditional_Families, last update November 30, 2019.

2 "Help: Adoptions and Multiple Parents," WikiTree: Where Genealogists Collaborate, https://www.wikitree.com/wiki/Adoptions_and_multiple_parents, last update November 30, 2019.

3 Lubiano 1992; Clifford 1993; Crenshaw et al 1996; Gooding-Williams 1993, 2013; Loseke 2007.

4 See Loseke 2007.

5 See Spradley 1979; and Caughey 1982, 1984, 2006. Person-centered ethnography provides a lens through which to explore the multiple systems of cultural meaning that individuals in different social locations employ in constructing identities and families. Cultural anthropologist John L. Caughey argues that all humans navigating complex contemporary societies are "multicultural" in the sense that we each draw on a broad range of cultural meaning systems to make sense of our lives. People in different social locations—shaped by race, ethnicity, tribal identity, gender, socioeconomics, sexuality, disability—have access to, and find useful and necessary, different systems of cultural meaning. This methodological approach facilitates an intersectional analysis at the level of individual experience. None of us is defined by "membership" in just one social category; rather, we each draw on multiple, and sometimes conflicting, cultural meaning systems and public narratives that inform our senses of self and family in society. This is not only important at the level of personhood, but also at the social level of understanding how various categorizations of identity intersect, overlap, contradict, and trouble each other. Defining identities through belonging in discrete social groups misrepresents the ways that people make sense of and navigate our social worlds, as well as the ways that power relations position different citizens in opposition to each other.

6 "Minority stress" research demonstrates the effects of stigma and discrimination on individuals and on couples and families. See Cao, Zhou, Fine, Liang, Li, and Mills-Koonce 2017.

7 I will discuss the controversy over the NYC school curriculum in more depth in chapter 4.

8 See Mink 1999; Patton 2000; Solinger 2001; Briggs 2012.

9 See Coontz 1992, 1997, 2005; and Stacey 1990, 1996.

10 See Dill 1988; Collins 1991; Roberts 1997; and Solinger 2005.

11 See Adams 1995; and Adams and DeLuzio 2012. In *BirthMarks*, I introduced the term "cultural eugenics" to illuminate the politics of assimilation and reproductive regulation articulated by politicians and policy pundits about transracial adoption laws in the 1990s. This is applicable to Indigenous people's histories in relation to the U.S. government as well.

12 I began exploring these questions in "Legitimacy and the Transfer of Children: Adoption, Belonging, and Online Genealogy" (2018).

13 Alexandria, Virginia, Property Records 1813.

14 See Collins 1990.

15 See Davis 1981; Dill 1988; Collins 1990; and Roberts 1997.

16 Davis 1981; Dill 1988; Collins 1990; Roberts 1997.

17 See Collins 1990 for a discussion of "other-mothering."

CHAPTER 3. MAKING FAMILY

1 Under US immigration law "a foreign-born child is an orphan if he or she does not have any parents because of the death or disappearance of, or abandonment or desertion by, or separation or loss from, both parents. A foreign-born child is also an orphan if his or her sole or surviving parent is not able to take proper care of the child and has, in writing, irrevocably released the child for emigration and adoption" (https://travel.state.gov/content/travel/en/Intercountry-Adoption/Adoption-Process/before-you-adopt/who-can-be-adopted.html#ExternalPopup, last accessed December 4, 2019).

2 This was the case among the women who participated in Mamo's research as well.

3 Roberts 1997; Briggs 1998; Ross 2006; Goodrow 2019.

4 Medical screening tests and policies at sperm banks are rigorous in some ways, and less so in others. Sue and Adrienne were told that this genetic condition could not have been caught by their tests. Another medical screening practice designed to eliminate the risk of AIDS and HIV transmission through sperm has ramifications beyond their transmission. Screening practices eliminate men who have had sex with other men in the past six months or who are intravenous drug users. Gay men are largely bared from donating sperm (Mamo 2004).

5 See Roberts 2012.

6 See Ladner 1977; Day 1979; Cole and Donley 1990; Patton 2000; and Briggs 2012.

7 For in-depth discussion of the market forces shaping private adoption, see sociologist Elizabeth Raleigh's *Selling Transracial Adoption: Families, Markets, and the Color Line* (2018).

8 In fact, the possibility of adopting as a single mother and passing as straight no longer exists in the transnational adoption system. Raleigh explains that "restrictions have become especially cumbersome over the past decade, as prime sending countries incrementally changed their policies, making it harder for nontraditional applicants to procure a baby" (2018, 103). Indeed, her research with social workers makes clear that by 2018 there were no countries accepting adoption applications from gays and lesbians.

9 Patton 2000; Briggs 2003; Patton-Imani 2012: Mayers 2016.

10 "American to Stand Trial over Guatemalan Adoptions," National Public Radio, April 27, 2017.

11 Christine Gailey's (2000) ethnographic research found that white adoptive parents frequently cited the severance of all ties in transnational adoption as a central benefit over domestic adoption. Raleigh's research found that social workers in private adoption agencies regularly relied on this as a marketing strategy for talking with prospective adoptive parents.

12 See Joyce 2013 for a cogent discussion of the role of conservative Christian churches in the movement for "child rescue."

13 See Coontz 2005.

CHAPTER 4. WHAT ABOUT THE CHILDREN?

1 A "queer time" analysis critiques the "normative narratives of time" (Halberstam 2008, 152) that support the reproduction of capitalism, including narratives of "progress" that deploy representations of children as images of the future. Edelman links this "reproductive futurism" with heteronormativity and sees it as a threat to the possibility of communal and other forms of "resistant" kinship. This is a useful framework for thinking about the ways sociopolitical narratives about children are deployed in family values debates. Yet Edelman's construction of queerness in opposition to reproductive or family timeframes cleaves too closely to polarized views of resistance versus assimilation. He romanticizes resistance as a means of stepping outside the logic of the system of power relations to embrace the "death drive" (Edelman 2004). Munoz's embrace of queer utopia offers a critique of Edelman based on his lack of attention to structural inequality. As Munoz points out, not all children are seen as those who must be protected; LGBTQ youth of color in particular demonstrate that intersections of race, gender, and socioeconomic status shape which children are envisioned as the future (2004).

2 Very little scholarly attention has been accorded queer families of color. Important exceptions include Magpantay 2006; Asencio 2009; Moore 2011; Acosta 2013; Harkins 2017; Tuthill 2016; and Tallbear 2019.

3 *If These Walls Could Talk 2* is a fictional HBO movie made in 2000 that explores lesbian relationships among women living in the same house in three historical moments: 1961, 1972, and 2000.

4 The structure of this story is grounded in a history of public discussions about the "pathology" of African American families.

5 A legacy of illegitimacy has haunted political discussions of families of color throughout US history. In the 1939 *The Negro Family in America*, sociologist E. Franklin Frazier argued that slavery had destroyed the nuclear Negro family, leaving a matriarchal system, unfit for assimilation and socialization into mainstream American society. This was the research undergirding Senator Daniel Patrick Moynihan's 1965 *The Negro Family: The Case for National Action*, which argues that large percentages of children born to Black unwed mothers had created a "tangle of pathology" that was being reproduced through generational cycles of a "culture of poverty." Chapter 4 of his book is called "The Tangle of Pathology." This sociopolitical narrative denies the existence of structural inequality by targeting individual, cultural, moral, and financial behavior, demonizing women in poverty, and denying the role of the state in sustaining economic inequality.

6 Anthropologist Oscar Lewis coined the term in a 1959 study of Mexican families, in which he argued that people living in conditions of poverty develop their culture or way of life in response to the exclusion from mainstream society they

experience. Social commentators have extrapolated Lewis's concept from the specificity of his study of poor Mexican families and used it to explain the causes and perpetuation of poverty in general. This generic "culture" is said to be characterized by female-headed households, laziness, lack of motivation, lack of a work ethic, and a present-time orientation.

7 See Patton 2000 for an in-depth discussion.

8 Scientific racism asserts biological inferiority, and the academic and legal shift toward the acceptance of cultural explanations for difference gradually superseded the biological racism that functioned to justify oppression against people of color in the antebellum and postbellum periods (Pascoe 1996). See Lerman and Weaver 2014 regarding the ideology that the civil rights movement ended racial discrimination in the United States.

9 See Roberts 1999.

10 Roberts 2002; Golden 1997.

11 See Solinger 2001; and Briggs 2012.

CHAPTER 5. NAVIGATING ILLEGITIMACY

1 RSV (respiratory syncytial virus) is a common respiratory illness that premature infants are particularly susceptible to. While most people experience it as a common cold, it can be life-threatening for infants born prematurely; thus they are typically given a shot to protect them from RSV during their first year.

2 The question of "survival skills" has been at the center of debates about whether or not white adoptive parents are able and willing to foster coping mechanisms in their children for dealing with the racism they will inevitably experience (Patton 2000).

3 See Trenka et al. 2006.

4 The difference between these two ways of framing racism has profound consequences for transracial adoptees' senses of self. My research with adult transracial adoptees (2000) demonstrates that children whose parents explained racism as a structural issue fared better than kids whose parents explained it through individual ignorance. A structural explanation allowed children of color to remove the focus from themselves to recognize that race was a system of oppression that all people of color experience. Children whose parents explained racism through individual ignorance often internalized the negative stereotypes about people of color they heard and distanced themselves from these ideas by identifying with whiteness.

5 Quiroz's 2007 research makes clear that the "colorblind" framework used in the past few decades to discuss adoption policy and law has encouraged people to see transracial adoption as evidence that society has moved beyond racism.

6 See *Wilcox v. Trautz*, 427 Mass. 326, 334 (1998); *Collins v. Guggenheim*, 417 Mass. 615, 618 (1994); *Feliciano v. Rosemar Silver Co.*, 401 Mass. 141, 142 (1987).

7 Supreme Court of Minnesota 1972; Supreme Court of Hawaii 1991.

CHAPTER 6. MAKING FAMILY LEGAL

1 Bernstein and Burke's analysis of news coverage of various responses to same-sex marriage in Vermont found that the Vermont Supreme Court decision in *Baker v. State of Vermont* (2000) was a turning point in news coverage of a "queer" perspective on same-sex marriage. "Once it became clear from the decision that the Court had charged the legislature with creating a remedy that would give same-sex couples the rights and benefits of marriage and that this charge included the possibility of enacting alternatives to marriage such as a comprehensive domestic partnership scheme, speakers in the *BFP* began to engage with queer arguments. Thus it was the *Baker v. State* decision that helped give queer arguments credibility and therefore standing in a way that they had not been able to garner prior to the decision" (2013, 329).

2 CNN 2004.

3 See Duggan 2003; and Bernstein and Taylor 2013b.

4 We located mothers to interview through word of mouth, approaching people at Pride, and through participant observation at the Albuquerque Metropolitan Community Church. We carried our camera at Albuquerque Pride and conducted short interviews with people. We then set up times to meet at people's homes for in-depth interviews.

5 Goldstein 2014.

6 See Gurr 2011.

7 Adams 1995; Adams and DeLuzio 2012; O'Sullivan 2016.

8 Baca Zinn 1990; Gutierrez 2009; Perales 2013.

9 "Hispanic" is the term they use to describe themselves.

10 Until very recently, it was not possible for a child in the United States to have more than two parents legally recognized. In 2013 California passed a law allowing the recognition of three parents. Courts have legalized third-parent adoptions on a case-by-case basis in Alaska, Louisiana, Massachusetts, Oregon, and Washington (Lovett 2012).

CHAPTER 7. IRRECONCILIABLE DIFFERENCES

1 Proposition 22 was passed in 2000, banning same-sex marriage throughout the state. As I discussed in chapter 4, this law was challenged in 2004, when officials at San Francisco City Hall began performing same-sex marriages. Four thousand marriage licenses issued to same-sex couples in San Francisco were voided by a California Supreme Court ruling on August 12, 2004, following a series of lawsuits. In September 2005 the California Senate passed a bill granting gays and lesbians the right to marry. However, Governor Schwarzenegger vetoed it, upholding the 2000 law limiting marriage to one man and one woman.

2 See Oliviero for an in-depth analysis of the iprotectmarriage organization's role in the Proposition 8 debate.

3 *Parker v. Hurley* 2007.

4 See Briggs for a discussion of this concept's legacy in US reproductive politics.

5 See Somerville for a critical history of this analogy.

6 "Discrimination," produced by No on Prop 8, October 30, 2008, http://www.youtube.com/.

7 https://slog.thestranger.com/2008/11/black_homophobia, last accessed December 13, 2019.

CHAPTER 8. QUEER IN THE "HEARTLAND"

1 Hotel Fort Des Moines, located downtown, is where presidential candidates typically stay while campaigning in Des Moines.

2 He resigned in 2012 over a very public disagreement with the NAACP's official stance supporting same-sex marriage.

3 See Wahneema Lubiano's 1992 incisive analysis of this issue in the Thomas-Hill hearings.

4 The term is drawn from Frantz Fanon's classic study of racial identity, *Black Skin, White Masks*, in which he says, "From the opposite end of the white world a magical Negro culture was hailing me. . . . Was this our salvation?" ([1952] 1993, 123). The linkage of "magical Negro culture" with "salvation" is particularly notable in this context. Sociologist Matthew W. Hughey explores the prevalence of this image in contemporary film, arguing that it articulates what scholars are calling the "new racism" (see Bonilla-Silva 2003). Hughey explains: "Within this milieu, I note the emergence of an explicitly positive, but latently racist character in Hollywood film—the "magical negro" ("MN"). The MN has become a stock character that often appears as a lower class, uneducated black person who possesses supernatural or magical powers. These powers are used to save and transform disheveled, uncultured, lost, or broken whites (almost exclusively white men) into competent, successful, and content people within the context of the American myth of redemption and salvation" (2009, 544).

CONCLUSION

1 *Obergefell v. Hodges* (2015) was a consolidation of cases from Michigan, Kentucky, Ohio, and Tennessee concerning same-sex marriage. The US Supreme Court addressed Constitutional questions concerning whether or not the Fourteenth amendment requires states to issue marriage licenses to same-sex couples and to recognize marriage licenses issued in other states. The Court answered yes on both counts.

2 http://series.hashtagsunplugged.com/lovewins, last accessed December 4, 2019.

BIBLIOGRAPHY

Abrajano, Marisa. 2010. "Attitudes on California's Proposal to Ban Same-Sex Marriage in 2008." *Political Research Quarterly* 63, no. 4:922–932.

Abu-Lughod, Lila. 1991. "Writing Against Culture." In *Recapturing Anthropology: Working in the Present*, edited by Richard G. Fox, 137–54. Sante Fe: School of American Research.

Acosta, Katie L. 2013. *Amigas y Amantes: Sexually Nonconforming Latinas Negotiate Family*. New Brunswick, NJ: Rutgers University Press.

Adams, David Wallace. 1995. *Education for Extinction: American Indians and the Boarding School Experience, 1875–1928*. Lawrence: University Press of Kansas.

———, and Crista DeLuzio. 2012. *On the Borders of Love and Power: Families and Kinship in the Intercultural American Southwest*. Berkeley: University of California Press.

Adoption and Safe Families Act (ASFA). 1997, pub. L., no. 105–89.

Alexandria, Virginia, Property Records. 1813. http://www.freedmenscemetery.org.

Alimahomed, Sabrina. 2010. "Thinking Outside the Rainbow: Women of Color Redefining Queer Politics and Identity." *Social Identities* 16, no. 2:151–68.

Allen, Jafari S. 2016. "Black/Queer Rhizomatics: Train Up a Child in the Way Ze Should Grow." In *No Tea, No Shade: New Writings in Black Queer Studies*, edited by E. Patrick Johnson, 27–47. Durham, NC: Duke University Press.

———. 2013. "Race/Sex Theory: Toward a New and More Possible Meeting." *Cultural Anthropology* 28, no. 3:552–55.

Anagnost, Ann. 2000. "Scenes of Misrecognition: Maternal Citizenship in the Age of Transitional Adoption." *Positions* 8:839–421.

Asencio, Marysol. 2009. "Migrant Puerto Rican Lesbians Negotiating Gender, Sexuality, and Ethnonationality." *NWSA Journal* 21, no. 3:1–23.

Baca Zinn. 1990. "Family, Feminism, and Race in America." *Gender & Society* 4, no. 1:68–82.

———, and Bonnie Thornton Dill. 1994. *Women of Color in US Society*. Philadelphia: Temple University Press.

Badgett, M. V. Lee. 2009. *When Gay People Get Married: What Happens When Societies Legalize Same-Sex Marriage*. New York: New York University Press.

———, and Jody L. Herman. 2011. "Patterns of Relationship Recognition by Same-Sex Couples in the United States." Report for the Williams Institute, University of California, Los Angeles.

Balsam, Kimberly F., Yamile Molina, Blair Beadnell, Jane Simoni, and Karina Walters. 2011. "Measuring Multiple Minority Stress: The LGBT People of Color Microaggressions Scale." *Cultural Diversity and Ethnic Minority Psychology* 17, no. 2:163–74.

Barker, Joanne. 2011. *Native Acts: Law, Recognition, and Cultural Authenticity* Durham, NC: Duke University Press.

Beckwith, Francis. 2008. "Bauman on *Heather Has Two Mommies*." www.whatswrong-withtheworld.net.

Bennett, William. 1995. Prepared Testimony by William Bennett before the Ways and Means Subcommittee on Human Resources, US House of Representatives. January 20.

———. 1996. "For the Sake of the Children." *Washington Post*, May 21, 1996.

Bernstein, Mary, and Mary Burke. 2014. "How the Right Usurped the Queer Agenda: Frame Co-optation in Political Discourse." *Sociological Forum* 29, no. 4:830–50.

———, and Verta Taylor. 2013a. "Marital Discord: Understanding the Contested Place of Marriage in the Lesbian and Gay Movement." In *The Marrying Kind: Debating Same-Sex Marriage within the Lesbian and Gay Movement*, edited by M. Bernstein and V. Taylor, 1–35. Minneapolis: University of Minnesota Press.

———, ———, eds. 2013b. *The Marrying Kind? Debating Same-Sex Marriage within the Lesbian and Gay Movement*. Minneapolis: University of Minnesota Press.

Bernstein, Robin. 2011a. *Racial Innocence: Performing American Childhood from Slavery to Civil Rights*. New York: New York University Press.

———. 2011b. "Children's Books, Dolls, and the Performance of Race; or the Possibility of Children's Literature." *PMLA* 126, no. 1:160–69.

Beyond Same-Sex Marriage. 2006. "A New Strategic Vision for All Our Families and Relationships." BeyondMarriage. http://www.beyondmarriage.org.

Bogage, Jacob. 2015. "Companies Celebrate the Supreme Court Same-Sex Marriage Ruling." *Washington Post*, June 26.

Bonilla-Silva, Eduardo. 2003. *Racism Without Racists: Color-blind Racism and the Persistence of Racial Inequality in America*. Lanham: Rowman & Littlefield.

Briggs, Laura. 1998. "Discourses of Forced Sterilization in Puerto Rico: The Problem with the Speaking Subaltern." *Differences* 10, no. 2:30–66.

———. 2003. "Mother, Child, Race, Nation: The Visual Iconography of Rescue and Politics of Transnational and Transracial Adoption." *Gender and History* 15:179–200.

———. 2006. "Making 'American' Families: Transnational Adoption and US Latin America Foreign Policy." In *Haunted by Empire: Geographies of Intimacy in North American History*, edited by A. Stolker, 344–64. Durham, NC: Duke University Press.

———. 2012. *Somebody's Children: The Politics of Transracial and Transnational Adoption*. Durham, NC: Duke University Press.

———. 2017. *How All Politics Became Reproductive Politics: From Welfare Reform to Foreclosure to Trump*. Berkeley: University of California Press.

Butler, Judith. 2002. "Is Kinship Always Already Heterosexual?" *differences* 13:14–44.

———. 1990. *Gender Trouble: Feminism and the Subversion of Identity*. New York: Routledge.

Cahill, Sean. 2009. "The Disproportionate Impact of Anti-Gay Policies on Black and Latino Same-Sex Couple Households." *Journal of African American Studies* 13:219–50.

———. 2005. "Welfare Moms and the Two Grooms: The Concurrent Promotion and Restriction of Marriage in US Public Policy." *Sexualities* 8, no. 2:169–87.

Cahn, Naomi. 2015. "The Uncertain Legal Basis for the New Kinship." *Journal of Family Issues* 36, no. 4:501–18.

California Ballot Proposition 8. 2008.

California Domestic Partnership Rights and Responsibilities Act. 2003.

Callahan, Cynthia. 2011. *Kin of Another Kind: Transracial Adoption in American Literature*. Ann Arbor: University of Michigan Press.

Canaday, Margot. 2011. *The Straight State: Sexuality and Citizenship in Twentieth-Century America*. Princeton, NJ: Princeton University Press.

Cao, Zhou, Fine, Liang, Li, and Mills-Koonce. 2017. "Sexual Minority Stress and Same-Sex Relationship Well-being: A Meta-analysis of Research Prior to the US Nationwide Legalization of Same-Sex Marriage." *Journal of Marriage and Family* 79, no. 5:1258–77.

Carp, Wayne E. 1998. *Family Matters: Secrecy and Disclosure in the History of Adoption*. Cambridge, MA: Harvard University Press.

Castro, Tony. 2008. "Call It an Election Year Twist of Fate." *Inland Valley Daily Bulletin*, October 30.

Caughey, John. 1982. "The Ethnography of Everyday Life: Theories and Methods for American Culture Studies." *American Quarterly* 34, no. 3:222–43.

———. 1984. *Imaginary Social Relationships: A Cultural Approach*. Lincoln: University of Nebraska Press.

———, ed. 2006. *Individuals and Cultures: A Life History Approach to the Study of American Identities*. Lincoln: University of Nebraska Press.

Chauncey, George. 2004. *Why Marriage? The History Shaping Today's Debate over Gay Equality*. New York: Basic Books.

Chavez, Karma. 2012. "Pushing Boundaries: Queer Intercultural Communication." *Journal of International and Intercultural Communication* 6, no. 2:83–95.

Clarke, Adele E., and Donna Haraway, eds. 2018. *Making Kin Not Population*. Chicago: Prickly Paradigm.

Clifford, James. 1986. "Introduction: Partial Truths." In *Writing Culture: The Poetics and Politics of Ethnography*, edited by James Clifford and George E. Marcus, 1–26. Berkeley: University of California Press.

———. 1993. "On Ethnographic Allegory." In *The Postmodern Turn: New Perspectives on Social Theory*, edited by Steven Seidman, 205–28. Cambridge: Cambridge University Press.

CNN. 2004. "Mayor Defends Same-sex Marriages: San Francisco Will Resume Issuing Licenses." http://www.cnn.com.

Cohen, Cathy. 1997. "Punks, Bulldaggers, and Welfare Queens: The Radical Potential of Queer Politics?" *GLQ* 3:437–65.

———. 2012. "Obama, Neoliberalism, and the 2012 Election: Why We Want More than Same-sex Marriage." *Souls* 14, nos. 1–2:19–27.

Cole, Elizabeth S., and Kathryn S. Donley. 1990. "History, Values, and Placement Policy Issues in Adoption." In *The Psychology of Adoption*, edited by David M. Brodzinsky and Marshall D. Schechter, 273–95. New York: Oxford University Press.

Colen, Shelley. 1995. "Like a Mother to Them: Stratified Reproduction and West Indian Childcare Workers and Employers in New York." In *Conceiving the New World Order: The Global Politics of Reproduction*, edited by F. D. Ginsburg and R. Rapp, 78–102. Berkeley: University of California Press.

Collins, Patricia Hill. 1991. *Black Feminist Thought: Knowledge, Consciousness, and the Politics of Empowerment*. New York: Routledge.

Congressional Record. September 9, 1992, vol. 138, no. 18.

Congressional Record. March 24, 1994, vol. 140, no. 35.

Congressional Record. September 10, 1996, S10116.

Conrad, Ryan, ed. 2014. *Against Equality: Queer Revolution, Not Mere Inclusion*. Edinburgh: AK Press.

Coontz, Stephanie. 2004. "The World Historical Transformation of Marriage." *Journal of Marriage and the Family* 66:947–79.

———. 2005. *Marriage, A History: From Obedience to Intimacy, or How Love Conquered Marriage*. New York: Viking.

Cooper, Davina. 2018. "Possessive Attachments: Identity Beliefs, Equality Law and the Politics of State Play Theory." *Culture & Society* 35, no. 2:115–35.

Cooper Davis, Peggy. 1997. *Neglected Stories: The Constitution and Family Values*. New York: Hill & Wang.

Cott, Nancy F. 2000. *Public Vows: A History of Marriage and the Nation*. Cambridge, MA: Harvard University Press.

Cox, Susan Soon-Keum, ed. 1999. *Voices from Another Place: A Collection of Works from a Generation Born in Korea and Adopted to Other Countries*. St. Paul, MN: Yeong & Yeong.

Crenshaw, Kimberly. 1989. "Demarginalizing the Intersection of Race and Sex: A Black Feminist Critique of Antidiscrimination Doctrine, Feminist Theory, and Antiracist Politics." *University of Chicago Legal Forum* 8:139–67.

———, Neil Gotanda, Gary Peller, and Kendall Thomas. 1996. *Critical Race Theory: The Writings the Formed the Movement*. New York: New Press.

Currah, Paisley. 1997. "Defending Genders: Sex and Gender Non-Conformity in the Civil Rights Strategies of Sexual Minorities." *Hastings Law Journal* 48:1363–85.

Dalton, Susan. 2001. "Protecting our Parent-Child Relationships: Understanding the Strengths and Weaknesses of Second-Parent Adoption." In *Queer Families, Queer Politics: Challenging Culture and the State*, edited by M. Bernstein and R. Reimann, 201–20. Minneapolis: University of Minnesota Press.

Daniel, Drew. 2010. "Trading Futures: Queer Theory's Anti-antirelational Turn." *Honoring Eve: A Special Issue on the Work of Eve Kosofsky Sedgwick* 52, no. 2:325–30.

Daniels, Cynthia R., and Erin Heidt-Forsythe. 2012. "Gendered Eugenics and the Problematic of Free Market Reproductive Technologies: Sperm and Egg Donation in the United States." *Signs: Journal of Women in Culture and Society* 37, no. 3:719–47.

———, and Janet Golden. 2004. "Procreative Compounds: Popular Eugenics, Artificial Insemination and the Rise of the American Sperm Banking Industry." *Journal of Social History* 38, no. 1:5–27.

Davis, Angela Y. 1981. *Women, Race, and Class.* New York: Vintage.

DeHaan, Linda, and Stern Nijland. 2000. *King and King.* Netherlands: Gottmer.

Denetdale, Jennifer Nez. 2006. "Chairmen, Presidents, and Princesses: The Navajo Nation, Gender, and the Politics of Tradition." *Wicazo Sa Review* 21, no. 1:9–28.

———. 2008. "Carving Navajo National Boundaries: Patriotism, Tradition, and the Diné Marriage Act of 2005." *American Quarterly* 60, no. 2:289–94.

———. 2009. "Securing Navajo National Boundaries: War, Patriotism, Tradition, and the Diné Marriage Act of 2005." *Wicazo Sa Review* 24, no. 2:131–48.

Dill, Bonnie Thornton. 1988. "Our Mothers' Grief: Racial Ethnic Women and the Maintenance of Families." *Journal of Family History* 13, no. 4:415–31.

———.1994. "Fictive Kin, Paper Sons, and Compadrazgo: Women of Color and the Struggle for Family Survival." In *Women of Color in US Society*, edited by Maxine Baca Zinn and Bonnie Thornton Dill, 149–70. Philadelphia: Temple University Press.

———, and Ruth Zambrana, eds. 2009. *Emerging Intersections: Race, Class, and Gender in Theory, Policy, and Practice.* New Brunswick, NJ: Rutgers University.

———, Maxine Baca Zinn, and Sandra Patton. 1999. "Race, Family Values, and Welfare Reform." In *A New Introduction to Poverty: The Role of Race, Power, and Politics*, edited by Louis Kushnick and James Jennings, 263–86. New York: New York University Press.

Diné Marriage Act. 2005.

Dinshaw, Carolyn, and Lee Edelman, Roderick A. Ferguson, Carla Freccero, Elizabeth Freeman, Judith Halberstam, Annamarie Jagose, Christopher Nealon, and Nguyen Tan Hoang. 2007. "Theorizing Queer Temporalities: A Roundtable Discussion." *GLQ* 3, no. 1:117–95.

Dobson, James. 2000. *The Complete Marriage and Family Home Reference Guide.* Carol Stream, IL: Tyndale Momentum.

———. 2006. Focus on the Family. web https://www.focusonthefamily.com.

Dorow, Sara K. 2006. *Transnational Adoption: A Cultural Economy of Race, Gender, and Kinship.* New York: New York University Press.

Dubinsky, Karen. 2010. *Babies Without Borders: Adoption and Migration across the Americas.* New York: New York University Press.

Du Bois, W. E. B. 1903. *The Souls of Black Folk.* Chicago: A.C. McClurg.

Duggan, Lisa. 2003. *The Twilight of Equality? Neoliberalism, Cultural Politics, and the Attack on Democracy.* Boston: Beacon.

Duster, Troy. 1996. "The Prism of Heritability and the Sociology of Knowledge." In *Naked Science: Anthropological Inquiry into Boundaries, Power, and Knowledge*, edited by Laura Nader, 119–30. New York: Routledge.

Edelman, Lee. 2004. *No Future: Queer Theory and the Death Drive*. Durham, NC: Duke University Press.

Edin, Katheryn, and Joanna M. Reed. 2005. "Why Don't They Just Get Married? Barriers to Marriage among the Disadvantaged." in "Marriage and Child Well-being," special issue, *Future of Children* 15, no. 2 (Fall):117–37.

Egan, Patrick J., and Kenneth Sherrill. 2009. "California's Proposition 8: What Happened, and What Does the Future Hold?" Commissioned by the Evelyn and Walter Haas, Jr. Fund in San Francisco. Released under the auspices of the National Gay and Lesbian Task Force Policy Institute. http://www.thetaskforce.org.

Egelko, Bob. 2008. "State's Top Court Strikes Down Marriage Ban." *SF Gate*, May 16.

Eligon, John. 2018. "Hate Crimes Increase for Third Consecutive Year, F.B.I. Reports." *New York Times*, November 13.

Eng, David L. 2003. "Transnational Adoption and Queer Diasporas." *Social Text* 76, no. 21:1–37.

———. 2010. *The Feeling of Kinship: Queer Liberalism and the Racialization of Intimacy*. Durham, NC: Duke University Press.

Eskridge, W. N. 1996. *The Case for Same-Sex Marriage: From Sexual Liberty to Civilized Commitment*. New York: Free Press.

Esposito, Jennifer. 2009. "We're Here, We're Queer, But We're Just Like Heterosexuals: A Cultural Studies Analysis of Lesbian-Themed Children's Books." *Educational Foundations* 23, nos. 3–4:61–78.

Essi, Cedric. 2018. "Queer Genealogies across the Color Line and into Children's Literature: Autobiographical Picture Books, Interraciality, and Gay Family Formation." *Genealogy* 2, no. 4:43.

Ettelbrick, Paula L. 1992. "Since When Is Marriage a Path to Liberation?" In *Lesbian and Gay Marriage: Private Commitments, Public Ceremonies*, edited by S. Sherman, 20–26. Philadelphia: Temple University Press.

Fanon, Frantz. [1952] 1993. *Black Skin, White Masks*. London: Pluto.

Fenton, Zanita E. 2014. "Bastards! . . . And the Welfare Plantation." *Journal of Gender, Race, and Justice* 17, no. 1:9–26.

Ferguson, Ann. 2007. "Gay Marriage: An American and Feminist Dilemma." *Hypatia* 22, no. 1:39–57.

Ferguson, Roderick. 2003. *Aberrations in Black: Toward a Queer of Color Critique*. Minneapolis: University of Minnesota Press.

———. 2005. "Of Our Normative Strivings: African American Studies and the Histories of Sexuality." *Social Text* 23, nos. 3–4:85–100.

———. 2014. "The Distributions of Whiteness." *American Quarterly* 66, no. 4:1101–6.

———. 2019. "The Pulse Nightclub and the State of Our World." *GLQ: A Journal of Lesbian and Gay Studies*, no. 24:36–38.

———, and Grace Hong. 2012. "The Sexual and Racial Contradictions of Neoliberal-ism." *Journal of Homosexuality* 59:1057–64.

Fleischer, David. 2010. "Behind the Numbers of Prop 8." *Los Angeles Times*, August 3.

Fotopoulou, Aristea. 2012. "Intersectionality Queer Studies and Hybridity: Method-ological Frameworks for Social Research." *Journal of International Women's Studies* 13, no. 2:19–32.

Foucault, Michel. 1978. *The History of Sexuality: An Introduction*. Translated by R. Hurley. New York: Pantheon.

Franke, Katherine. 2015. *Wedlocked: The Perils of Marriage Equality*. New York: New York University Press.

Frankenberg, Ruth. 1993. *White Women, Race Matters: The Social Construction of Whiteness*. Minneapolis: University of Minnesota Press.

Frazier, E. Franklin. 1939. *The Negro Family in the United States*. Chicago: University of Chicago Press.

Fujiwara, Lynn. 1999. "Asian Immigrant Communities and the Racial Politics of Wel-fare Reform." In *Whose Welfare*, edited by Gwendolyn Mink, 100–131. Ithaca, NY: Cornell University Press.

Gailey, Christine Ward. 2000. "Ideologies of Motherhood and Kinship in US Adop-tion." In *Ideologies and Technologies of Motherhood: Race, Class, Sexuality, Nation-alism*, edited by Helena Ragone and France Winddance Twine, 11–55. New York: Routledge.

Garden, Nancy. 2004. *Molly's Family*. New York: Farrar, Straus & Giroux.

Gates, Gary, M. V. Lee Badgett, and Deborah Ho. 2008. "Marriage, Registration, and Dissolution by Same-Sex Couples in the US." Report for the Williams Institute, University of California, Los Angeles.

———, M. V. Lee Badgett, Jennifer Ehrle Macomber, and Kate Chambers. 2007. "Adop-tion and Foster Care by Gay and Lesbian Parents in the United States." Report for the Williams Institute and the Urban Institute, University of California, Los Angeles.

Gates, Gary, and C. Ramos. 2008. "Census Snapshot: California's Lesbian, Gay, Bisexual Population." Report for the Williams Institute and the Urban Institute, University of California, Los Angeles.

Gavigan, Shelley A. M. 1995. "A Parent(ly) Knot: Can Heather Have Two Mommies?" In *Legal Inversions: Lesbians, Gay Men, and the Politics of the Law*, edited by Didi Herman and Carl Stychin, 87–102. Philadelphia: Temple University Press.

Ghaziani, Amin. 2008. *The Dividends of Dissent: How Conflict and Culture Work in Lesbian and Gay Marches on Washington*. Chicago: University of Chicago Press.

Ginsburg, Faye D., and Rayna Rapp, eds. 1995. *Conceiving the New World Order: The Global Politics of Reproduction*. Berkeley: University of California Press.

Glenn, Evelyn Nakano et al., eds. 1994. *Mothering: Ideology, Experience, and Agency*. New York: Routledge.

Goldstein, Alyosha. 2014. *Formations of United States Colonialism*. Durham, NC: Duke University Press.

Gonzalez, Susan. 2001. "Director Spike Lee Slams 'Same Old' Black Stereotypes in Today's Films." *Yale Bulletin and Calendar*, March 2.

Gooding-Williams, Robert. 1993. "Look, a Negro!" In *Reading Rodney King/Reading Urban Uprising*, edited by Robert Gooding-Williams, 157–77. New York: Routledge.

———. 2006. *Look, a Negro!: Philosophical Essays on Race, Culture, and Politics* New York: Routledge.

Goodrow, Gabrielle. 2019. "Biopower, Disability, and Capitalism: Neoliberal Eugenics and the Future of ART Regulation." *Duke Journal of Gender Law & Policy* 26, no. 2:137–55.

Gordon-Reed, Annette. 2008. *The Hemingses of Monticello: An American Family*. New York: W. W. Norton.

Graham, Tiffany C. "The Shifting Doctrinal Face of Immutability." *Virginia Journal of Social Policy & the Law* 19, no. 2:169–204.

Green, Adam Isaiah. 2006. "Until Death Do Us Part? The Impact of Differential Access to Marriage on a Sample of Urban Men." *Social Perspectives* 49:163–89.

Gurr, Barbara. 2011. "Mothering in the Borderlands: Policing Native American Women's Reproductive Healthcare." *International Journal of Sociology of the Family* 37, no. 1:69–84.

Gutierrez, Elena R. 2009. *Fertile Matters: The Politics of Mexican Reproduction*. Austin: University of Texas Press.

Halberstam, Judith. 2005. *In a Queer Time and Place: Transgendered Bodies, Subcultural Lives*. New York: New York University Press.

_____. 2010. "The Kids Aren't Alright!" Bullybloggers, July 15. http://www.bullybloggers.wordpress.com.

Hall, Ryan. 2005. "Same-Sex Marriage Do or Don't? Navajo Man Speaks Out for Homosexual Marriage." *Farmington Daily Times*, May 2.

Hames-García, Michael. 2013. "What's After Queer Theory? Queer Ethnic and Indigenous Studies." *Feminist Studies* 39, no. 2:384–404.

Haraway, Donna. 2016. *Staying with the Trouble: Making Kin in the Chthulucene*. Durham, NC: Duke University Press.

Harkins, Jessica A. F. 2017. "Same-Sex Marriage in the Cherokee Nation: Toward Decolonial Queer Indigeneities." In *Sovereign Acts: Contesting Colonialism across Indigenous Nations and Latinx America*, edited by Frances Negrone-Muntaner, 175–98. Tucson: University of Arizona Press.

Harmon, Steven. 2008. "Support Is Weak for Same-Sex Ballot Measure." *East Bay Times*, August 27.

Harris-Perry 2011. *Sister Citizen: Shame, Stereotypes, and Black Women in America*. New Haven, CT: Yale University Press.

Hartman, Saidya V. 2007. *Lose Your Mother: A Journey along the Atlantic Slave Route*. New York: Farrar, Straus & Giroux.

———. 2019. *Wayward Lives, Beautiful Experiments: Intimate Histories of Social Upheaval*. New York: W.W. Norton.

Haslanger, Sally, and Charlotte Witt, eds. 2005. *Adoption Matters: Philosophical and Feminist Essays*. Ithaca, NY: Cornell University Press.

Haule, Kristin. 2016. "It's Complicated: The Unusual Way *Obergefell v. Hodges* Legalized Same-Sex Marriage." *Loyola of Los Angeles Law Review* 49:561–73.

Hequembourg, Amy L. 2007. "Becoming Lesbian Mothers." *Journal of Homosexuality* 53, no. 3:153–80.

Herman, Didi, and Carl Stychin, eds. 1995. *Legal Inversions: Lesbians, Gay Men, and the Politics of the Law*. Philadelphia: Temple University Press.

Herrnstein, Richard J., and Charles Murray. 1994. *The Bell Curve: Intelligence and Class Structure in American Life*. New York: Free Press.

Higginbotham, Evelyn. 1992. "African-American Women's History and the Metalanguage of Race." *Signs* 17, no. 2:251–74.

Hondagneu-Sotelo, Pierrette. 1996. "Unpacking 187: Targeting Mexicans." In *Immigration and Ethnic Communities: A Focus on Latinos*, edited by Refugio I. Rochin, 93–103. East Lansing, MI: Julian Samora Research Institute.

Hughey, Matthew W. 2012. "Racializing Redemption, Reproducing Racism: The Odyssey of Magical Negroes and White Saviors." *Sociology Compass* 6, no. 9:751–67.

Jerng, Mark C. 2010. *Claiming Others: Transracial Adoption and National Belonging*. Minneapolis: University of Minnesota Press.

Johnson, E. Patrick, and Mae G. Henderson, eds. 2005. *Black Queer Studies: A Critical Anthology*. Durham, NC: Duke University Press.

Johnson, Richard Greggory, III. 2014. "African Americans, Proposition 8, and the Importance of Social Movements." *JHHSA* 37, no. 2:242–59.

Jordan, Mary. 1992. "Guidance on Gays Divides Parents; N.Y. Schools Chancellor Under Attack for 'Rainbow' Curriculum." *Washington Post*, December 8.

Josephson, Jyl J. 2005. "Citizenship, Same-Sex Marriage, and Feminist Critiques of Marriage." *Perspectives on Politics* 3:269–84.

Joyce, Kathryn. 2013. *The Child Catchers: Rescue, Trafficking, and the New Gospel of Adoption*. New York: Public Affairs.

Kearl, Michelle Kelsey. 2015. "Is Gay the New Black?: An Intersectional Perspective on Social Movement Rhetoric in California's Proposition 8 Debate." *Communication and Critical/Cultural Studies* 12, no. 1:63–82.

Keeling, Kara. 2014. "Queer OS." *Cinema Journal* 53, no. 2:152–57.

———. 2009. "Looking for M—Queer Temporality, Black Political Possibility, and Poetry from the Future." *GLQ* 15, no. 4:565–82.

Kennedy, Tammie M. 2014. "Sustaining White Homonormativity: *The Kids Are All Right* as Public Pedagogy." *Journal of Lesbian Studies* 18:118–32.

Kim, Eleana. 2010. *Adopted Territory: Transnational Adoption and the Politics of Belonging*. Durham, NC: Duke University Press.

Kimport, Katrina. 2012. "Remaking the White Wedding? Same-Sex Wedding Photographs' Challenge to Symbolic Heteronormativity." *Gender & Society* 26:874–98.

———. 2013a. "Being Seen through Marriage: Lesbian Wedding Photographs and the Troubling of Heteronormativity." In *The Marrying Kind? Debating Same-sex Mar-*

riage with the Lesbian and Gay Movement, edited by M. Bernstein and V. Taylor, 291–316. Minneapolis: University of Minnesota Press.

———. 2013b. *Queering Marriage: Challenging Family Formation in the United States.* New Brunswick, NJ: Rutgers University Press.

Kissen, Rita M. 1999. "Children of the Future Age: Lesbian and Gay Parents Talk about School." In *Queering Elementary Education: Advancing the Dialogue about Sexualities and Schooling*, edited by William J. Letts and James T. Sears, 165–76. Lanham, MD: Rowman & Littlefield.

Kohm, Lynne Marie. 2007. "Tracing the Foundations of the Best interests of the Child Standard in American Jurisprudence." *Journal of Law & Family Studies* 10, no. 2:337–76.

Korte, Gregory. 2015. "Obama: Gay Marriage Ruling is 'A Victory for America.'" *USA Today*, June 26.

Ladd-Taylor, Molly, and Lauri Umansky, eds. 1998. *"Bad Mothers": The Politics of Blame in Twentieth-Century America*. New York: New York University Press.

Ladner, Joyce A. 1977. *Mixed Families: Adopting across Racial Boundaries*. Garden City, NY: Anchor/Doubleday.

Lerman, Amy E., and Vesla M. Weaver. 2014. *Arresting Citizenship: The Democratic Consequences of American Crime Control*. Chicago: University of Chicago Press.

Lester, Jazmine Z. 2014. "Homonormativity in Children's Literature: An Intersectional Analysis of Queer-Themed Picture Books." *Journal of LGBT Youth* 11:244–75.

Letts, William J., and James T. Sears. 1999. *Queering Elementary Education: Advancing the Dialogue about Sexualities and Schooling*. Lanham, MD: Rowman & Littlefield.

Lewin, Ellen. 1993. *Lesbian Mothers: Accounts of Gender in American Culture*. Ithaca, NY: Cornell University Press.

———. 1998. *Recognizing Ourselves: Ceremonies of Lesbian and Gay Commitment*. New York: Columbia University Press.

Lewis, Oscar 1959. *Five Families: Mexican Case Studies in The Culture of Poverty*. New York: Basic Books.

Liem, Deann Borshay, dir. 2000. *First Person, Plural*. New Day Films.

Lipsitz, George. 2006. *The Possessive Investment in Whiteness: How White People Profit from Identity Politics*. Rev. ed. Philadelphia: Temple University Press.

Loseke, Donileen. 2007. "The Study of Identity as Cultural, Institutional, Organizational, and Personal Narratives: Theoretical and Empirical Integrations." *Sociological Quarterly* 48, no. 4:661–88.

Lorde, Audre. [1978] 1997. "A Litany for Survival." In *The Collected Poems of Audre Lorde*, 255. New York: W. W. Norton.

Lovett, Ian. 2012. "Measure Opens Door to Three Parents or Four." *New York Times*, July 12.

Lowe, Lisa. 1996. *Immigrant Acts: On Asian American Cultural Politics*. Durham, NC: Duke University Press.

Lubiano, Wahneema. 1992. "Black Ladies, Welfare Queens, and State Minstrels: Ideological War by Narrative Means." In *Race-ing Justice, En-Gendering Power: Essays* on *Anita Hill, Clarence Thomas, and the Construction of Social Reality*, edited by Wahneema Lubiano and Toni Morrison, 323–63. Toronto: Random House.

———. 1996. "Like Being Mugged by a Metaphor: Multiculturalism and State Narratives." In *Mapping Multiculturalism*, edited by Avery F. Gordon and Christopher Newfield, 64–75. Minneapolis: University of Minnesota Press.

Magpantay, Glenn D. 2006. "The Ambivalence of Queer Asian Pacific Americans Toward Same-Sex Marriage." *Amerasia Journal* 32, no. 1:109–17.

Mamo, Laura. 2007. *Queering Reproduction: Achieving Pregnancy in the Age of Technoscience*. Durham, NC: Duke University Press.

———, and Eli Alston-Stepnitz. 2015. "Queer Intimacies and Structural Inequalities: New Directions in Stratified Reproduction." *Journal of Family Issues* 36, no. 4:519–40.

Manalansan, Martin F., IV, Chantal Nadeau, Richard T. Rodríguez, and Siobhan B. Somerville. 2014. "Queering the Middle: Race, Region, and a Queer Midwest." *GLQ* 20:1–2.

Marre, Diana, and Laura Briggs, eds. 2009. *International Adoption: Global Inequalities and the Circulation of Children*. New York: New York University Press.

Massachusetts Supreme Court. 2003. *Goodridge v. Department of Health*.

———. 2007. *Parker v. Hurley*.

May, Vivian M. 2015. *Pursuing Intersectionality, Unsettling Dominant Imaginaries*. Milton Park: Taylor & Francis.

Mayers, Leifa. 2016. "The 'Orphan' Child: Politics of Vulnerability and Circuits of Precarity." *Feminist Formations* 28, no. 1:60–85.

McKinley, Jesse. 2008. "Same-Sex Marriage Ban Is Tied to Obama Factor." *New York Times*, September 21.

McPherson, Tara. 2014. "Designing for Difference." *differences: A Journal of Feminist Cultural Studies* 25, no. 1:177–88.

Mink, Gwendolyn 1995. *The Wages of Motherhood: Inequality in the Welfare State, 1917–1942*. Ithaca, NY: Cornell University Press.

———. 1999. *Whose Welfare?* Ithaca, NY: Cornell University Press.

———. 2001. "Violating Women: Rights Abuses in the Welfare Police State." In "Reforming Welfare, Redefining Poverty," special issue, *Annals of the American Academy of Political and Social Science* 577:79–93.

Moore, Mignon. 2011. *Invisible Families: Gay Identities, Relationships, and Motherhood among Black Women*. Berkeley: University of California Press.

———. 2019. "Reflections on Marriage Equality as a Vehicle for LGBT Transformation." In *Queer Families and Relationships After Marriage Equality*, edited by Michael W. Yarbrough, Angela Jones, and Joseph Nicholas DeFilippis, 73–79. London: Routledge.

Moreira, Luciana. 2018. "Queer Motherhood: Challenging Heteronormative Rules beyond the Assimilationist/Radical Binary." *Journal of International Women's Studies* 19, no. 2:14–28.

Morrison, Toni. 1992. *Playing in the Dark: Whiteness in the Literary Imagination*. New York: Vintage.

Moynihan, Daniel Patrick. 1965. *The Negro Family: The Case for National Action.* Washington, DC: United States Department of Labor.

Muñoz, José Esteban. 2009. *Cruising Utopia: The Then and There of Queer Futurity.* New York: New York University Press.

Murray, Melissa. 2012a. "Marriage as Punishment." *Columbia Law Review* 112, no. 1:1–65.

———. 2012b. "What's So New About the New Illegitimacy?" *American University Journal of Gender, Social Policy & the Law* 20, no. 3:387–436.

———. 2016a. "*Obergefell v. Hodges* and Nonmarriage Inequality." *California Law Review* 104:1207–58.

———. 2016b. "Rights and Regulation: The Evolution of Sexual Regulation." *Columbia Law Review* 116, no. 2:573–623.

Myers, Steven Lee. 1992. "Values in Conflict: Schools Diversify." *New York Times,* December 13.

Naples, Nancy. 1997. "The 'New Consensus' on the Gendered 'Social Contract': The 1987–1988 US Congressional Hearings on Welfare Reform." *Signs* 22, no. 4:907–45.

National Center for Lesbian Rights. 2004. "Adoption by Lesbian, Gay and Bisexual Parents: An Overview of Current Law." http://www.nclrights.org.

National Public Radio. 2017. "American to Stand Trial over Guatemalan Adoptions." https://www.npr.org.

Navajo Times. 2005. "Gay, Close Kin Marriage Banned." April 28.

Nelson, Kim Park. 2009. "Mapping Multiple Histories of Korean American Transnational Adoption." Working Paper Series, Washington, DC: US Korea Institute at AIIS.

Newman, Leslea. 1989. *Heather Has Two Mommies.* New York: Alyson.

———. 2009. "*Heather Has Two Mommies* Turns 20." *Publishers Weekly,* October 19.

Nieves, Evelyn. 2004. "California Judge Won't Halt Gay Nuptials; New Mexico Court Briefly Follows San Francisco's Lead." *Washington Post,* February 20.

Novy, Marianne. 2004. *Imagining Adoption: Essays on Literature and Culture.* Ann Arbor: University of Michigan Press.

Oliviero, Katie. 2013. "Yes on Proposition 8: The Conservative Opposition to Same-Sex Marriage." In *The Marrying Kind: Debating Same-Sex Marriage within the Lesbian and Gay Movement,* edited by M. Bernstein and V. Taylor, 1–35. Minneapolis: University of Minnesota Press.

Omi, Michael, and Howard Winant. 2015. 3rd ed. *Racial Formation in the United States.* New York: Routledge.

Ong, Aihwa. 1996. "Cultural Citizenship as Subject-Making." *Current Anthropology* 37, no. 5:737–62.

Ortiz, Ana Teresa, and Laura Briggs. 2003. "The Culture of Poverty, Crack Babies, and Welfare Cheats: The Making of the 'Healthy White Baby Crisis.'" *Social Text* 21, no. 3:39–57.

O'Sullivan, Meg Devlin. 2016. "'More Destruction to These Family Ties': Native American Women, Child Welfare, and the Solution of Sovereignty." *Journal of Family History* 41, no. 1:19–38.

Pallotta-Chiarolli, Maria. 1999. "'My Moving Days': A Child's Negotiation of Multiple Lifeworlds in Relation to Gender, Ethnicity, and Sexuality." In *Queering Elementary Education: Advancing the Dialogue about Sexualities and Schooling*, edited by William Letts and James Sears, 71–82. Lanham, MD: Rowman & Littlefield.

Pascoe, Peggy. 1996. "Miscegenation Law, Court Cases, and Ideologies of 'Race' in Twentieth-Century America." *Journal of American History* 83, no. 1:44–69.

Patterson, David. 2008. "Letter to the Editor." *East Bay Times*, October 17.

Patton, Sandra. 2000. *BirthMarks: Transracial Adoption in Contemporary America*. New York: New York University Press.

Patton-Imani, Sandra. 2012. "Orphan Sunday: Narratives of Salvation in Transnational Adoption." *Dialog: A Journal of Theology* 51, no. 4:294–304.

———. 2018. "Legitimacy and the Transfer of Children: Adoption, Belonging, and Online Genealogy." *Genealogy* 2, no. 37:1–19.

Perales, Monica. 2013. "On Borderlands/La Frontera: Gloria Anzaldúa and Twenty-Five Years of Research on Gender in the Borderlands." *Journal of Women's History* 25, no. 4:163–73, 371–72.

Perry, Samuel L. 2016. "Transracial Adoption, Neoliberalism, and Religion: A Test of Moderating Effects." *Journal of Family Issues* 37, no. 13:1843–68.

Polikoff, Nancy. 2008. *Beyond Straight and Gay Marriage: Valuing All Families under the Law*. Boston: Beacon.

Price, Kamala. 2010. "What Is Reproductive Justice? How Women of Color Activists Are Redefining the Pro-Choice Paradigm." *Meridians: feminism, race, transnationalism* 10, no. 2:42–65.

———. 2018. "Queering Reproductive Justice in the Trump Era: A Note on Political Intersectionality." *Politics & Gender* 14:581–601.

Quiroz, Pamela A. 2007. *Adoption in a Color-blind Society*. New York: Rowman & Littlefield.

Radke, Jim. 2008. "Zealots Won't Stop With Marriage." *Chico Enterprise-Record*, November 1.

Raleigh, Elizabeth. 2018. *Selling Transracial Adoption: Families, Markets, and the Color Line*. Philadelphia: Temple University Press.

Register, Cheri. 1991. *"Are Those Kids Yours?": American Families with Children Adopted from Other Countries*. New York: Free Press.

Reuser, Sue. 2008. "Indoctrination Has Begun." *Chico Enterprise-Record*, October 26.

Reyna, Karen. 2008. "If Prop. 8 Is Defeated, You Will Have No Right to Protect Your Children in the Public Classroom from the Teaching that Homosexuality Is Normal and Acceptable. Just Ask the Wirthlin family of Massachusetts." *Contra Costa Times*, October 18.

Rich, Adrienne. 1980. "Compulsory Heterosexuality and Lesbian Existence." *Signs* 5:631–60.

Richards, Sarah. 2012. "'What the Map Cuts Up the Story Cuts Across': Narratives of Belonging in Intercountry Adoption." *Adoption & Fostering* 36, nos. 3–4:104–11.

Richardson, Matthew. 2013. *The Queer Limit of Black Memory: Black Lesbian Literature and Irresolution*. Columbus: Ohio State University Press.

Rincon, Maria, and Brian Trung Lam. 2011. "The Perspectives of Latina Mothers on Latina Lesbian Families." *Journal of Human Behavior in the Social Environment* 21:334–49.

Rivers, Daniel Winunwe. 2013. *Radical Relations: Lesbian Mothers, Gay Fathers, and Their Children in the United States since World War II*. Chapel Hill: University of North Carolina Press.

Roberts, Dorothy. 1997. *Killing the Black Body: Race, Reproduction, and the Meaning of Liberty*. New York: Pantheon.

———. 1999. "Poverty, Race, and New Directions in Child Welfare Policy." *Washington University Journal of Law & Policy* 1:63–76.

———. 2002. *Shattered Bonds: The Color of Child Welfare*. New York: Basic Books.

———. 1996. "The Priority Paradigm: Private Choices and the Limits of Equality." *University of Pittsburgh Law Review* 57:363–404.

Roman, Leslie G. 1997. "Denying (White) Racial Privilege: Redemption Discourses and the Uses of Fantasy." In *Off White: Readings on Race, Power, and Society*, edited by Michelle Fine, Lois Weis, Linda C. Powell, and L. Mun Wong, 270–82. New York: Routledge.

Ross, Loretta. 2006. "Understanding Reproductive Justice: Transforming the Pro-Choice Movement." *off our backs* 36, no. 4:14–19.

———. 2018. "Reproductive Justice as Intersectional Feminist Activism." *Souls: A Journal of Black Politics, Culture, and Society* 19, no. 3: 286–314.

Savage, Dan. 2008. "Black Homophobia." https://slog.thestranger.com/2008/11/black_homophobia.

Sears, James T. 1999. "Teaching Queerly: Some Elementary Propositions." In *Queering Elementary Education: Advancing the Dialogue about Sexualities and Schooling*, edited by William J. Letts and James T. Sears, 3–14. Lanham, MD: Rowman & Littlefield.

Shannahan, Dervla. 2010. "Heather Has Two Mommies and They're Both Caucasian and Moneyed: Unsaids in International 'Queer' Children's Literature." *Dark Matter*, September 28.

Shin, Michael. 2009. "Show Me the Money! The Geography of Contributions to California's Proposition 8." California Center for Population Research On-Line Working Paper Series.

Shome, Raka. 2011. "'Global Motherhood': The Transnational Intimacies of White Femininity." *Critical Studies in Media Communication* 28, no. 5:388–406.

Skrentny, John. 2013. *After Civil Rights: Racial Realism in the New American Workplace*. Princeton, NJ: Princeton University Press.

Smith, Miriam. 2008. *Political Institutions and Lesbian and Gay Rights in the United States and Canada*. New York: Routledge.

Solinger, Rickie. 1992. *Wake Up Little Susie: Single Pregnancy and Race Before Roe v. Wade*. New York: Routledge.

———. 2001. *Beggars and Choosers: How the Politics of Choice Shapes Adoption, Abortion, and Welfare in the United States*. New York: Hill & Wang, 2001.

_____ 2005. *Pregnancy and Power: A Short History of Reproductive Politics in America*. New York: New York University Press.

Somerville, Siobhan. 2000. *Queering the Color Line: Race and the Invention of Homosexuality in America*. Durham, NC: Duke University Press.

Spindelman, Marc. 2016. "Obergefell's Dreams." In "Colloquium: *Obergefell v. Hodges*," *Ohio State Law Journal* 77, no. 5:1039–108.

Spradley, James P. 1979. *The Ethnographic Interview*. New York: Holt, Rinehart & Winston.

Stacey, Judith. 1996. *In the Name of the Family: Rethinking Family Values in the Postmodern Age*. Boston: Beacon.

———. 2004. "Cruising to Familyland: Gay Hypergamy and Rainbow Kinship." *Current Sociology* 52:181–197.

———. 2011. *Unhitched: Love Marriage, and Family Values*. New York: New York University Press.

———. 2018. "Queer Reproductive Justice?" *Reproductive Biomedicine and Society Online* 7:4–7.

———, and T. J. Biblarz. 2001. "(How) Does the Sexual Orientation of Parents Matter?" *American Sociological Review* 66:159–83.

State of Iowa. 2007. An Act Relating to the Iowa Civil Rights Act and Discrimination Based Upon a Person's Sexual Orientation or Gender Identity.

Stone, Amy L. 2012. *Gay Rights at the Ballot Box*. Minneapolis: University of Minnesota Press

———, and Jane Ward. 2011. "From 'Black people are not a homosexual act' to 'gay is the new Black': mapping white uses of Blackness in modern gay rights campaigns in the United States." *Social Identities* 17, no. 5:605–24.

Stults, Christopher B., Sandra A. Kupprat, Perry N. Halkitis, Kristen D. Krause, and Farzana Kapadia. 2017. "Perceptions of Safety Among LGBTQ People Following the 2016 Pulse Nightclub Shooting." *Psychology of Sexual Orientation and Gender Diversity* 4, no. 3:251–56.

Sullivan, Maureen. 2004. *The Family of Woman: Lesbian Mothers, Their Children, and the Undoing of Gender*. Berkeley: University of California Press.

Supreme Court of the State of Iowa. 2009. *Varnum v. Brien*.

Supreme Court of the State of Massachusetts. 2008. *Parker V. Hurley*.

Supreme Court of the State of Virginia. 1967. *Loving v. Virginia*.

Supreme Court of the United States. 2015. *Obergefell v. Hodges*.

Sycamore, Matilda. 2004. http://mattildabernsteinsycamore.com.

Taylor, Verta, Katrina Kimport, Nella Van Dyke, and Ellen Ann Andersen. 2009. "Culture and Mobilization: Tactical Repertoires, Same-Sex Weddings, and the Impact on Gay Activism." *American Sociological Review* 74:865–90.

Taylor, Verta, Katrina Kimport, Nella Van Dyke, and Ellen Ann Anderson. 2013. "Mobilization through Marriage The San Francisco Wedding Protest." In *The Marrying*

Kind: Debating Same-Sex Marriage within the Lesbian and Gay Movement, edited by M. Bernstein and V. Taylor, 1–35. Minneapolis: University of Minnesota Press.

Tsosie, Cecelia. 2004. "Letter to the Editor." *Farmington Daily Times,* March 9.

Trenka, Jane Jeong, Julia Chinyere Oparah, and Sun Yung Shin, eds. 2006. *Outsiders Within: Writing on Transracial Adoption.* Boston: South End.

Tuthill, Zelma. 2016. "Negotiating Religiosity and Sexual Identity Among Hispanic Lesbian Mothers." *Journal of Homosexuality* 63, no. 9:1194–210.

US Court of Appeals for the First Circuit. 2008. *Parker v. Hurley.*

US State Department. https://www.uscis.gov.

US House of Representatives. 1996. US House Judiciary Committee Report on the Defense of Marriage Act.

US Congress. 1994. Multiethnic Placement Act.

———. 1996. Defense of Marriage Act.

———. 1996. Interethnic Placement Act.

———. 1997. Adoption and Safe Families Act.

US Department of Justice, Immigration and Naturalization Service. 2000. Child Citizenship Act of 2000.

US Department of State. "Adoption Guidelines—Identifying a Child." http://www.state.gov.

Vermont Supreme Court. 1999. *Baker v. Vermont.*

Volkman, Toby Alice, ed. 2005. *Cultures of Transnational Adoption.* Durham, NC: Duke University Press.

Von Drehle, David. 2004. "Legal Confusion Over Gay Marriage; Who Is, and Who Isn't, Wed Is Subject of Great Debate." *Washington Post,* February 27.

Wallace Adams, David, and Crista DeLuzio 2012. *On the Borders of Love and Power: Families and Kinship in the Intercultural American Southwest.* Berkeley: University of California Press.

Walters, Suzanna. 2014. *The Tolerance Trap: How God, Genes, and Good Intentions Are Sabotaging Gay Equality.* New York: New York University Press.

Walther, Caroline S. 2014. "Skin Tone, Biracial Stratification, and Tri-racial Stratification among Sperm Donors." *Ethnic and Racial Studies* 37, no. 3:517–36.

Ward, Jane. 2008a. *Respectably Queer: Diversity Culture in LGBT Activist Organizations.* Nashville, TN: Vanderbilt University Press.

———. 2008b. "White Normativity: The Cultural Dimensions of Whiteness in a Racially Diverse LGBT Organization." *Sociological Perspectives* 51, no. 3:563–86.

———, and Beth Schneider. 2009. "The Reaches of Heteronormativity: An Introduction." In "Heteronormativity and Sexualities," special issue, *Gender and Society* 23, no. 4:433–39.

Warren, Deirdre M., and Katrina R. Bloch. 2014. "Framing Same-Sex Marriage: Media Constructions of California's Proposition 8." *Social Science Journal* 51:503–13.

Watson, Julia. 1996. "Ordering the Family: Genealogy as Autobiographical Pedigree." In *Getting a Life: Everyday Uses of Autobiography,* edited by Sidonie Smith and Julia Watson, 297–323. Minneapolis: University of Minnesota Press.

Weber, Shannon. 2015. "Daring to Marry: Marriage Equality Activism After Proposition 8 as Challenge to the Assimilationist/Radical Binary in Queer Studies." *Journal of Homosexuality* 62:1147–73.

Weeks, Jeffrey. 2008. "Regulation, Resistance, Recognition." *Sexualities* 11:787–92.

Wegar, Katarina. 1997. *Adoption, Identity, and Kinship: The Debate over Sealed Birth Records*. New Haven, CT: Yale University Press.

Weil, Francois. 2013. *Family Trees: A History of Genealogy in America*. Cambridge, MA: Harvard University Press.

Weston, Kath. 1991. *Families We Choose: Lesbians, Gays, Kinship*. New York: Columbia University Press.

Whitehead, Jaye Cee. 2012. *The Nuptial Deal: Same-Sex Marriage and Neoliberal Governance*. Chicago: University of Chicago Press.

Witosky, Tom, and Marc Hanson. 2015. *Equal Before the Law: How Iowa Led Americans to Marriage Equality*. Iowa City: University of Iowa Press.

Wolfson, Evan. 2004. *Why Marriage Matters: America, Equality, and Gay People's Right to Marry*. New York: Simon & Schuster.

Xhonneus, Lies. 2016. "Queer Kin in the Oevre of Rebecca Brown: De-Naturalizing Biological Kinship." *Women's Studies* 45:20–38.

Yarbrough, Michael W., Angela Jones, and Joseph Nicholas DeFilippis, eds. 2019. *Queer Families and Relationships After Marriage Equality*. London: Routledge.

Yngvesson, Barbara. 2002. "Placing the 'Gift Child' in Transnational Adoption." *Law and Society Review* 36:227–56.

———. 2005. "Going 'Home': Adoption, Loss of Bearings, and the Mythology of Roots." In *Cultures of Transnational Adoption*, edited by Toby Alice Volkman, 25–48, Durham, NC: Duke University Press.

———. 2010. *Belonging in an Adopted World: Race, Identity, and Transnational Adoption*. Chicago: University of Chicago Press.

Yoshino, Kenji. 2015. "A New Birth of Freedom?: *Obergefell v. Hodges*." *Harvard Law Review* 129, no. 1:147–79.

INDEX

abortion, 277n4

Acosta, Katie L., 278n5

Adams, David Wallace, 185

adoption: as allegory, 250–55; birth certificates and, 11, 53–54; birth mother and, 12–13, 100–102, 131–32, 187–88; in California, 167–75; family legitimacy and, 9–15, 40–43, 250–55; family-making and, 95–102; family trees and, 10–15, 49–51, 71–73, 79–80, 250–55; in Florida, 132–33, 141–42; home study and, 97–99; immigration and, 129, 280n1; in Iowa, 98; law and, 95–98, 140–42, 283n10; neoliberalism and, 126–33, 253–54; origin stories and, 155–56; orphan-salvation myth in, 99–102; parental rights and, 11, 53–57; poverty and, 99–102, 124–32; queer mothering and, 10–15, 34, 40–43; race and, 40–43, 128–29, 133, 153–56, 236–39, 252–55; race-matching in, 128; racism and, 128; reproductive politics and, 12, 155–56; risk assessment and, 131–32; salvation and, 237–39; social location and, 11, 95–102, 140–45; stratified mothering and, 40–43; transnational, 97–102, 153, 280n8, 280n11; whiteness and, 40–43, 236–38

advertising, 203–4

AFDC. *See* Aid to Families with Dependent Children

African American homophobia, 215–16

Africanism, 46–47

Aid to Families with Dependent Children (AFDC), 63–64, 123, 127, 129

Alexander, Elizabeth, 270

allegories, 198–201, 248–49; adoption, 250–55; ethnographic, 53–57; genealogical, 66–76; sociopolitical, 57–66, 123

Allen, Jafari S., 267–68, 270

alternative insemination, 83–93. *See also* sperm donors

Anderson, Ellen Ann, 167–68

Arresting Citizenship (Lerman and Weaver), 35–36

assimilation: family trees and, 69; marriage and, 174–75, 177–78, 181–83; politics and, 167, 174–75, 177–78, 181; resistance compared to, 44–45, 106

assisted reproduction: alternative insemination, 83–93; family legitimacy and, 169; family-making and, 81–94; fertility and, 83–85; healthcare and, 84–85; health relating to, 90, 280n4; power relations and, 93–94; race and, 93–94; with sperm donors, 85–94, 280n4

Baker v. Vermont (1999), 159, 283n1 (chapter 6)

BarbouRoske, Dawn, 229–30

Barker, Joanne, 69–70

Bauman, Michael, 115–16

belonging: citizenship and, 19, 25–26; family legitimacy and, 26–34; identity and, 20–21, 73–74, 279n5; illegitimacy and, 20–21; nation and, 36–37, 76–77; Proposition 8 and, 195–201; religion, race, and, 26–34; representational, 25

Bennett, William, 127, 256

Bernstein, Mary, 167, 236, 238, 283n1 (chapter 6)

Bernstein, Robin, 155–56

biological racism, 282n8

biology, 51, 53, 73–75, 126–27, 206

birth certificates, 39, 169, 200; adoption and, 11, 53–54

birth mothers, 12–13, 100–102, 131–32, 187–88

Black man "threat," 154–55

Black Skin, White Masks (Fanon), 284n4

Bluest Eye, The (Morrison), 76–77

books, children's, 20, 58–66, 113–18, 148–49, 203–6, 250

border crossings, 166, 178–84, 241–44

Briggs, Laura, 61, 130, 140, 162, 257–58

Bryant, Anita, 142

Burke, Mary C., 167, 283n1 (chapter 6)

Bush, George W., 165

California: adoption in, 167–75; citizenship in, 120; Domestic Partnership Rights and Responsibilities Act in, 168–69, 171–72, 200; education in, 203; family legitimacy in, 167–75, 200; Proposition 8 in, 195–218; Proposition 22 in, 283n1 (chapter 7); Proposition 187 in, 120; same-sex marriage in, 21, 167–75, 177–78, 194, 195–218, 283n1 (chapter 7); San Francisco, 167–75

Callahan, Cynthia, 253, 254

Cambodia, 99

Canaday, Margot, 36

Carter, Mandy, 226–27

Castro, Tony, 210

Caughey, John L., 279n5

Chavez, Karma, 269

Child Citizenship Act (2000), 133

children: books for, 20, 58–66, 113–18, 148–49, 203–6, 250; in foster care, 129–32, 186–87; gender and children's toys, 147; illegitimacy of, 159–60, 250–51; nation and, 61; Proposition 8 and, 198, 201–9; same-sex marriage and, 4, 9–10, 201–9, 221–25, 249–51; slavery and, 73–75; stigma and, 250–51; in *Varnum v. Brien,* 224–25. *See also* adoption

"Children of the Rainbow" curriculum, 115

child socialization, 278n5; citizenship and, 113–18, 122–23, 153–56; education and, 145–53; family structure and, 153–56; illegitimacy and, 153–56; race and, 153–56

child trafficking, 99, 100

child welfare policies, 41; AFDC and, 63–64, 123, 127, 129; Child Citizenship Act and, 133; family legitimacy and, 184–89; illegitimacy and, 156–60; parental rights and, 156–60; poverty and, 126–32; queer mothering and, 130–33; race and, 133, 156–60, 184–89; stratified reproduction and, 184–89

choice: culture and, 126–27; discrimination and, 159–62; equality and, 158–59, 232–35, 263–65; illusion of, 260–66; power relations and, 38, 45; race and, 232–35; structural inequality and, 45, 55; women and, 45, 62–63

citizenship: belonging and, 19, 25–26; in California, 120; child socialization and, 113–18, 122–23, 153–56; criminal justice and, 35–36; cultural, 36–37; dependency and, 118–23; family legitimacy and, 1–20, 23–47, 62–63; identity and, 24; illegitimacy and, 118–23; immigration and, 119–20, 122; lived experience of, 25, 47; marriage equality and, 23–24, 40–43; motherhood and, 238; narratives on, 118–23; politics and, 23–24; Proposition 8 and, 196, 198, 200–201; race and, 118–19; reproduction and, 24–25, 45–46, 276n5; same-sex marriage and, 5–6, 40–43; social location and, 14,

119; socioeconomic status and, 23–24; welfare reform and, 118–23

civil rights, 8, 24, 44, 61; in Iowa, 231–33, 240; Proposition 8 and, 209–13

Clark, Brad, 230–31

class. *See* socioeconomic status

Cohen, Cathy, 13–14, 269

colonization: family trees and, 68–69, 71, 72–73, 188–89; race and, 184–89; stratified reproduction and, 184–89

colorblindness, 235–39, 276n9; politics and, 24, 69–70, 106–7, 209–10; queer legitimacy and, 17, 24; racism and, 282n5

color evasiveness, 24

compulsory marriage, 260–66

coparenting, 102–6

criminal justice, 35–36

critical race theory: family legitimacy and, 24–25, 52; same-sex marriage and, 9, 24–25

cultural citizenship, 36–37

cultural eugenics, 126–27, 279n11

cultural values, 124–26

culture: choice and, 126–27; family legitimacy and, 175–84; family-making and, 110–11, 149; gender and, 66–68; poverty and, 124–28, 281n6

Currah, Paisley, 26, 192

Davis, Peggy Cooper, 9, 52

Death Pension, 35

Defense of Marriage Act (DOMA), 4, 15, 57; family legitimacy and, 109–24, 134–35, 139–40, 179, 255–56; illegitimacy and citizenship relating to, 118–23; *Obergefell v. Hodges* and, 255–56; reproductive politics and, 61, 63; welfare reform and, 116–18

dehumanization, 72–75

Deluzio, Crista, 185

Denetdale, Jennifer Nez, 68, 181, 182

dependency and citizenship, 118–23

Des Moines, Iowa. *See* Iowa

Dill, Bonnie Thornton, 63, 153, 184

Diné Marriage Act (2005), 165–66, 179–82, 259–60

disability, 120–22

discrimination, 1–3, 150, 233–34, 256–57, 260, 269–70; choice and, 159–62; law and, 2–3, 210; race and, 50, 96, 209–10; sameness and, 209

diversity experiences: education and, 146–53; same-sex marriage and, 275n4

DNA, 49, 50

DOMA. *See* Defense of Marriage Act

Domestic Partnership Rights and Responsibilities Act (2003), 168–69, 171–72, 200

double consciousness, 152–53

Dubinsky, Karen, 100

Du Bois, W. E. B., 152–53

Duggan, Lisa, 252

Edelman, Peter, 124, 281n1

education: in California, 203; "Children of the Rainbow" curriculum, 115; children's books and, 20, 58–66, 113–18, 203–5; child socialization and, 145–53; diversity experiences and, 146–53; family structure and, 145–53; illegitimacy and, 145–53; Improving America's School Act and, 60; politics and, 113–18

Eng, David L., 17, 238–39, 253, 254, 276n6

equality: choice and, 158–59, 232–35, 263–65; in Iowa, 226–27, 230–35; marriage, 23–24, 40–43, 160–62, 224; neoliberalism and, 46–47; race, choice, and, 232–35

Equality Iowa, 226–27, 235

ethnography, 17–18, 19; family trees and ethnographic allegories, 53–57; person-centered, 56, 279n5; stratified reproduction and, 81

eugenics: cultural, 126–27, 279n11; family-making and, 90–92

Families We Choose (Weston), 81

family definitions, 1–2, 13–14, 80

Family Equality Council, 211–12

family legitimacy: adoption and, 9–15, 40–43, 250–55; assisted reproduction and, 169; belonging and, 26–34; border crossings and, 166, 178–84, 241–44; in California, 167–75, 200; child welfare policies and, 184–89; citizenship and, 1–20, 23–47, 62–63; critical race theory and, 24–25, 52; culture and, 175–84; Diné Marriage Act and, 165–66, 179–82, 259–60; DOMA and, 109–24, 134–35, 139–40, 179, 255–56; Domestic Partnership Rights and Responsibilities Act and, 168–69, 171–72, 200; family-making and, 83; family trees and, 49–57, 247–55; health and, 142, 170–71; in Iowa, 1–3, 15, 23, 31, 34–35, 189–92, 221–45, 275n1; law and, 2–4, 21, 34–39, 52–53, 57–58, 165–93, 247–49; legal access and, 38–39; narrative, stratified reproduction, and, 57–66; nation and, 10; Native Americans and, 175–83; in New Mexico, 175–80; parental rights and, 53–57; patriarchy and, 16, 247–48, 254; politics and, 23–24, 52–53, 109–35, 165–67, 268–70; privatization of care and, 122–23, 128, 153–56, 162–63, 217, 253–58; Proposition 8 and, 195–98; queering family trees and, 10–15; queer legitimacy, 15–20; queers of color and, 14–15, 134–35, 137–39; race and, 14–15, 24–25, 40–43, 74–75, 138–39, 208–18; religion and, 174, 179–82, 258–59; reproductive politics and, 184–89; rights and, 43–47; slavery and, 74–75, 281n5; "slippery laws" and, 37–40; social location and, 15–17, 109–11; socioeconomic inequality and, 37–39; socioeconomic status and, 23–24; structural critiques of, 43–47; structural inequality and, 34–37, 45–46; taxes and, 38–39, 189–90, 261; whiteness and, 40–43, 134–35; YMCAs and, 1–3, 17–18, 264, 275n1. *See also* illegitimacy

family-making: adoption and, 95–102; assisted reproduction and, 81–94; culture and, 110–11, 149; eugenics and, 90–92; family legitimacy and, 83; genetics and, 90–94; grafting family trees and, 102–6; illegitimacy and, 134–35; kinship and, 102–6, 248, 270; politics and, 268–70; queers of color and, 91–97

Family Pride Week, 17–18, 19, 58, 88

family structure: child socialization and, 153–56; education and, 145–53; illegitimacy and, 139–45, 156–63; marriage and, 160–62

family trees: adoption and, 10–15, 49–51, 71–73, 79–80, 250–55; assimilation and, 69; colonization and, 68–69, 71, 72–73, 188–89; ethnography and, 53–57; family legitimacy and, 49–57, 247–55; family-making and grafting of, 102–6; genealogy and, 49–53, 66–76; grafted trees and adoption as allegory, 250–55; grafted trees and radical roots, 267–71; inheritance and, 51; language and, 13; nation and, 76–77; patriarchy and, 49, 51, 68–69; politics and, 57–66; queer legitimacy and, 10–15, 49–77; queer mothering and, 79–80; race and, 66–75; reproduction and, 79–80; social order and, 57–66; with WikiTree, 49–50, 71

family values: narrative on, 58–61, 63, 66, 109–11, 281n1; politics and, 109–13; reproductive injustice and, 112–13

Fanon, Frantz, 284n4

fathers, 156–60. *See also* sperm donors

Fenton, Zanita E., 119, 157

Ferguson, Roderick, 134

fertility: assisted reproduction and, 83–85; stratified reproduction and, 81

fictive kin, 81–82, 105–6

Florida, 132–33, 141–42

foster care, 129–32, 186–87

Franke, Katherine, 263–64

Frankenberg, Ruth, 24

Frazier, Franklin, 281n5

Fujiwara, Lynn H., 125–26

Gailey, Christine, 280n11

"gay agenda," 60–61, 113

gender: children's toys and, 147; culture and, 66–68; *Heather Has Two Mommies* and, 116; marriage and, 175–78; politics and, 72–73, 116–18; race and, 8–9, 39–40, 72–73; race-gender blaming, 213–18; welfare reform and, 116–18

gendered racism, 8–9

genealogy: DNA and, 49, 50; family trees and, 49–53, 66–76; genealogical allegories, 66–76; identity and, 70–71; of illegitimacy, 51–52, 139; inheritance and, 51; intersectionality and, 267–68; as narrative, 69, 79–80; nuclear family ideal and, 51; queer legitimacy and, 64–69, 75–76; sperm donors and, 89–92; white heteronormativity and, 75–76. *See also* family trees

genetics: DNA and, 49, 50; family-making and, 90–94

Gingrich, Newt, 127

god-parenting, 104

Goldstein, Alyosha, 183–84

Gooding-Williams, Robert, 62

Goodrich v. Department of Public Health (2003), 160–61

Gordon-Reed, Annette, 74

Guatemala, 97, 100

Haiti, 100, 189

Hall, Ryan, 180–81

Hancock, Melton D., 60–61

Haraway, Donna, 270

Harris-Perry, Melissa, 25

Hartman, Saidya, 248

hate, 260, 263–66

Haule, Kristin, 257

health: assisted reproduction relating to, 90, 280n4; family legitimacy and, 142, 170–71; RSV and, 142, 282n1

healthcare: assisted reproduction and, 84–85; law and, 37–38, 64–65, 138; Medicaid as, 64–65; queer legitimacy and, 37–38, 64–65, 261; reproductive politics and, 64–65

Heather Has Two Mommies (Newman), 20, 59–61, 148–49, 204–6; gender and, 116; illegitimacy and socializing the future, 113–18

The Hemingses of Monticello (Gordon-Reed), 74

Hequembourg, Amy L., 270, 278n13

Higginbotham, Evelyn Brooks, 42

home study, 97–99

homophobia, 29, 146–47; hate and, 260, 263–65; race and, 215–16; religion and, 179–80; violence and, 260, 263, 264

Hughey, Matthew W., 284n4

Hurley, Chuck, 232

identity: belonging and, 20–21, 73–74, 279n5; categories and fluidity of, 275n3; citizenship and, 24; double consciousness and, 152–53; genealogy and, 70–71; intersectionality of, 7, 8; motherhood and, 3–4, 275n3; nation and, 122–23; neoliberalism and, 46; race and, 28–31, 152–54, 284n4; religion and, 26–31; social location relating to, 6–7, 31, 279n5; structural inequality and, 36

IFPC. *See* Iowa Family Policy Center

If These Walls Could Talk 122, 281n3

ignorance, 282n4

illegitimacy: belonging and, 20–21; of children, 159–60, 250–51; child socialization and, 153–56; child welfare policies and, 156–60; citizenship and, 118–23; education and, 145–53; family-making and, 134–35; family structure and, 139–45, 156–63; fathers and, 156–60; genealogy of, 51–52, 139; *Heather Has Two Mommies* and, 113–18; as injury, 156–60; law and, 118–23, 156–60; marriage and, 116, 119, 122–23, 160–62; poverty relating to, 124–31; queers of color and, 112, 153–56, 281n5; race and, 119, 121–23, 125–26, 153–60; reproduction and, 20, 62–64, 103–13; reproductive injustice and, 113–26; welfare reform and, 112–13, 124–25; white supremacy and, 119
immigration: adoption and, 129, 280n1; citizenship and, 119–20, 122; reproductive politics and, 63–64
Improving America's School Act (1994), 60
inheritance: Death Pension and, 35; family tree and, 51; genealogy and, 51
intersectionality: genealogy and, 267–68; of identity, 7, 8; in law, 39–40; in reproductive politics, 12; in stratified reproduction, 81, 106–7, 186–88; in structural inequality, 39–40, 106–7
invalids, 121–23
Iowa: adoption in, 98; civil rights in, 231–33, 240; equality in, 226–27, 230–35; Equality Iowa, 226–27; family legitimacy in, 1–3, 15, 23, 31, 34–35, 189–92, 221–45, 275n1; license day in, 239–44; One Iowa, 227–32, 235–39; race in, 226–28, 232–39; religion in, 232–33; same-sex marriage in, 2–3, 18, 54–55, 137–38, 190–92, 220, 221–45, 260–61; *Varnum v. Brien* and, 192, 223–27; whiteness in, 235–39
Iowa Family Policy Center (IFPC), 232

Jackson, Samuel L., 210–11
Jerng, Mark C., 253

Kearl, Michelle Kelsey, 211
Kempthorne, Dirk, 116
Killing the Black Body (Roberts), 24
Kimport, Katrina, 167–68
King and King (2000), 203–4
kinship: family-making and, 102–6, 248, 270; fictive kin, 81–82, 105–6; law and, 103–4; social order and, 16; stratified reproduction and, 81–82
Kissen, Rita M., 146–47

Lambda Legal, 223–26, 261
language: family trees and, 13; metalanguage of whiteness, 40–43; queering family trees and, 13; race and, 41–43
Latinx, 104, 150–53, 210; religion and, 35–36, 278n5
Lavender Moms, 168
law: adoption and, 95–98, 140–42, 283n10; border crossings and, 166, 178–84, 241–44; criminal justice system and, 35–36; Death Pension and, 35; discrimination and, 2–3, 210; family legitimacy and, 2–4, 21, 34–39, 52–53, 57–58, 165–93, 247–49; healthcare and, 37–38, 64–65, 138; illegitimacy and, 118–23, 156–60; Improving America's School Act and, 60; inconsistencies in, 3, 7; intersectionality in, 39–40; kinship and, 103–4; legal access and, 38–39; politics and, 26; Proposition 8 and, 198–201; reproductive politics and, 7, 53–66; "slippery laws," 37–40; social location and, 11; socioeconomic inequality and, 37–39; stratified reproduction and, 57–66; structural inequality and, 34–37. *See also* same-sex marriage
legal access, 38–39
legible, 2, 18, 20–21, 36, 60, 62, 70, 80, 91, 93, 257, 274, 284, 292–93, 336

Lerman, Amy E., 35–36, 40–41

Lewis, Oscar, 281n6

LGBTQ families: public dialogues about, 276n5; race and, 15–16, 276n5; religion and, 26–34, 258–59; same-sex marriage and, 7–9; socioeconomic status and, 276n5; structural inequality and, 7–9. *See also specific topics*

liberalism, 46

liberal tolerance, 149–50

"A Litany for Survival" (Lorde), 265

lived experience: of citizenship, 25, 47; of family legitimacy, 79–80; of reproductive politics and law, 53–56

Lorde, Audre, 265

Loseke, Donileen, 35, 58, 278n9

Lott, Trent, 122

love, 29, 148, 242–43, 264

Loving v. Virginia (1967), 209, 210, 260, 262–63, 276n6

Mac Donald, Heather, 120–21, 124–25

"magical negro," 235–39, 284n4

male role models, 156–60

Mamo, Laura, 89

marriage: assimilation and, 174–75, 177–78, 181–83; compulsory, 260–66; equality, 23–24, 40–43, 160–62, 224; family structure and, 160–62; gender and, 175–78; illegitimacy and, 116, 119, 122–23, 160–62; nation and, 5; as patriarchal institution, 6–7, 257; politics and, 116–18, 122–23, 165–67; privacy and, 161; race and, 137–39, 160–62; rights separated from, 6; social order and, 5, 43–44; structural critiques of, 43–47; welfare reform and, 118. *See also* same-sex marriage

Massachusetts: reproductive politics in, 84; same-sex marriage in, 15, 135, 140–41, 144–45, 159–62, 192

May, Vivian M., 52

Mayers, Leifa, 101, 237–38, 239, 251

McKinley, Jesse, 210

McPherson, Tara, 69

media, 229; reproductive politics and, 63

Medicaid, 64–65

"The Metalanguage of Race" (Higginbotham), 42

Mink, Gwendolyn, 118

Minnesota, 1–2, 82, 275n1

Missouri, 241–44

Molly's Family (2004), 204–6

Moore, Mignon, 29–30, 258–59

Morrison, Toni, 46–47, 76–77

motherhood: adoption and stratified mothering, 40–43; citizenship and, 238; identity and, 3–4, 275n3; politics and, 238–39; race and, 235–39; sexual identity and, 3–4, 275n3; socioeconomic status and, 7. *See also* queer mothering

mothers: birth, 12–13, 100–102, 131–32, 187–88; recognizing multiple mothers, 10–15

Moynihan, Daniel Patrick, 281n5

multicultural societies, 279n5

Munoz, Jose, 281n1

Murray, Charles, 117–18

Murray, Melissa, 45–46, 158–60, 224, 251, 255–56, 263

Nadleehi history, 66–69, 175–83

narrative, 35, 278n9; on citizenship, 118–23; cultural values and, 124–26; family legitimacy, stratified reproduction, and, 57–66; on family values, 58–61, 63, 66, 109–11, 281n1; genealogy as, 69, 79–80; nuclear family ideal and, 57, 63, 82, 225–26, 247, 254; orphan-salvation myth as, 99–102; power relations and, 59, 63, 65–66, 135, 152, 266, 269–71; racial, 61–62, 154–56, 208–9, 236–38; of racism, 282n4, 284n4; reproductive politics and, 62–63; resistance and, 76–77; of sameness, 222–24, 236–37; welfare reform and, 120–22, 124–26

nation: belonging and, 36–37, 76–77; children and, 61; family legitimacy and, 10; family trees and, 76–77; family values and, 58–61; identity and, 122–23; marriage and, 5; *Obergefell v. Hodges* and, 255–60; race and, 46–47; reproductive politics and, 58–66
National Gay and Lesbian Task Force Policy Institute, 216–17
Native Americans, 66–70, 175–83, 185
nature and nurture, 80–81
Navajo tradition, 66–69, 165, 175–83
neoliberalism: adoption and, 126–33, 253–54; equality and, 46–47; identity and, 46; liberalism compared to, 46; politics and, 126–33, 269–70; race and, 127–30; welfare reform and, 126–33
Newman, Leslea, 20, 59–60, 113–18, 148–49, 204–6
New Mexico, 66–67, 175–80, 185–89
Newsom, Gavin, 167–68
Nickles, Don, 122–23
nuclear family ideal, 6, 105; genealogy and, 51; narrative and, 57, 63, 82, 225–26, 247, 254; race and, 225–26

Obama, Barack, 210, 214, 215
Obergefell v. Hodges (2015): DOMA and, 255–56; nation, social order, and, 255–60; queer legitimacy in, 4–5, 6, 35, 248–64, 284n1
One Iowa, 227–32, 235–39
Ong, Aihwa, 36–37
origin stories, 155–56
orphan-salvation myth, 99–102
O'Sullivan, Meg Devlin, 185

parental rights: adoption and, 11, 53–57; child welfare policies and, 156–60; family legitimacy and, 53–57
Parker v. Hurley (2008), 203–5
pathology and race, 281n5

patriarchy, 8; family legitimacy and, 16, 247–48, 254; family trees and, 49, 51, 68–69; marriage, as patriarchal institution, 6–7, 257; religion and, 232–33
Patterson, David J., 209
Perales, Monica, 238
Perez v. Sharp (1948), 209
person-centered ethnography, 56, 279n5
Playing in the Dark (Morrison), 46–47
Polikoff, Nancy, 44
politics: assimilation and, 167, 174–75, 177–78, 181; citizenship and, 23–24; colorblindness and, 24, 69–70, 106–7, 209–10; education and, 113–18; family legitimacy and, 23–24, 52–53, 109–35, 165–67, 268–70; family-making and, 268–70; family trees and, 57–66; family values and, 109–13; "gay agenda" and, 60–61, 113; gender and, 72–73, 116–18; law and, 26; marriage and, 116–18, 122–23, 165–67; motherhood and, 238–39; neoliberalism and, 126–33, 269–70; privatization of care and, 122–23, 128, 153–56, 162–63, 217, 253–58; of queer mothering, 14–15; race and, 72–73; reproductive injustice and, 112–13; women and, 62–63. *See also* reproductive politics
poverty: adoption and, 99–102, 124–32; child welfare policies and, 126–32; culture and, 124–28, 281n6; illegitimacy relating to, 124–31; social location and, 123; welfare reform and, 124–25
power relations: assisted reproduction and, 93–94; choice and, 38, 45; narrative and, 59, 63, 65–66, 135, 152, 266, 269–71; queer legitimacy and, 17, 38; race and, 41–43, 46–47; structural inequality and, 38, 77, 269–71
pregnancy, 83–84
privacy, 161
privatization of care, 122–23, 128, 153–56, 162–63, 217, 253–58

Proposition 8: belonging and, 195–201; children and, 198, 201–9; citizenship and, 196, 198, 200–201; civil rights and, 209–13; family legitimacy and, 195–98; law and, 198–201; passing of, 201–9, 213–18; race-gender blaming for passing of, 213–18; race relating to, 209–18; religion and, 201–4, 218; same-sex marriage and, 195–218; voting patterns in, 216–17

Proposition 22, 283n1 (chapter 7)

Proposition 187, 120

"Punks, Bulldaggers, and Welfare Queens" (Cohen), 13–14

queer definition, 14, 275n3

queer legitimacy: colorblindness and, 17, 24; genealogy and, 64–69, 75–76; healthcare and, 37–38, 64–65, 261; in *Obergefell v. Hodges*, 4–5, 6, 35, 248–64, 284n1; power relations and, 17, 38; by queering family trees, 10–15, 49–77; recognition and passing, 15–20; structural inequality and, 36–37

queer mothering, 3–4; adoption and, 10–15, 34, 40–43; assisted reproduction and, 81–94; child welfare policies and, 130–33; coparenting and, 102–6; family trees and, 79–80; negative representations of, 4–5; passing as straight, 97–98, 280n8; politics of, 14–15; pregnancy and, 83–84; questioning who's "real mom," 205–7; same-sex marriage and, 6–7; social location and, 14; stratified mothering and, 40–43

queers of color, 9–10, 276n5; family legitimacy and, 14–15, 134–35, 137–39; family-making and, 91–97; illegitimacy and, 112, 153–56, 281n5

Quiroz, Pamela A., 282n5

race: adoption and, 40–43, 128–29, 133, 153–56, 236–39, 252–55; assisted reproduction and, 93–94; child socialization and, 153–56; child welfare policies and, 133, 156–60, 184–89; choice, equality, and, 232–35; citizenship and, 118–19; civil rights and, 8, 24, 44, 61; colonization and, 184–89; color evasiveness and, 24; critical race theory, 9, 24–25, 52; discrimination and, 50, 96, 209–10; family legitimacy and, 14–15, 24–25, 40–43, 74–75, 138–39, 208–18; family trees and, 66–75; gender and, 8–9, 39–40, 72–73; homophobia and, 215–16; identity and, 28–31, 152–54, 284n4; illegitimacy and, 119, 121–23, 125–26, 153–60; in Iowa, 226–28, 232–39; language and, 41–43; LGBTQ families and, 15–16, 276n5; *Loving v. Virginia* and, 209, 210, 260, 262–63, 276n6; "magical negro" and, 235–39, 284n4; marriage and, 137–39, 160–62; motherhood and, 235–39; nation and, 46–47; neoliberalism and, 127–30; nuclear family ideal and, 225–26; pathology and, 281n5; politics and, 72–73; power relations and, 41–43, 46–47; Proposition 8 relating to, 209–18; religion, belonging, and, 26–34; reproduction and, 24–25, 72–73, 155–56, 184–89; reproductive politics and, 7, 61–62, 64–65, 155–56, 253; same-sex marriage and, 160–62; sexuality and, 64–66, 73–74; socio-economic status and, 8, 39–40; sperm donors and, 91–94; stratified reproduction and, 184–89; structural inequality and, 72–74; *Varnum v. Brien* and, 223–26. See also colorblindness; queers of color; whiteness

race-gender blaming, 213–18

race-matching, 128

racial narrative, 61–62, 154–56, 208–9, 236–38

racism, 69, 72–73, 212–13; adoption and, 128; biological or scientific, 282n8; Black man "threat" and, 154–55; color-blindness and, 282n5; in film, 284n4; gendered, 8–9; hate and, 265–66; ignorance and, 282n4; "magical negro" and, 235–39, 284n4; narratives of, 282n4, 284n4; survival skills, 153, 282n2

Ratliff, Keith, 232–33

religion: family legitimacy and, 174, 179–82, 258–59; homophobia and, 179–80; identity and, 26–31; in Iowa, 232–33; Latinx and, 35–36, 278n5; LGBTQ families and, 26–34, 258–59; patriarchy and, 232–33; Proposition 8 and, 201–4, 218; race, belonging, and, 26–34; sin and, 26, 28–34, 174, 180, 232–35, 238

representational belonging, 25

reproduction: assisted, 81–94, 169, 280n4; citizenship and, 24–25, 45–46, 276n5; family trees and, 79–80; fertility and, 81; illegitimacy and, 20, 62–64, 103–13; nature and nurture and, 80–81; race and, 24–25, 72–73, 155–56, 184–89; slavery and, 72–75; stratified, 55–56, 57–66, 81–82, 106–7, 184–89

reproductive futurism, 111, 113–18, 281n1

reproductive injustice: family values and, 112–13; illegitimacy and, 113–26; 1990-2000, 103–13; politics and, 112–13; welfare reform and, 112–13

reproductive politics, 277n4; adoption and, 12, 155–56; DOMA and, 61, 63; family legitimacy and, 184–89; healthcare and, 64–65; immigration and, 63–64; intersectionality in, 12; law and, 7, 53–66; lived experience of, 53–56; in Massachusetts, 84; media and, 63; narrative and, 62–63; nation and, 58–66; race and, 7, 61–62, 64–65, 155–56, 253; same-sex marriage and, 7–8; structural inequality and, 7–8, 25, 45–46; welfare reform and, 63–64

resistance: assimilation compared to, 44–45, 106; narrative and, 76–77

respiratory syncytial virus (RSV), 142, 282n1

rhizomes, 267–68

rights: family legitimacy and, 43–47; marriage separated from, 6. See also civil rights; parental rights; specific topics

risk assessment, 131–32

Rivera, Lisbeth Melendez, 103–4

Roanhorse, Sherrick, 180–81

Roberts, Dorothy, 24, 47, 72

Ross, Loretta, 25

RSV. See respiratory syncytial virus

salvation, 235–39, 284n4

sameness: discrimination and, 209; narrative of, 222–24, 236–37

same-sex marriage: in Baker v. Vermont, 159, 283n1 (chapter 6); in California, 21, 167–75, 177–78, 194, 195–218, 283n1 (chapter 7); children and, 4, 9–10, 201–9, 221–25, 249–51; citizenship and, 5–6, 40–43; critical race theory and, 9, 24–25; Diné Marriage Act and, 165–66, 179–82, 259–60; diversity experiences and, 275n4; Goodrich v. Department of Public Health and, 160–61; in Iowa, 2–3, 18, 54–55, 137–38, 190–92, 220, 221–45, 260–61; LGBTQ families and, 7–9; Loving v. Virginia and, 209, 210, 260, 262–63, 276n6; in Massachusetts, 15, 135, 140–41, 144–45, 159–62, 192; Navajo tradition and, 165, 175–83; in New Mexico, 175–80; Obergefell v. Hodges and, 4–5, 6, 35, 248–64, 284n1; Proposition 8 and, 195–218; protection of, 7; public dialogues about, 4–5, 276n6; queer mothering and, 6–7; race and, 160–62; reproductive politics and, 7–8; "slippery laws," 37–40; social location and, 6–7, 139–45, 165–67; structural inequality and, 7; in Varnum

v. Brien, 192, 223–27; in Vermont, 15, 135, 140, 159–62, 283n1 (chapter 6). *See also* Defense of Marriage Act
same-sex marriage timelines: 1990-2000, 108; 2000-2003, 136; 2004-2006, 164; 2004-2010, California, 194; 2005-2009, Iowa, 220; 2009-2015, 246
San Francisco, California, 167–75
Savage, Dan, 215–16
"Save Our Children" campaign, 142
Schubert, Frank, 210
scientific racism, 282n8
Sears, James T., 147–48
settler colonialism, 83, 86–87, 144, 220, 223–24, 229, 239, 296, 336
sexuality: identity and motherhood, 3–4, 275n3; race and, 64–66, 73–74; structural inequality and, 36
Shalala, Donna, 124
Shannahan, Dervla, 148–49
Shin, Michael, 217–18
shootings, 260, 263, 264
Simms, Rudy, 230
sin, 26, 28–34, 174, 180, 232–35, 238
SisterSong, 277n4
slavery: children and, 73–75; family legitimacy and, 74–75, 281n5; reproduction and, 72–75
"slippery laws," 37–40
social institutions, 34–37, 57. *See also* structural inequality
socialization. *See* child socialization
social location: adoption and, 11, 95–102, 140–45; border crossings and, 166, 178–84, 241–44; citizenship and, 14, 119; family legitimacy and, 15–17, 109–11; identity relating to, 6–7, 31, 279n5; law and, 11; poverty and, 123; queer mothering and, 14; same-sex marriage and, 6–7, 139–45, 165–67
social order: family trees and, 57–66; kinship and, 16; marriage and, 5, 43–44; *Obergefell v. Hodges* and, 255–60

socioeconomic inequality, 7–8; family legitimacy and, 37–39; law and, 37–39; structural inequality and, 46
socioeconomic status: citizenship and, 23–24; family legitimacy and, 23–24; LGBTQ families and, 276n5; motherhood and, 7; race and, 8, 39–40. *See also* poverty
sociopolitical allegories, 57–66, 123
Solinger, Rickie, 7, 62
Sommerville, Siobhan, 14, 24
sperm donors, 280n4; choosing, 85–94; genealogy and, 89–92; race and, 91–94
Spindelman, Marc, 255
stigma, 25; children and, 250–51
stratified mothering, 40–43
stratified reproduction, 55–56; child welfare policies and, 184–89; colonization and, 184–89; ethnography and, 81; fertility and, 81; intersectionality in, 81, 106–7, 186–88; kinship and, 81–82; law and, 57–66; race and, 184–89
structural inequality: choice and, 45, 55; denial of, 5; family legitimacy and, 34–37, 45–46; identity and, 36; inequality in social institutions, 34–37, 57; intersectionality in, 39–40, 106–7; law and, 34–37; LGBTQ families and, 7–9; poverty and illegitimacy as, 124–26; power relations and, 38, 77, 269–71; queer legitimacy and, 36–37; race and, 72–74; reproductive politics and, 7–8, 25, 45–46; same-sex marriage and, 7; sexuality and, 36; social reality of, 25; socioeconomic inequality and, 46
Supreme Court cases: *Baker v. Vermont*, 159, 283n1 (chapter 6); *Goodrich v. Department of Public Health*, 160–61; *Loving v. Virginia*, 209, 210, 260, 262–63, 276n6; *Obergefell v. Hodges*, 4–5, 6, 35, 248–64, 284n1; *Parker v. Hurley*, 203–5; *Perez v. Sharp*, 209; *Varnum v. Brien*, 192, 223–27

Sycamore, Matilda (Matt) Bernstein, 174–75

TANF. *See* Temporary Assistance for Needy Families
taxes, 38–39, 189–90, 261
Taylor, Camilla, 229
Taylor, Verta, 167–68
Temporary Assistance for Needy Families (TANF), 118, 127, 129
Tober, Diane, 90
toys, 147
transnational adoption, 97–102, 153, 280n8, 280n11
Tsosie, Cecelia, 179–80

VA. *See* Veteran's Administration
values: cultural, 124–26; family, 58–61, 63, 66, 109–13, 281n1
Van Dyke, Nella, 167–68
Varnum v. Brien (2009): children in, 224–25; race and, 223–26; same-sex marriage in, 192, 223–27
Vermont: in *Baker v. Vermont* (1999), 159, 283n1 (chapter 6); same-sex marriage in, 15, 135, 140, 159–62, 283n1 (chapter 6)
Veteran's Administration (VA), 35
violence, 260, 263, 264
Volpalka, Sandy, 226
voting patterns, 216–17

Ward, Jane, 17, 211
Watson, Julia, 68
Weaver, Vesla M., 35–36, 40–41
Weber, Shannon, 177–78
welfare reform, 20; citizenship and, 118–23; disability and, 120–22; DOMA and, 116–18; gender and, 116–18; illegitimacy and, 112–13, 124–25; marriage and, 118; narrative and, 120–22, 124–26; neoliberalism and, 126–33; poverty and, 124–25; reproductive injustice and, 112–13; reproductive politics and, 63–64
Weston, Kath, 81
white heteronormativity, 75–76
"white man's burden," 239
whiteness: adoption and, 40–43, 236–38; family legitimacy and, 40–43, 134–35; in Iowa, 235–39; metalanguage, 40–43
white supremacy, 8, 67, 106, 119, 247, 252, 265–66
whitewashing, 7, 237
WikiTree, 49–50, 71
Wilkerson, James, 200
Williams Institute study (2009), 173–74
women: choice and, 45, 62–63; politics and, 62–63

YMCAs: family legitimacy and, 1–3, 17–18, 264, 275n1; inclusion in, 1–2, 275n1

Zinn, Maxine Baca, 63

ABOUT THE AUTHOR

Sandra Patton-Imani is a Professor of American Studies at Drake University. She earned her MA and PhD in American Studies, with a graduate certificate in Women's Studies, at the University of Maryland, College Park. She is the author of *BirthMarks: Transracial Adoption in Contemporary America* and a number of scholarly articles on adoption, race, gender, and family.